South Sudan: Fragile & Fragmented State

Dynamics of Violent Actors and Challenge of Disarmament of Ex-Combatants

PhD Marial Mach Aduot

Bor Publishers - Australia

A catalogue record for this work is available from the National Library of Australia

First published by Bor Publishers in 2020
Copyright © 2020 PhD Marial Mach Aduot

Bor Publishers,
Perth, Western Australia
Phone: 08 9439 4704
Email: admin@borpublishers.com
Web: www.borpublishers.com
ABN: 45 867 024 044

ISBN: 978-0-6482848-6-4

Legal & Disclaimer

DEDICATION

This book is dedicated to my parents, my siblings and my community, Panda Palek globally

TABLE OF CONTENTS

Foreword viii

Preface xi

Acknowledgments xvii

Definition of Abbreviations and Acronyms xix

Chapter One: Limited Statehood and the Challenges of the DDR in South Sudan 26

1.1 South Sudan: A Country without State 29

1.2 A Nation Challenged: Ethno-Political Loyalty Places Tribe before the Country 36

1.3 Internal Uncertainty 50

1.4 Problems of Legitimacy and Inner Justification of State in South Sudan 54

1.5 Dynamics of Power in South Sudan 62

1.6 Inducting the Rebels to the Government in South Sudan 66

1.7 Decentralisation of Violence 70

1.8 Conclusion 72

Chapter Two: Ethnicity and Political Discourse of Violence in South Sudan 74

2.1 Civil War in South Sudan: Is it an Ethnic Conflict? 84

2.2 Instrumentalists on Conceptualisation of Violent Conflicts 96

2.3 Ethno-Political Violence and Proliferation of Arms in South Sudan
.... 101

2.4 Ethno-Political Factionalism and the Proliferation of Arms in
South Sudan.. 113

2.5 An Impact of Armed Group's Insecurity Surrounding the DDR
.... 118

2.6 Self-Defence and the Militarisation of Identities in South Sudan
.... 120

2.7 Conclusion 124

Chapter Three: The Autopsy of the Sudan Comprehensive Peace
Agreement (CPA): Its Shortcomings and Their Effects on the DDR in
South Sudan... 126

3.1 A Bumpy Road to the Negotiated Settlement of Sudanese's Civil
War 133

3.2 The Breakthrough: 2001-2002 Momentum for Negotiated
Settlement... 141

3.3 IGAD Mediation: An Assessment of Peacemaking and its Effect
on DDR 146

3.4 Shifting the Peacemaking Strategy to the Principals' Haggling. 155

3.5 Implementing Exclusive CPA and the Impasses of the DDR in
South Sudan... 161

3.6 Conclusion 168

4: Conclusive Summary.. 170

References 192

Foreword

When Marial Mach Aduot informed me in the year 2014 about an opportunity he got in Australia to write a PhD thesis on the politics of Post -War in South Sudan, I was inspired by his dream, and since that time, we have shared many ideas on the politics of South Sudan and other writings he undertook. The dream of being part of the global Community platform in communicating one's ideas to the rest of the world in writing has been a shared objective since we were in Kakuma Refugee Camp in Kenya. Writing a book about South Sudan's politics at the time the country is engaged within itself, neighbours and the International Community on how to manage its affairs particularly the security sector could not be timely than it is today.

Many Writers and Researchers have written many books both in pre-Independence and post-Independence South Sudan, however, Marial's book, South Sudan: A fragmented State gives details account of how the failure of DDR policy in South Sudan becomes a key factor in an overall failure of the Security sector reforms. The book unlocks the debate further by vividly shed light on how the CPA fell short of addressing the DDR policy and hence independent South Sudan could not enjoy the peace it has been hunting for in decades.

The situational analysis of the security sector reforms is well captured in the book, and that will help the academics, researchers and policymakers in South Sudan and beyond to understand why and how the processes of DDR fell short of public expectations despite the SPLA/M well-established policy of a secure, free and a prosperous nation that belongs to all South Sudanese regardless of race, religion or tribe. The book is a manifestation of the reality between the country we fought for and the one we have at hand. The lack of strong Authority and legitimacy to govern the state made independence no different from the fragility that gave more actors an upper hand in tilting the decisions of the state. Tribal elements end up shaping the decisions of the state, and hence the country remain vulnerable to fragmentation.

The book talks about our history and present state of affairs as far as our security is a concern. It is a critique of those in power or out of power, including the opposition who have failed to come together and confront the beast within us. The book assesses the ironies and contradictions of the post-independence South Sudan security policies with particular reference to DDR.

Marial's book exposes the glaring mistakes made by the current regime in handling the state power and directing the security policies in a manner that no journalistic or academic account has ever done in South Sudan. The failure of the leadership to transform South Sudan into a vibrant Country with socioeconomics policies as envisioned by the founders of the liberation struggles is a point of contention in the debate put forward in the book. As we enter into a transitional period, we face a question of power, its use and misuse. The ability of the state to organised power to protect citizens and territory of South Sudan seems to have vanished and yet remain an integral part of our future discussion.

We are now on our way to the state of lawlessness characterised by inequality, corruption and tribalism that we thought we left behind in Sudan. As citizens of the new state, we have allowed complacency of being independence to pervades our country and when things get wronged at the political stage the way they have been, we keep complaining that it is those around the President that are misleading him. What have we done legally to challenge that state of affairs? The book is a must-read for those who want to understand the current states of affairs in South Sudan political sphere. The second edition of this book will have to focus on simplifying it to nonacademic to be on the same page of understanding because the current edition is highly technical.

Michael Thon Mangok

B.A – Communication, M.A – Diplomacy – M.A -Political Science |
Journalist and political Analyst in South Sudan |

Preface

In societies with socio-political stability, state principles and authority are enduring. While stability can be misleading, the prospects for a sense of relative peace and security could countervail violence. Even with a little persuasion, law enforcement agencies can prevent casual use of force, and that is the idea of a functioning state. The functioning state is characterised by the existence of cohesive socio-political capacity and is viewed by internal and external actors as legitimate. This study argues that South Sudan emerged as a fragile and fragmented; 'a country without a state' (Johnson, 2016, p. 16). This argument emphasises how the legacies of protracted civil war, between North and Southern rebels, various violent ethno-political factionalism in South/ern Sudan, and the enactment of politico-military policies present severe challenges. In this context, it worth arguing that South Sudan faces two challenging tasks: state-building and nation-building. The domestic dimension of sovereignty is punctuated by different degrees of violence and deficiency of the state's capacities. In that case, South Sudan lacks normative conceptualisation of the state as the effective domestic extensiveness of sovereignty.

This book examines the challenges of building effective state and instruments of governance in South Sudan. This emphasis explores the deficiency of the state as an organising system of public authority within a state has led to decentralisation of violence at every level of South Sudanese state. In the conceptual context, the book argues that there is a real danger of failing to rebuild the emerging state to become the ultimate authority capable of maintaining the structure of the socio-political function. The theoretical emphasis on the relationship between peace and functioning state is vested in the international relation's understanding of the state as an omnipotent actor that upholds a claim to a legitimate monopoly over the use of force in a given territory (Weber, 1946; Lake, 2008).

Based on this rationale, academics like (Waltz, 1979; Keohane, 1984) defined the state as a collective unit of global politics. As they focused on state functions and their interactions, these scholars regarded the states as the fundamental instrument of power (Bull 1977; Reus-Smit, 1999; Wendt, 1999). Sovereign states, in this context, are perceived as indispensable objects of international politics. Therefore, states stood as an essential component of both peace and violence (Wendt, 1999). Deriving from this understanding, the international community has adopted a state building approach which associated the capacity for the prevention of war with the capacity of state's institutions (Lemay-Hébert, 2012). According to Copnall, (2014, p. 25), South Sudan is 'a state in search of a nation: a new country on the map populated by the people without a particularly strong common identity'.

This argument implied lacks a consolidated statehood. Hence, formal institutions or structures of governance are too fragile and unable to perform political and security responsibilities associated with statehood. In this case, the authority to mobilised ethno-political armies and the use force is instead arrayed through 'a system of relations linking rules, not with the 'public' or 'even with the ruled, but with patrons, associates, clients, supporters, and rivals, who constitute the 'system' (Jackson and Rosberg, 1982, p. 19). The fragility of central authority means the South Sudanese state is unable to control the hostile behaviours of the ethno-political identities. At the opposite of sufficient sovereign authority lies limited statehood, which can manifest itself with lack the capacity to implement and enforce collective decisions, including the monopoly of the use of force. As such, determining the reason why armed groups resisted the disarmament requires an emphasis that South Sudanese state lacked a practical capacity to enforce central decisions.

The first chapter will apply the concept of political instability: defining South Sudan as a country where the behaviour of elites changes the political system into a chaotic scene of violent competition among factions. This challenge has overcome an effort to rebuilds South Sudanese state based on the objectives, and rationales of the state-centric political and security arguments. This inability to overcomes the fury of political divisions and violence reinforced the group's quest for survival, and a perception of security as zero-sum, hence, fuelling armed bargaining, and an internal arms race. In that case, South Sudanese state become just another actor among different armed actors (Waltz, 1979). This rising of other violent actors within the weaker state has raised questions on the efficiency of the state-centric approach in post-war situations.

I argue in the study that the state-building theories ignored, or obscure issues involved in the making of the state from the rubbles of war (Ray, 1997). With that, the international policymakers justify their stances under the conceptual definition of strength and weakness of the state. The United Nations' agencies that intervene in post-war states viewed 'state' in two core assumptions; 'as the apparatus of government, or as the social system subject to that government' (Giddens, 1985, p. 17). Because of the perception of state 'as the apparatus of government, or as the social system' (Giddens, 1985, p. 17), the post-war interveners see the state as 'a unitary entity with a collective preference' (Lake, 2009, p. 43). The complicated question, in this case, arises when analysing a country like South Sudan, which emerged as the result of the long civil war. What is critical in South Sudan is the challenges of several false starts attributed to Africans countries when they emerged from the colonial system. The doctrines of the South Sudanese state are new, and the nation-building processes suffer from a terminal decline given its long attachment to violence, socio-political and national identity autonomy.

Indeed, the current crises in South Sudan remind us of overt and salience unresolved socio-political crisis. The question is how the state-building and peace-building approaches are contrary to the reality in South Sudan? Although many crises afflicting South Sudan are not new, the post-independent violence has its roots in the history of socio-political uncertainties over the absence of state and long-established ethno-political contest over power and resources. I argue, therefore, that the violence is fuelled by the power-struggling which have created an enormous challenge to political order. Hence, we need an understanding of various structures, interests and expectations and how these interrelated problems impeded positive peace and state-building dynamic.

These challenges come as a result of upgrading what was virtually a contested territory into a sovereign state. This transition is not the same as when the unitary state fought the war and started to rebuild after the war. South Sudan is a new country founded on the wreckages of war, ethnic division, and governed by the rebels who have been relying on the rogue pattern of institutions.

While the Sudan People Liberation Movement/Army has successfully negotiated peace and steered the Southern region into becoming a fully sovereign state, observers believed it is not as effectual in setting up a functioning political system capable of addressing political and ethnic conflicts from flaring to the civil war (Lyman, 2013). The testimony to this accusation is the prevalence of different armed conflict among ethno-political factions. These issues hinted that South Sudan was not destined for the transition to a peaceful society, but it was destined for war, a notion not considered during the CPA and post-secession arrangements. In this case, I do not just need to join the firestorm of critics of the post-war reconstruction efforts, in providing solutions to the post-war issues. This study reflects on the states of South Sudan's stateness, using the fact that it was unlike other post-war countries.

South Sudan was meant to be built from scratch, not to be rebuild. Hence, this book will cast the South Sudanese state as the new and overly militarised state; a consequent of perennial relying on the use force to settle disputes. South Sudan's upheavals are rooted in the institutional deficiency that makes the state prone to violence. All these challenges are condoned and often ignored by peace and conflict prevention mechanism which I described as a rubber-bandages strategy, that does not have any plan for dealing with societal issues that gradually stocked enmity among the group.

Acknowledgments

This academic journey involved the sacrifices and contribution of many people. I was born in war-torn South/ern Sudan during the civil war with the Sudanese Government, and learned to write on the ground with no writing materials in Kakuma Refugee Camp in Kenya. It was not an easy path to come this far, and that warrants a list of those worthy of acknowledgment. First thanks go to the humanitarian and the Australian community, which has given me security and a home. Second, there have been unimaginable contributions from family members, friends, and a group of academics. At this milestone, I expressed thanks to my chief supervisor, Dr Costas Laoutides, whose work is indispensable. On a personal note, I am indebted to the contributions rendered by my family. My sisters, Atong Mach Aduot, Yom Mawut Gai, and Aluel Majier Gai. Their unswerving supports would have been in vain without the guiding hands of a matriarch, Akon Achiek Wai.

The same can be said for those who have supported me in different ways. Those thanks go to General Mac Paul, Ayuel Martin Majier & Dr Mach Martin Majier, Mabior Maler Ajok, Ayuel Gai Ayuel, David Mabior Lual, Yuot Ayuen Yuot, Lual Andrew Makuei and Dr Clifton Evers, Dr Anne Bunde-birouste, and Alexander Balmer. With that being said, it does not withstand the support given by Anyang Gurech, Michael Thon Magok, Ayuel Mading Ayuel, Geu Ngong Athel, Peter Majak Kuol, and Agot Alier Leek, Jok Aguto Akuot, Panchol Mathiang Mach, Akoy Wut Lual, Guguei Gai Kuei and Garang Ateny Reng & Nicodemus Ajak Bior, to name a few. To my friends who have witnessed my journey to this stage: Achan Deng Kudum, Abul Manyoun Mayen, Deng-thie Mading Deng, Bishop; David Achiek Mach Luala, & Rev. Bol Amol, Angar Chating Abiel, David Ayuel Machar Thiong, Juach Garang Bul, to name a few. Your contribution pushed me this far. Last, I would like to convey my appreciation to content readers, Dr Kate Hall & Dr Leanne Kelly, and the entire team of academics of the Faculty, all the interviewees and institutions that provided access to first-hand information, I am grateful to you all. Without whom the preparation of this thesis would not have been possible. I am thrilled with all these contributions.

Definition of Abbreviations and Acronyms

AAA: Abyei Administrative Area

AAA: Addis Ababa Agreement

AU: African Union

BCSSAS: Bureau for Community Security and Small Arms
Control

BFPS: Bergdorf Foundation for Peace Support

BICC: Bonn International Centre for Conversion

CCI: Compagnie des Constructions Internationales

CDR: Commander

CIDCM: Centre for International Development and Conflict
Management

Col: Colonel

CPA: Comprehensive Peace Agreement

DDR: Disarmament, Demobilisation & Reintegration

DFID: Department for International Development

DOP: Declaration of Principles

ECOMOG: Economic Community of West African States
Monitoring Group

ECOWAS: Economic Community of West African States

ELF: Eritrean Liberation Front

EPRDF: Ethiopian People's Revolutionary Democratic Front

EU: European Union

FDLR: Forces Démocratiques de Libération du Rwanda

Gen: General

GoS: Government of Sudan

GoSS: Government of South/ern Sudan

HRW: Human Rights Watch

ICC: International Criminal Court

ICG: International Crisis Group

ICISS: International Commission on Intervention and State Sovereignty

IDDRS: Integrated DDR-Standards

IDP: Internally Displaced People

IGAD: Intergovernmental Authority on Development

ILO: International Labour Organisation

INGOs: International Non-Governmental Organisations

IOM: International Organisation for Migration

IPA: International Peace Academy

IPF: International Partners Forum

IRIN: Integrated Regional Information Network

LRA: Lord's Resistance Army

MOU: Memorandum of Understanding

NANS: National Alliance for National Salvation

NCC: National Constitutional Conference

NCP: National Congress Party

NDA: National Democratic Alliance

NDDRC: National Disarmament, Demobilisation and Reintegration Council

NGOs: Non-Governmental Organisations

NIF: National Islamic Front

NRA: National Resistance Army

NSA: Non-State Actors

OAGs: Other Armed Groups

OECD: Organisation for Economic Co-operation and Development

OLS: Operation Lifeline Sudan

PKO: Peacekeeping Operation(s)

PMHC: Political-Military High Command

PRIO: Peace Research Institute of Oslo

PSO: Peace Support Operation(s)

RUF: Revolutionary United Front

SAF: Sudanese Armed Forces

SALW: Small arms and light weapons

SAS: Small Arms Survey

SIDDR: Stockholm Initiative on DDR

SPLA-IO: Sudan People's Liberation Army-In-Opposition

SPLM/A: Sudan People's Liberation Movement/Army

SRSG: Special Representative of the United Nations Secretary-General

SSDA/M: South Sudan Democratic Army/Movement

SSDDRC: South Sudan DDR Commission

SSDF: South Sudan Defence Forces

SSLM: South Sudan Liberation Movement

SSNLM: South Sudan National Liberation Movement

SSPS: South Sudan Police Service

SSR: Security Sector Reform

UCDP: Uppsala Conflict Data Program

U.N.: United Nations

UNDP: United Nations Development Programme

UNDPKO: United Nations Department of Peacekeeping Operations

UNITA: National Union for the Total Independence of Angola

UNMIS: United Nations Mission in Sudan

UNMISS: United Nations Mission in South Sudan

UNSC: UN Security Council

USA: United States of America

USAID: US Agency for International Development

WB: World Bank

Chapter One: Limited Statehood and the Challenges of the DDR in South Sudan

After casting their ballots in favour of secession, on January 9th, 2011, the vision of an independent South Sudanese state became a reality in the minds of millions yearning for change. When South Sudan declared its independence, it was a euphoric moment, "accompanied by headlines proclaiming the birth of a nation" (Leopold, 2011, p. 22). Euphoria aside, the road is riddled with impediments, not the least of which is the legacy of the civil war and building a functioning state from scratch, and drawing leaders from ill-prepared ex-insurgents, let alone a state composed of different ethnic identities in perpetual conflict with each other. Although South Sudan fulfilled "the declarative requirements of a state in international law" (Wassara, 2015, p. 635), the question of what kind of state had been born was not answered. First, the independence proclamation comes with responsibilities, such as taking control of the new state's public administration. Meeting these tasks requires nascent South Sudan to stand on the following pillars: "political unity, a disciplined military, equitable service delivery and a vibrant Civil Society" (Jok, 2011, p. 1).

This argument gives states the ability to navigate as the symbol of authority. Through this conception, sovereignty becomes the avenue in which states project their political legitimacy and authority. What is intriguing about this is states' autonomy, which defies other authorities and understands sovereign nations as ultimate actors in defining their affairs in the domestic or international scene. Therefore, states are primarily all-powerful within their boundaries. Sovereign states "control of their domestic and foreign policy institutions such as war and diplomacy" (Kayaoglu, 2010, p. 193). In contrast, South Sudan "was born prematurely into a conflict society where fragility is manifested through multiple challenges" (Wassara, 2015, p. 635). It has poor infrastructures, "a volatile political climate, limited capacity for governance, weak state institutions, violent ethnic divisions and an uncertain regional and international political atmosphere" (Jok, 2011, p. 2). What is the cause of fragility is the first question many would ask? Several reasons will be presented to address this question.

This research is moving towards an explanation that the DDR fall short in South Sudan because it was a state-based approach in a situation where the state was at its infancy. Hence, the challenges facing the DDR in South Sudan include building the state and its institutions from scratch and turning ex-insurgent leaders into bureaucrats (Thomas, 2015). So, chaotic violence "in South Sudan should not have come as a surprise after donors sought to build a state without addressing its more profound problems of internal conflict" (Clark, 2014, p. 2). This study argues that South Sudan existed only in sovereign entitlement but lacked a functional capacity to entice or coerce the dominated into obeying the authority of the state. Despite this volatile climate, the DDR initiatives were based on the international community's assumption that building political and economic capacity would help achieve peace and security, thereby neglecting fundamental problems such as nation-building and an ethno-political rivalry (Larson *et al.*, 2013).

The present proliferation of arms across South Sudan is a repetition of a history of violent insubordination of the state. Thus, the world's newest state remained "very much a territory comprising many ethnic groups who see themselves as rivals and not as co-citizens" (Ogunyemi, 2015, p. 12). This chapter will explore further the argument that the main reason South Sudan plunged into civil war after the failure of the DDR is the absence or the limitation of statehood (Wassara, 2002; 2007). The idea of limited statehood resembles but is not equivalent to Migdal's (1988) "weak states" and Jackson's (1990) "quasi-states". In particular, quasi-states differs from fragile statehood. The literature on fragile states is oriented towards developed statehood and the liberal ideal (Rotberg, 2004; 2007). Benchmarks of capable states have been discussed in previous chapters, such as democratic governance (Leibfried and Zürn, 2005). It is one thing to be endowed with sovereignty, and it is another for the state to function as "institutionalised rule with the ability to rule authoritatively" (Weber, 1980, n.p [1921]). It is imperative to say that the "institutionalised rule" denoted a "consolidated statehood", a condition lacking in South Sudanese state as it emerged without "the tools needed to build a sovereign state" (Wassaraa, 2015, p. 635).

My assumption of what Wassaraa referred to above as "the tools needed to build a sovereign state" could range from a civil population that views their government as legitimate, and the South Sudanese state that has stable political and economic institutions. In contrast, South Sudan emerged out of a protracted civil war. While most states do not always govern hierarchically, consolidated states can at least authoritatively make and enforce a collective decision about the use of force. South Sudan had a crisis because its "mode of hierarchical steering remains incomplete as the government cannot cast a consolidated shadow of hierarchy" over violent non-state actors (Risse, 2011, p. 2). This deficiency culminated in the crisis of decentralised internal sovereignty in the hands of multiple violent actors. My thesis uses the crisis of internal sovereignty to argue that while South Sudan maintains rightful entitlement to its sovereignty, it never possessed the legitimacy for superimposing structures. The notion of vertical governance lies in the functions of the state. Even if South Sudan had a monopoly over legitimate means of violence, there would have been questions about how it used that force, whether it is legitimate in the eyes of its citizens.

Whether state control over the use of violence provides security for citizens as a public good, and does so irrespective of political grouping, is a question that can render the idea of a consolidated state open to criticism. Nazi Germany was a consolidated state. Instead of providing collective protection, they used violence to terrorise the population. South Sudan, in contrast, has been described as a violent place where people feared their government (Hutton, 2014). While Hutton reflected on the history of violence in the SPLM/A, he did not link the collapse of DDR to the fear that violence instilled, which caused the groups to deplore the state. Besides, Nyaba (2019, p. 152) stressed that "the current brand of leaders in South

Sudan have shown that they are unable to make claims to represent national leadership". As South Sudan's government have not protected its citizens, ethno-political groups developed a mindset of self-defence (Pugh and Sidhu, 2003). Against this backdrop, widespread rebellions emerged. "We are better off having our Rocket-Propelled Grenade (RPG)", one participant argued (P27/14/12/2017).

This statement reflected the absence of collective protection and the role of multiple armed actors. Those who resisted the DDR believe it jeopardises their socio-political welling and interests, hence use force to undermine the disarmament (Stedman, 1995). One can argue that South Sudan has no overarching system of government to overshadow and violence. This view allows this chapter to emphasise how informal armed structures contributed to the decentralisation of the use of force, thus describing South Sudan as "a country without the state" (Hanzich, 2011, p. 38). This chapter will explain that the failure of DDR was partly due to the dynamics of armed structures that governed different ethno-political regions without any check from a central authority. The transition from peace and independence has not motivated the SPLM/A elites to invest in state institutions that would have allowed them to maintain a higher degree of legitimate power to mitigate violence. Decades of civil war with the North "have resulted in a hyper-militarisation of South Sudan" (Kuntzelman, 2013, p. 106). The "influx of arms has produced security threats wherein civilians settle disputes by the gun instead of in a court" (2013, p. 106).

Hence, the lack of a legitimate and functioning authority to control arms has made it impossible to conduct the DDR in South

Sudan. Thus, existing violent ethno-political divisions created varying competing interests, which underpinned the proliferation of arms. In this case, the South Sudanese state is unable to carry out the essential duties of a state, and it has been ranked as the most fragile state since its inception. Such state, in the view of this project, has the legal accoutrements of sovereign statehood, but the nation-state formation has disintegrated, and the state's capability to govern vertically in its sovereign territory has failed. My project argues that there is a divide between the state's authority and OAGs (Abdel Salam and De Waal, 2001). These problems influence the behaviour of groups, including their response to the DDR. While scholars have studied the influence of ethnicity on violence, they have limited these studies to an analysis of ethnic manipulation (Horowitz, 1985; Posner, 2005). They did not analyse the unique nature of ethnolinguistic security structures, and their impacts on the DDR.

1.1 South Sudan: A Country without State

In societies with socio-political stability, the state values and authority are enduring. Although stability can be misleading, the prospects for a relative peace could countervail violence. Even with a little persuasion, law enforcement agencies can prevent informal use of force, and that is the idea of a functioning state (Malejacq, 2016). The functioning state is characterised by the existence of cohesive socio-political capacity and is viewed by internal and external actors as legitimate (Hagmann and Péclard, 2010). This study argues that South Sudan emerged as a "state without a country" (Johnson, 2016, p. 16). This emphasises how the legacies of protracted civil war, the enactment of politico-military policies, and political violence present severe challenges. South Sudan faces two challenging tasks: state-building and nation-building. In contextualising these challenges in South Sudan, Johnson (2016) demonstrated the difference between ex-liberation movements who assumed power in Uganda and Eritrea with the SPLM/A.

The difference Johnson presented is that the movement in Uganda, for instance, "entered the government offices of functional post-colonial institutions" (2016, p. 16). Given the institutional platform they inherited, some of these movements have demonstrated the resilience and political stability that prevent non-state actors from shaping or shifting the internal sovereignty and use of force. Throughout the CPA, there was doubt as to whether the South Sudanese government understood the difference between state and state-building and the costs of pursuing one over the other (Deng, 2013). The literature on these two concepts shows a divergence in definitions, but there are contextual emphases. According to Wassara (2013, p. 41; also, Wassara and Kurimoto, 2017) "state-building provides for the construction of functional institutions of control over a defined territory, to hold the monopoly of power over economic, political and social structures". This argument echoes Fukuyama's emphasis that refers to state-building "as the creation of new government institutions and the strengthening of old ones" (2004, p. 18). The above definitions show the focus on institutions.

In the context of South Sudan, however, institutional construction alone cannot address the violent fragmentation of domestic authority. Despite the weakness of public administration, there are socio-economic and political issues which inadvertently provide factions "with opportunities that allow them to shift their sources of power and reinvent themselves at the expense of state centralisation" (Malejacq, 2016, p. 87). Given the functional context of the DDR, a suitable definition of state-building is provided as: "the purposeful action to develop the capacity, institutions and legitimacy of the state in relation to an effective political process for negotiating the mutual demands between state and societal groups" (OECD, 2008, p. 14). The OECD's approach is perhaps better for understanding the challenges of the DDR because it is not based on the mandate of international peacebuilding alone, but also the impact of the intrusiveness of informal armed actors in the political process. This emphasis surpassed perception of state-building by focusing on strengthening state capacity to rule and its legitimacy as a state through service delivery.

With that being said, Wassara, (2013) analysed the policy development of post-war and secession South Sudan and categorised those policies according to short, medium, and long-term priorities. In the interim period, South Sudan planned to focus on the humanitarian crisis resulting from the swelling number of refugees returning after the referendum. This plan was aimed at public infrastructures like hospitals and schools, to boost economic activities. Institution of other state features like an interim constitution and security laws formed part of the short-term priority. The medium plan was based on economic recovery and political stability. Finally, the long-term strategy was the formulation of "development visions based on sustainable trajectories of growth" (Omondi, 2013, p. 2). In the current setting, whatever was envisioned as 'sustainable trajectories of growth' has not been achieved. There are many reasons to cite South Sudan's continuing struggle with war, but it "appears to verify that the subject of promoting ethnic cohesion was excluded in the priorities for development planning of South Sudan" (Omondi, 2013, p. 3).

Thus, the priorities were lacking a strategy for nation-building. Nation-building "is a process of socio-political development, which, ideally—usually over a longer historical span—allows initially loosely, linked communities to become a common society with a nation-state corresponding to it" (Hippler, 2005, p. 6). This process includes instruments such as "economic integration, political centralisation, creation of common interest, and common citizenship" (2005, p. 6). Similarly, Call referred to "nation-building as actions undertaken usually by national actors, to forge a sense of common nationhood, usually to overcome ethnic differences; usually to counter alternate sources of identity and loyalty" (2007, p. 3). These definitions imply the construction of a collective identity among different ethno-political identities that, at present, see themselves as distinct and political rivals. This process is easier said than done, but some researchers have offered simple solutions. Dobbins *et al.,* argue that "nation-building always requires the integration of national and international effort" (2007, p. 22). Other than Germany and Japan, Dobbins cited no successful cases of nation-building in situations similar to South Sudan.

Although the German and Japanese cases were different from South Sudan, they are still used to set the standards for post-conflict transformation. While the decisive intervention and responsibility taken by the international community is vital, its capacity is often limited, and the bulk of the responsibility for fostering the national identity and unity still lies with the states in question. Aware of this role, Jok Madut presented some factors that would threaten South Sudan's transformation into statehood: tribalism, nepotism, corruption, exclusion on ethnic bases and the "lack of a respectable constitution that spells out a clear social contract between government and citizens" (2011, p. 4). In his assessment, the ethnic composition was going to "be a liability" for war if it is not managed (Jok, 2011, p. 3). Jok was not pre-empting war over power relations. But he sensed that becoming a nation-state will expose the gap in ethnic differences (Stedman, 1997). In the following chapter, I will explore the function of ethno-political leaders in instigating violence and explain how the framing of one group as enemy led to mobilisation for war.

This strategy is a detriment to the DDR when political war and conflict may be part of a greater struggle for survival or recognition. Jok (2011) sensed that the war in South Sudan was avoidable, but when it occurred, the nascent state had no strategy for preventing it. This argument raised questions as to why it was difficult to prevent the war, and the answer lies with the SPLM's political history of violence. As one would expect, guerrilla fighters who spent most of their lives waging war were not necessarily the ones best suited for the task of governing South Sudan. Johnson argues that while many liberation movements "had been governing liberated areas, these were still military administrations and not political governments based on at least some principles of the rule of law" (2016, p. 16). She attributes the troubles of South Sudan to the fact that the SPLM/A had never developed a system capable of preventing ethnic strife. This emphasises that the SPLM elites in the post-secession period posed as bureaucrats but functioned like insurgents. These informalized politics are the antithesis of a rule-based system of governance. This project argues that a country without a state is in a far more precarious position than a fragile state.

It is a situation where a lack of capacity is faced with the absence of nationalism. South Sudan is comprised of multi-ethnic identities, which have not adjusted to the role of the state. These identities were marshalled to war due to the "presence of an aggressive and often predatory other, be it the central government in the North or a rival faction in the South that serves to unify those under attack" (Frahm, 2012, p. 2). Fighting a common enemy was essential in defining the South Sudanese unity pre-independence. When South Sudan seceded, Deng emphasised the lack of a common enemy and wondered "what will hold it together now that the North-South divide longer serves to mute intraregional differences [and] ethnic fragmentation" (Frahm, 2012, p. 2; citing Deng; 2005, p. 65). The reflection from this argument is that "if exclusion from power and relative resource deprivation serves to heighten the cultural identity solidarity of subordinate groups" (Markakis 1999, p. 75), then the demise of "Northern oppression may strain the sense of togetherness in South Sudan" (Frahm, 2012, p. 2).

As one of the world's weakest countries, Frahm concluded that "South Sudan is not in a position to buy loyalty with hand-outs to the population" (Frahm, 2012, p. 2). This thesis states that the success of the DDR is based on public trust and loyalty to the state. If the state (South Sudan) is not able to secure loyalty from a group or provide them with security, the failure of the DDR needs to be measured along with the absence of state and institutional deficiency. While scholars of African politics explain the problem of South Sudan from the perspective of collapsed states, this project argues the situation is more akin to an absence of state (Kalyvas and Kocher, 2007). This context fitted South Sudan because it shares political authority with other violent structures. Thus, the fact that South Sudan remained delimited by non-state armed groups' exercise of parallel authority, is neither an accident nor indicative of wickedness inherent within those groups. Such a situation is not peculiar to South Sudan but shared among states where liberation movements came to power "claiming to represent the interest of all people and a total monopoly in advocating the public interest" (Melber, 2009a, p. 453; also, 2009b).

This problem started with a myopic sense of legitimacy based on the 'dominant syndrome' (Bratton and Masunungure, 2008) and militarised operation that conjured perceptions of state repression. As a contingent act of a fearful group, the state-led DDR can be seen as illegal retribution enforcement that must be resisted (Rodney, 1972). That reaction to the DDR is attributed to the "psychological fixedness" that permeates society's attitudes towards self-security (Reed, 2016). Group fixedness to self-security led to the withdrawal of trust in the state's protection. This context created the resilience of an informal security logic, according to which armed actors shape the use of force. While such a situation tends to carry on from civil wars, it is more noticeable in South Sudan (Jok, 2017). The notion of post-war state-building is simple: a stronger state is expected to monopolise the use of force. To date, the role of state capacity to maintain peace has been theorised narrowly, by overlooking the relationship between institutional qualities and the cause of war. In an orthodox institutionalist outlook, South Sudan is a failed state.

1.2 A Nation Challenged: Ethno-Political Loyalty Places Tribe before the Country

As South Sudan received swift recognition for its claim to nationhood because of the promulgation of its membership in the U.N., there were immediate challenges awaiting the nascent state, among them nation-building. Frahm emphasises this particular predicament: "having never existed as a sovereign state and with its citizens being a minority group in Sudan, collective action among the South Sudanese has historically been shaped in response to the hostile nation-building pursued by various governments in the North" (2012, p. 22). One participant echoed this view that: "at one point, we disagreed along ethnic lines, but the SPLM/A was the hope we had" (P30/01/03/2018). The rebel leaders were there to serve a directive function. These directive functions are presented in three phases: "diagnostic, which includes the formulation of the problem facing the collective, prescriptive, which entails the formulation of the responses and actions, and mobilisation, which involves garnering support for political action" (Tucker, 1981, p. 15).

Thus, the SPLM/A leaders could mobilise the Southern Sudanese for violence because they have a framing function. As cited in Chapter One, the SPLM/A sought to change the face of politics and policies of the regime in the North (Lesch, 1998), whereby the descent into the war was described as "a natural reaction of the oppressed" (Garang, 1984, n.p.). The SPLM leaders diagnose the problem and prescribe action, thus formulating the discourse upon which they built the solidarity and resulting mobilisation for violence. This argument hinted that a "unity of purpose" was an invaluable asset that cooled internal division among South/ern Sudanese during their war with the North. Therefore, the 'external threat' framework was influential in constructing South Sudanese political entity (Sharkey, 2008). With that, Southern leaders were able to execute the north-south war "because they have an implementing function – they have power over support for an organisation, and thus have control over resources for action" (Brosche and Honlung, 2017, p. 201). We can describe mobilisation as "the process in which individuals are motivated and recruited to take action for a common goal" (Gurr, 2000, p. 74).

Given the fact that Southern leaders framed the North as the oppressor, they were able to create binary oppositions, formulated in "us versus them" terms. This characterisation was meant to construct an affiliation toward the SPLM/A. To use the context of collective action against the North, the SPLM/A presented itself as a protector of the oppressed, and thus "provide[s] collective incentives through appeals to identity solidarity which will benefit the entire group" (Olson 1965, p. 51). Despite these efforts, in any situation where a larger unit of base measurement is used, such a situation is still dealing with social and political fragmentation. It would have been significant during the CPA to understand how South Sudanese framing of the North was not only crucial in shaping a climate conducive for war but would also lead to a massive armament. Instead, the CPA did not provide a retrospective analysis of this armament, or the legacy of civil war (Rogier, 2005). The CPA and its post-war processes insufficiently account for the eventualities of the internal fragmentation and factionalism in South Sudan.

As the fear of the North diminished, Southern ethnicities descended into a void of state and feared each other. It was with great difficulty that a region like South Sudan, "emerging from decades of war and conflict, could undertake the task of statehood and nationhood" (Nyaba, 2019, p. 14). Second, the liberation leaders still suffered from war fatigue and mindset. Third, the culture of peace and state as a supreme authority, in terms of political institutions, had yet to permeate the populations. Besides, the art of government centred on the rule of law would be a challenge for the SPLM cadres. Some leaders, now in charge of South Sudan, entered the war of liberation at a tender age, in terms of political maturity. This situation would not have been an issue if the SPLM had organised itself in a way that provided development to its leaders. The immediate task of SPLM/A requires skills different from the ones they would have had when they inherited the power in South Sudan. Peacetime sensibilities are different from the war of liberation. When South Sudan's government fell short of becoming the coordinator of societal affairs, ethno-political friction began and led to boiling points that propelled South Sudan into another war.

Despite having fought together, the power struggle between the Dinka and the Nuer inflamed inter-ethnic conflict (Stringham and Forney, 2017). The idea of "Dinka domination" predated the current problems. It goes back to the first Southern Sudanese transitional government following the signing of the Addis Ababa Agreement (AAA) in 1972. The leaders who split from the main SPLM/A in the late 1990s fought for control, citing Dinka dominance, in a process akin to warlordism. Rather than defining what a warlord is, this project focuses on the impact of the mindsets on the DDR by arguing that the framing of the Dinka as the oppressor serves as a strategy for mobilisation and resistance to the disarmament in South Sudan. While the securitisation of identities does not always result in war, it became a catalyst for leaders who mobilise for war. Without a central authority, informal systems substitute for state authority by occupying niches, where the central government is inadequate, and discharged authority (Pendle 2015).

While several academics have explored rebel-civilian interactions and how legitimation of violence impacts civilian views of rebels (Arjona, 2016; Terpstra and Frerks, 2017), this chapter expands the debate that the SPLM/A factions used citizens discontents to wage war. If the fear of the North muted ethnic conflict among South

Sudanese, there was nothing to prevent them from disintegration now that the North was no longer a threat. This process leads to "oligopolies of violence, buoyed by a fluctuating number of partly competing and partly cooperating actors" (Mehler, 2004, p. 540). These groups are divided further into sub-groups or sections (Stubbs, 1934; Stubbs and Morison, 1938). Despite years of civil war with the North, there is a general perception that such unity of purpose has failed to forge the unity of Southern ethnic groups into a nation-state due to a lack of social capital and cohesion. Putnam describes social capital "as informal and organised reciprocal networks of trust", (Putnam, 1993, p. 170), while Fukuyama (2001, p. 7), defines it as "informal norms that promote co-operation between individuals and groups". An ethnic group's social capital involves specific socio-political and economic resources accessible by individuals through their membership in that group (Bankston and Zhou, 2002).

Hence, an ethnic group's social capital is "found in the closed system of social networks inherent in the structure of relations between persons and among persons within a collectivity" (Bankston and Zhou, 2002, p. 824). This social capital is not a solitary unit. However, it is characterised by its function. While social capital has various characteristics, it encompasses various facet of socio-political constructs. It enables a specified action within the social structure Coleman defines action "as occurring within a social setting and is rooted in the structure of social relations" (1988, p. 98). In this case, social capital existing in political interactions is significant in "creating human capital" (1988, p. 116). In sociological theory, social capital is different from human capital because it does not focus on the requisite for formal political organisation. Instead, its lies in a shared feeling that enables "groups to set up institutions that members can access" (Coleman, 1988, p. 98). Swift (1996) has noted social capital among the core bases for survival in ethnic settings. Firm beliefs in social, cultural connection and fears make it even more likely for ethnic groups to build exclusive political and security settings.

This mindset contrasts with settlement approaches that emphasise the importance of a state. Jok Madut, (2010; 2017) considers resources within ethnic-political identities in South Sudan as the most significant factor in improving the chances of mobility. For the elites in South Sudan, the tribal/ethnic group can be the process by which one competitor obtain political and moral support. As stated before, ethnic groups make available certain social resources that armed youths and elites can access and utilise. One of the main problems challenging peace and disarmament in South Sudan is larger established groups' distinct political and security institutions, which provide a ready-made military support for competing elites. Warner argues that "such groups had repeatedly requested formal or observer status for the IGAD peace process and the failure to accommodate them meant that the CPA firmly entrenched parties with no democratic legitimacy in power" (Warner, 2013, p. 40). The effect on these armed groups was evident in the war between the SPLM/A and its adversaries in the south during, and after the war of liberation.

Following the secession in 2011, the state institutions were built on an implicit intransigence, an intensity of ethnic divisions and political violence. To manage ethno-political conflict, the DDR must come from an authority that is trusted by armed groups. The GoSS is not trusted nor regarded as legitimate by those who oppose it, and with that, the tendency to mobilise around an exclusionist group grows because the insecurity is widespread. Regardless of the increasing acknowledgment of the immense influence of social capital in violence, an understanding of how it enhances informal structures, which in turn, undermined DDR, is inadequately researched. For years, the international community had striven to build institutions after the CPA until when South Sudan became independent in 2011(The World Bank, 2011). That ambitious task proved too difficult because an attempt to facilitate political dialogue and DDR did not overcome the mistrust that characterises the exclusive nature of groups' political and security structures. To some extent, it is an epitome of a poorly understood trend of competing structures.

The challenges are propelled by the developing role of armed structures and local authorities in fostering local and ethnicities forms of political order and security (Lyons, 2002a; 2002b). Whether the informal mosaic of ethno-political authorities that have arisen in South Sudan constitutes nation or state-building is arguable. Conversely, the inadequacy of top-down DDR to prevent violence should not hide the success of local systems of governance within South Sudanese societies, although such governance is not occurring in South Sudan now. The intention of this argument is not to describe parallel systems operating across South Sudan. Instead, it is to study the link between these informal authorities and increases arms proliferation. It appears that these armed groups have realised the importance of informal structures, given that they have played a crucial part in the battles against the North and factional wars (Idris, 2014). Despite the security role played by these groups, they have also become the critical impediment to the DDR (Turse, 2016). The rise of these self-protective groups emerged from the SPLM/A's mistakes. The SPLM become involved in governance in liberated areas (Terpstraa and Frerks, 2017).

Initiated in 1994, the SPLM/A's *Civil Authority of New Sudan* (CANS), descended into many troubles, similar to legitimacy problems facing the incumbent government in Khartoum at the time. As the rebels "raised the expectations of civilians" living in their liberated areas, the question of distribution and representation emerged, something SPLM/A leaders were not keen to emphasise, but that was not the only problem (Branch and Mampilly, 2005, p. 7). A military-style of governance inexorably permeates the CANS. Some argue that "despite SPLA claims to the contrary, the military still had power; there is a "fusion" of powers in the SPLA" (Johnson, 1998, p. 67), CANS' administrative system was not democratic, but "rather a militaristic top-down approach" (Riehl, 2001, p. 11). The organisational legitimacy of CANS was not through public consent, but it was engendered through a military means. An "organisational legitimacy refers to the extent to which the array of established cultural accounts provides explanations for [an organisation's] existence" (Meyer and Scott, 1983, p. 201). Even if the SPLM was relying on coercion to implement what some described as a "jungle law", the movement was unyielding in efforts to demilitarise its politics and gain legitimacy to increase population compliance.

However, some problematic issues remained unaddressed, and they are still affecting the DDR today (Nyaba, 2019). First, the costs for SPLA relying on coercion is high. Based on fear and defence, the effects of violence inflicted on one group by the supposed authority last as long as the victims' recalls. Second, because it was a military installation, and still, by and large, a rebel in government, the issue of political equity remained unanswered. Additionally, unanswered were questions regarding how the armed groups' forms of legitimation and their mutually opposing interests affected compliance to the CPA-and post-secession DDR in South Sudan. While political leaders' systematic exploitation of informal armies exacerbates armament and the arms race, the role of informal structures and inter-ethnic "violence has not been part of the mainstream process and dialogue around political solutions or the DDR" (Wild, Jok and Patel, 2018, p. 2). The standard DDR policy imposes a bureaucratic order without engaging these hybrid systems.

Peacebuilders must know that "the state is not given, but forged and remade through processes of negotiations, contestations and bricolage by local, national and transnational actors" (Hagman and Péclard 2010, p. 544). This research sees the shortcoming of the disarmament DDR as a lack of incorporation of competing governance mechanisms in policy design and the informal structures that prevented the emergence of a centralised use of force (Heger and

Salehyan, 2007). Where there are no alternatives to informal structures, the DDR will not rescue the situation. In this case, the depleted relationship between hostile structures and the DDR work in opposite directions (Kohnert, 2010; Hoffman and Graham, 2009). The context-based structures of conflict have substantial effects for procedures that seek to enhance development and peace. If armed political factions are involved in governance as they have in South Sudan, their consciousness of the issues of politics and security become self-centred (Diamond, 2002; Schedler, 2001).

Persson's *et al.*, (1997, p. 164) emphasise that "if men were angels, no government would be necessary, and if angels were to govern men, neither external nor internal controls on government would be necessary". This dilemma is paramount in South Sudan. De Waal (2014) has shown how those in charge of the system and the system itself could not be trusted for its lack of extra guarding proceeding from legitimacy bestowed on the state and mature institutions to control the governed, and the state. The South Sudanese state was created to hold a legitimate monopoly of violence. However, this objective resides in the realm of wishful thinking. While the South Sudanese state, in its own self-interest, may protect some ethno-political groups, such security or protection is inadequate, highly unreliable, and often nothing but a mockery of security. As will be argued in Chapter Five, the security system in South Sudan remained a fragile system unable to achieve prescribed duties, which was also complicit in crimes against the very public the state was duty-bound to protect. Preoccupied with the unsuitable model of liberal peace, the

DDR operators failed to apply the precautionary principles cited in Chapter Three, principles that are regularly misapplied in the recent intervention in South Sudan.

The hybrid model holds that, if a DDR causes great permanent harm notwithstanding a lack of contextual understanding, those who support the DDR should shoulder the burden. If we look at the DDR in the Republic of South Sudan, the failure might lie with some "genuine struggle" for survival (Richards, 2002). Thus, any attempt to build a pyramid model of security undercuts in-country "tools for political transformation, whereby local and national peacemakers work to resolve their conflicts through the creation of joint instruments" (Siebert, 2014, p. 25). This criticism inspired the hybrid theory's argument that all state-based methods have political implications for the DDR because they do not focus on the "opposing tenets and legitimacies" (Di Maggio and Powell, 1991, p. 267). The conflicting relationship between different armies and systems does not require good institutions to control behaviours within the state. This fluid political interaction "occurs when non-state actors engage in forms of organised violence and have the capacity to provide public goods under-provided by public authority, allowing them to emerge as legitimate alternative 'centres of social organisation" (Hall and Biersteker, 2002, p. 17).

What causes the hybridity is the lack of appropriate socio-political conditions upon which groups base their security (Ansorg, 2017). This hints that the DDR in South Sudan did not create a security system to enhance peace and trust-building. In international relations theory, there are at least four drivers of mistrust: "the security dilemma; the challenge of peaceful/defensive self-images; ambiguous symbolism; and ideological fundamentalism" (Wheeler, 2012, p. 3). In inter-state relations, this security uncertainty "can be overcome in a way that promotes cooperation, and even trust, mitigating or transcending the international uncertainty that can otherwise severely inhabit inter-states cooperation" (Keating and Wheeler, 2013, p. 56). These scholars argue that inter-state security dilemmas can be redressed through political alliance or cooperation. This security cooperation is impractical in South Sudan's domestic context, where the inner legitimacy of the state resembled what Hobbes' (1906) described as the state of nature. Thus, the resistance to the DDR is based on the dilemma caused by the state's failure to meet its functional roles.

Irrespective of these challenges, the disarmament programme in South Sudan was approached in a way that requires the disarmament of one-party, and the arming of the other, which is the state. The basis for disarming the non-state actors and other loose groups in the post-war context is built on the Realist argument that states are the paramount actors bestow with sovereignty and authority. While the prospects for effective DDR and state-building appeared to be useful in some countries, they are bleak in South Sudan. This project argues that the post-war disarmament and SSR programmes have constantly ignored the existence of functional and violent equivalents to a fragile state in South Sudan. South Sudan had violent systems of governance without government, and they accumulate arms and armies in the absence of a strong, and centralised state hierarchy. During the fieldwork conducted for this project, the author of the thesis identified functional equivalents to the hierarchy of the state, as factional ethno-political armies and will discuss the extent they impeded the state monopoly of force.

As mentioned by one participant: "I do not care whether they are government soldiers. What I know they were Dinka in uniform". He added that their group resisted the DDR "because it leaves them vulnerable" (P12/04/09/2017). This participant does not see the DDR as the way of ensuring the legitimate state control over the use of force, but a tool for strengthening a supposed position of the Dinka. This suspicion affected DDR. The question worth asking is whether these fears are warranted, and the response is affirmative, those fears are real. This project will show in next chapter that South Sudanese's government has not empowered diverse identities and citizens to participate in governance, or to "stand for election and hav[e] freedom of expression towards any government policy" (Rousseau, 1913, p. 60). The failure to cultivate "self-rule", whereby all citizens are involved in deciding what is best for their community, hinders public trust in their government. Without socio-political, economic and security parity, as it is the case in South Sudan, ordinary citizens become competitors as the central authority disintegrates. In South Sudan, however, it is not because the army is a Dinka vehicle of domination.

It is because the state is incapable of rendering collective services; hence, each individual or group has developed a mentality of self-help. Therefore, resistance to the DDR is the signal that the groups are acting in self-defence. The literature on the state monopoly of violence, upon which the disarmament is based, has not focused on informal armies and their modes of socio-political coordination and the involvement in the design and application of public security. Second, those who militated against the DDR have an offensive motivation in mind: they seek to change the existing situation to their advantage. This is because the South Sudanese, not just competing political elites, but also ethnic identities, doubted each other's motives and intentions, and it is the failure of the CPA to mandate inclusive trust-building. Trust-building efforts seek to delimit the levels of mutual mistrust and hostility, such as through Kydd's model of Costly Signalling (Kydd, 2005; 2007). Neither the North-South conflict nor the post-secession transitions met these conditions. Without an understanding of informal structures' influence within the peripheries, DDR strategy remains inadequate, regardless of the efforts directed towards its success.

As a result, the DDR became an impossible task in South Sudan as the country's socio-political system became captive to OAGs. One prominent leader confirmed this argument, asking "before we became a country, what were we? We were just a bunch of tribal groups who shared the same region" (P17/04/09/2017). Further, this participant highlights that "there was nothing national about these groups to unify them apart from their collective fear of the North". This argument reflects the problem of 'amalgamation', including security. It suggests that South Sudan is built on "socio-political crises and paradoxes'; thus 'an arena of tribal groups bunched together in one territory" (Berlin, 2001). This situation hinders the DDR because ethnic loyalty comes with a fragmented system of governance that incubates conflict-breeding elements like tribalism and power struggle. South Sudan suffers from socio-political fragmentation (Williamson, 2006). The problems of the DDR are not the existence of armed groups' per se, but it is their behaviours during the interim periods and pre-2011, which are cause for concern.

As armed groups fragment and coalesce, given the situation, that behaviour obstructs true state-building. While national loyalty and nationalism are equally as problematic, it is the legitimacy of the state as a bearer of the means of force that became unacceptable in South Sudan (El-Affendi, 2001). In this situation, the DDR became worthless, as it could not buy loyalty with economic/political handouts. My thesis suggests that local defence systems merge from reactions to the imminent insecurity and that the rise of self-defence mentalities come with effects. As noted by a participant, "when the conflict occurs, it is always along tribal lines" (P5/04/08/2017). This assertion reflects a divided society where political identity lies in ethnic groups. This attitude repels a trusting relationship and inner certainty that often sustained or re-created rebel groups (Ruzicka and Wheeler, 2010). Because of the close interconnections between the South Sudanese army and rebel factions, DDR is not merely a military issue but goes to the heart of the dynamics of conflict.

1.3 Internal Uncertainty

Uncertainty in the civil war situations refers to the difficulty facing the state in determining obedience, known as conformity, to contracted political and security covenants. It is a problem of 'hidden action': the difficulty in monitoring the activities and behaviours of the internal agency to which the task, such as the DDR, has been allocated (Arrow–Debreu, 1985). In fragmented states, DDR does not ensure what Arrow–Debreu described as contingent contracts that would make indemnification rendered by the process of the DDR conditional. In this situation, the state's weakness, and fragmentation of its security systems, and also the instability of the armed groups, do not allow the creation of the real-world political and security contracts. In the absence of the real-world political and security contracts, there is nothing to make would-be disarmed Ex-Combatants confirmed to the DDR. Enlisting for the DDR dependent upon the occurrence of public protection. However, it is also challenging because it increases the prospect for an opportunistic warring group to evade contractually assigned tasks, such as to disarm and disband (Williamson, 1981).

Second, the inflow and outflow of arms and fighters' thwart efforts to write political contracts that provide acceptable and compatible incentives to both warring parties and their subjects (Anderson and Rolandsen, 2014). These problems are worse in South Sudan, where the quality of outputs by the state is overshadowed by its own inadequacies to meet sovereign responsibilities and keep resentful parties in check. At that point, a state-centric analysis of how the DDR is the solution to the conflict is no longer sufficient. This project argues that the use of violence cannot be perceived from a monolithic context, that is, as the prerogative of a formal system when that country is not in control of a sovereign territory. The projection of the state as an omnipresent and rational entity seemed to conflate state failure with the lack of the system and state-building with institution-building (Herring and Rangwala, 2006). Thus, the international community is confused by theories that offer ambiguous prescriptions for designing of the DDR in places where the security of the groups is conducted in uncertainty.

This institutional approach leaves the DDR unguided when it comes to solving the security problems of the violent non-state hierarchies. As South Sudan experienced a protracted war, political mobilisation has been occurring along conflict lines (Paris, 2004). Violent non-state hierarchies emphasised differences rather than similarities to recruit fighters and sowed fear in them, to the detriment of the DDR. The failure to tailor the DDR to the situation, where the use of force has never lain with states, may result in the building of a fragile state that is unable to monopolise the force (Baker, 2008). While domination of force does not exist as such, resistance to the DDR affords a mechanism for OAGs to increase their political power. Thus, a group that internalises its sources of defence and external supply of arms increases its security relative to other groups. Ironically, preferred methods for self-defence undermine the very nature of security NSAs need as violence spreads. Thus, understanding the status-quo of OAGs requires a recognition of the rules governing their use (Kettl, 2009; Ikenberry, 2000). The merit of this argument is that political adjustment alone cannot put South Sudan on a sustainable violence-reducing path.

That task is impossible in South Sudan because the DDR faces complex political emergencies. The South Sudanese state does not tower over its subjects, and yet the DDR was conceived as if the rights and obligations are aggregated to the state. This narrow conceptualisation may lead to an artificial construct of the state institutions, but disarmament and demobilisation may not prevail unless the state finds ways of translating its raw power into acceptable power. Determining what signifies acceptable power requires assessing the salient features of grievances in South Sudan. That assessment is essential in elaborating how these features of grievances allowed ethno-political groups or factions to deride the government as incapable or illegitimate; therefore, frustrating its attempt to disarm them. While such signals of violence among South Sudanese were excused in the CPA to meet the schedule for a turbulent transition, the new rules of the game were deferred in South Sudan. The SPLM, with its unyielding, top-down system, seized power and wielded it arbitrarily.

This practice led to the marginalisation of some groups who resorted to the use of force. "When people rebel, they do so because their needs are not met" (P21/21/07/2017), stated one participant. For state-builders, these those rebels are meant to be co-opted. However, the marginal groups see the government as a branch of liberation cadres from the Dinka majority who dominated the war of liberation, and because that structure ascended to the government, it replicated an ethnically dominated state (Staniland, 2012; Eke, 1995). Those who feel excluded resisted the DDR and raised questions about the effectiveness of the DDR in the absence of broader state reform (Barnett, 2006). This perception of delegitimising South Sudanese state in the eyes of many OAGs and leading to persistence of violence. The DDR failed due to the absence of a state of "inner justification" (Hall, 2013). Hence, the shifting front lines produce violence as a means of production and predation. This situation renders the simplistic state-building paradigm problematic because it presents one-size-fits-all solutions (Chandler, 2010).

1.4 Problems of Legitimacy and Inner Justification of State in South Sudan

While state-building is interconnected to the state, there is a slight reflection on the nature or type of the state, which is frequently assumed as a given construct, that requires no further re-evaluation (Hameiri 2010; 2013; Bellina *et al.*, 2009; Sørensen, 2001). The numerous functions of modern states may be divided into three categories: security, representation of citizens and welfare of those citizens. These are the ideals on which all post-war peacebuilding efforts are based. Irrespective of whether these responsibilities are carried out directly by the state or not, the perception is that the state remains ultimately in charge. The sovereign state is described as "the image of a coherent, controlling organisation in a territory, which is a representation of the people bounded by that territory" (Migdal, 2001, p. 15). This argument assumes that South Sudan's capacity to ensure the public welfare could be built but does not consider that political institutions and society are constructively and firmly interconnected.

If state legitimacy is defined descriptively, it refers to an individual or group's beliefs about the justness of the state authority.

Here, the political legitimacy of the South Sudanese state cannot just be about the righteousness of political organisations and the decision-making about the use of force, but the policies made for the benefit of the entire population. That has never been the view of the South Sudanese towards their nascent state (Warner, 2016). The South Sudanese state is depicted as a Khartoum under different flag: "South Sudanese had high expectations for their country and were very eager to have a free state where they can express views without any interference. Unfortunately, what they see was the opposite of what they had desired. The state is highly corrupt and poorly managed" (P16/03/08/2017). While the political legitimacy of the South Sudanese state cannot be taken for granted, there are more questions than answers when it comes to how the rulers sanctioned the sovereign power of the state. If the SPLM was a guerrilla dictatorship, as cited in the introduction, one would expect that the South Sudanese state may have a statutory power to rule, issue instructions and, perhaps, to implement these orders using forcible means.

However, those rights have been challenged violently because the government has not demonstrated legitimate political authority or fulfilled its political obligations. Indeed, Herbst (2000, p. 134) contends that "one of the most common patterns of authority in Africa is for states to control their political cores but [have] highly differentiated control over the outlying areas". As a result, the absence of governance outside major towns is not an issue as such. The problems correlated with inadequate governance become dire when the masses start to call on the state for services, including protection. Centeno (2002, p. 8) contended that "many of the deaths produced by political violence have resulted from the inability of the state to impose its authority definitively and permanently". While the definition of the state makes it seem the public must obey its authority indefinitely, it is the deliverability of services that affect how people respond to its demands. This argument separated state function from its normative account of legitimacy. Gurr (1970, p. 235) stated that "if dissident coercive control is substantially less than the regime's coercive control in both scope and degree, dissidents are not likely to be able to organise and sustain an internal war".

As mentioned earlier, the South Sudanese state is not powerful relative to the various rebel groups. Thus, the public commitments towards state monopoly of force arise only if further conditions hold, including collective security. De Waal (2017) blamed this condition for the failure of the DDR in South Sudan because the SA in the CPA and after the secession "were determined by a combination of the leaders' calculations over their internal power base along with their expectations of ongoing or anticipated armed conflicts" (p. 180). Given this condition, relations between the government and most groups, mainly non-Dinka identities, have been problematic. The rise of a supposedly ethno-political dictatorship hinders the descriptive meaning of legitimacy in South Sudan where political groups have described their state as a replica of the oppressive Northern style of government. These armed actors reacted in defiance towards the DDR as they protested the incapability of the state and opposing the legitimacy that discounts any recourse to normative principles of legitimacy and legitimisation (Mommsen, 1989).

In Weber's view, "the basis of every system of authority, and correspondingly of every kind of willingness to obey, is a belief, a belief by virtue of which persons exercising authority are lent prestige" (1964, p. 382). The question is, what happens when a state is too divided and fragile to carry out the above functions. Where would the state gain its legitimacy when citizens and non-state groups feared their own state? These questions problematise the state's legitimacy. Weber differentiates three primary bases of legitimacy, referred to as the recognition both of a state's "authority and of the need to obey the state's commands" (1964, p. 382). In that case, legitimacy is "an important explanatory category for social science because faith in a social order produces social regularities that are more stable than those that result from self-interest or from habitual rule-following" (Weber, 1964, p. 124). In contrary to this emphasis, the normative legitimacy of the state and its rulers implies some scale of inner justification; an emphasis on whether a political system has political obligations towards their dependents (Rawls, 1993).

On a commonly held alternative stance, legitimacy of state/government is attached to the justness of political authority. South Sudan may be an effective illegitimate state. If the authority to govern and to be obeyed depended on meeting public interests, South Sudanese state failed that obligation. As long they meet these needs, state or informal systems are authoritative. As argued in previous chapters, South Sudan constituted to have political spaces where the state failed to consolidate authority. It means that the post-secession South Sudanese state maintains what is described as "de jure sovereignty [rightful entitlement] but no longer possess the right to the means of violence or the legitimacy for superimposing de facto authority" (Lilyblad, 2014, p. 75). Nevertheless, within these ethno-political areas, it is probable to observe the state-based rules of organisations, such as the tribal governing system without the actual government (Raz, 1986). Legitimate authority assigned by the independence of South Sudan does not create political obligations (Dworkin, 1986). This is because the South Sudanese, "have not transitioned from anything", they are stuck in the "ethnic setting, and the guerrilla mentality" (P30/21/12/2018).

In this sense, the state is not a given, nor are the institutional concentrations of power synonymous with legitimacy (King and Kendall, 2003). The entrenching of informal armies and authorities in South Sudan mean that legitimacy comprises, not in accomplishing normative provisions of the state, but in believing in its legitimacy of the state (Cox, 1983; 1987). What arises in this situation are competing political theatres where formal and informal authorities traverse, and often contradict each other violently (South, 2018). This situation requires peacebuilders "to develop greater context-sensitivity and to move away from the idea of a single model of the state rooted in the Westphalian tradition" (Jarstad and Belloni, 2012, p. 4). The resistance to the disarmament lies with the question of competing legitimacies. Like Weber's definition of the state, Schuppert argues that informal structures like ethnic armies "rests on three monopolies: 'legitimate violence, taxes, and legislation'" (2013, p. 65). South Sudan's armed structures are involved in these realms. Thus, Bozus (2013, p. 27) calls for a better understanding of the situation "where the authority of the state and more non-state actors overlap".

Bozus sees this as a way of convincing a self-protecting group to join the DDR. These arguments were not applied in South Sudan where there is a limited statehood, and where the state is 'weak and subordinate' (Clapham, 1996, p. 140). The entire system hinges on a loosely confederated nationalism where there is never a reflexive rationalisation of inter-ethnic relations. An analysis of South Sudan's security trajectories must be seen through the role played by non-state actors. Scholars critical of state-based DDR contend that 'the state control' has programmed practitioners to think "it is possible to conduct state-building operations from the outside without entering the contested sphere of nation-building" (Lemay-Hébert, 2009, p. 21). While the overall interjectory of state approaches is positive, the idea that the state may alone use force is hypocritical where the state is absent or not trusted. Legitimacy depends less on the theoretical principle and more on the inward functions of states. Thus, any talk of DDR must contextualise ex-fighters' doubt in the government's "ability to share resources and provide services" (Hutton, 2014, p. 11).

This perception of dominance by excluded elites caused friction, which increased to boiling point in 2013. As the war resumed, South Sudan disintegrated. This readjustment of priorities complicated the political relationship required to control the informal use of force.

Commenting on this point, Chandler (2012) argues that DDR depends on how the structures of the groups and politics of the emerging states are read. These groups must voluntarily subscribe to the state, and in doing so, move away from their ethnic loyalties. It is this problem that Samatar and Samatar (2008, p. 4) discuss when they redefine "the parameters of the state debate", explaining political and economic debacles in Africa as caused by "the self-inscribed inability of the state". They found it sensible to be cautious of those self-inscribed inabilities. If the state were part of the problem, Samatar and Samatar argued that strengthening it cannot produce a sustainable solution because the engrained limits of authority "place the state on the margins of a political theory" (2008, p. 4). This analysis derived from the belief that "economic and political issues are better understood through other lenses than those provided by theories of the state" (Hyden, 1996, p. 30).

This thesis argues that the idea that peace depends on the efficacy of the state ignores the idea that there is no "violence without disharmonies" (Knopf, 2016). There are three contexts in which to view South Sudan: post-rebellion politics, organisation of institutions and loyalty. The SPLM's cadres bring the credibility of liberation with them, and the credibility of individual leaders (De Waal, 2014). While emerging guerrillas appeared to be in control, their governments risk being unregulated, thus "promoting policies that may not be compatible" with the transitional system (O'Leary, 2010, p. 9). Hence, the governing systems enacted in South Sudan are incredibly centralised with the ranked ex-guerrillas wielding unchecked power.

Such a system encourages the politics of dominance and exclusion (Bogaards and Boucek, 2010). As emphasised previously, the SPLM is not democratic but holds power "because the playing field is heavily skewed" in its favour (Levitsky and Way, 2010, p. 51). South Sudan may not have moved toward an authoritarian system because that requires the rulers to design a suppressive system without being overthrown.

What is true is that South Sudan remained hybrid with different systems claiming legitimacy, and attitudes of armed groups hinder all the efforts to ensure state control. This is not because South Sudan lacks a condition that can sustain "the continuity of state-initiated pacification" (Elias, 2000 [1939]: pp. 445–6), but because are people not attuned to the state. In this stage, the DDR must answer how to engage opposing NSAs acceptably. Only by striving to recognise and engage informal actors can peacebuilders hope to support sustainable DDR (Richmond, 2013). The role of informal structures can be studied with reference to rebel rulership and governance (Mampilly, 2011). Armed conflict may be down to "a decision problem, competitive situation, and a conflict situation where the parties understand that they influence each other payoffs perceptibly" (Stahl, 1972, p. 14). While Mampilly ignored these groups' legitimacy, he argues that "armed groups are motivated to provide elements of governance and service delivery, in order that civilians may embrace a specific rebel organisation" (2011, p. 64).

Disregarding the representativeness of informal political and security system "deny the facts on the ground and foreclose engagement with such authorities, who may provide as good or better care for civilians under their control than those of the de jure government" (South, 2018, p. 54). South Sudan is described as "the government in Juba", denoting the limitation of state control over vast rural authorities (Jok, 2017). The context of the above arguments reflected the fragility of South Sudanese state. However, my thesis argues that it is also because of a violent devolution of government, meaning that the countryside is susceptible to governance by armed ethno-political factions who meet the requirements for establishing authority. When the informal armies substitute for the state by occupying areas where state authority is lacking, it becomes harder to conduct the DDR when NSAs "engage in organised violence" (Hall and Biersteker, 2002, p. 16). Even though this project is not about what the legitimacy entails, the causal agent of resistance is grounded in contested legitimacy. This political order propelled South Sudan to a situation of static violent struggle among the dynamics of power.

1.5 Dynamics of Power in South Sudan

When analysing the violence in South Sudan, the best starting point, introspective of the fragility of the state, may lie in the uncovering the dynamics of power (World Bank, 2013). It is apparent that most liberation movements have adhered to military and political traditions, and in most cases, these constituted a serious divergence and disconnect between theory and practice of good governance. A political setting in such a situation lacked rulers' fidelity to principles. According to Nyaba, the SPLM/A lacked a political and ideological base where "difference is managed through democratic political and ideological struggle" (2019, p. 97). He emphasised that willingness to engage in debate "helps to clarify and sharpen the points of difference, rendering it easy to resolve them" (Nyaba, 2019, p. 97). In his view, the SPLM has been operating in contrast to its liberation promises, and hence adhered to both military-political traditions. Nyaba stressed that:

> The SPLM/A leadership imposed strict military order and discipline, which betrayed the falsehood that one was both a soldier and a politician. They tried to justify this falsehood with a rejoinder that the decision the individual took to enlist in the liberation movement was a political decision. The soldier/politician individual in the SPLM was the personification of a robot soldier, having no conscience and, therefore, was not a revolutionary engaged in a war of liberation. Speaking of the purpose for the military-political set-up in the SPLM, it cannot be anything less than an intention to monopolise and personify the SPLM/A's power and public authority (Nyaba, 2019, pp. 97-8).

Nyaba's criticism acknowledged that "in a political movement the power and authority rest with the political leadership, which in itself is an institution" (2019, p. 98). However, he emphasised that the SPLM had never had a political practice where power and authority are institutionalised in the form of practical and open political institutions. In his view, "the SPLM/A leadership refused to construct institutions and instruments of power and authority apart from the dysfunctional *Political-Military High Command* (PMHC)", which he argues was form without content (Nyaba, 2019, p. 97). In Nyaba's (2019) interpretation, PMHC "had no rules for the conduct of its business". Thus, transferring that mindset and conduct to the government, when the SPLM/A became the ruling party worsened a situation that played out negatively in many episodes.

What is essential in this argument is the lack of space, for those who dared to dissent. As a result, the politics of rebellion remained static, and little has changed in the SPLM's operational behaviour and political procedures, despite ascending to the government (Deng, 2012). Propelled by the influences of liberation, the SPLM supposedly won the 2010 election with over 90 per cent of the elected seats in the legislative assembly (De Waal, 2012). The road map for this election derived from the post-war reconstruction efforts. However, this well-developed formula did not bring about stability in South Sudan, as it failed to reflect the history. Because of the historical "struggle over the claims to status, power and scarce resources" (Coser, 1957), the question of how SPLM dominance affected the violence is pertinent. If the SPLM-led government remained a network of self-serving elites, as presented above, the personal rule and competition to break the cycle of domination could be applied without difficulty to analytical objectives of the war.

The project argues that that war and resistance to the DDR were inevitable in South Sudan given the fact that the post-liberation regime has been depicted as a despotic system dominated by ethnic-affiliated politico-military elites who pursued an agenda of political corruption through violent (Deng, 2010b; Lacher, 2012). This mindset has driven previous military dictatorships; for example, Idi Amin and

Mobutu who pilfered resources and brutalised their people until they plunged their states into an abyss of ruin. While bad leadership can create conflict, it is insufficient motivation for citizen-led violence, and thus provides an insubstantial explanation for instability. Given Nyaba's arguments and the historical repercussions of Idi Amin and Mobutu's reigns, it worth noting that bad leadership is not only about acting alone. The leader may or may not be the only one in the realm of power; the presidency is often not the point in the despotic system dominated by ethnic-affiliated politico-military elites. Instead, it is the leader as a protagonist that matters. In South Sudan, poor leadership and competition for corrupt power drive conflict (Deng, 2009). This observation blames the dynamics of political violence for the proliferation of arms.

While "the Big-Tent strategy" bridged some gaps between the dominant groups within the SPLM/A and dissidents, it did not create fundamental reform. *The Big-Tent strategy'* was adopted by President Kiir's as a policy of amnesty and to integrate dissidents into the SPLM/A to create a conducive environment for peace and security, but the attempt failed (Copnall 2014). The groups remained aloof, maintaining their past ethno-political allegiances. As a result, the DDR hinged on a shaky foundation, precisely because the SPLA remained ethnically segmented. As mentioned by one participant: "there is a lot of killing by the tribal army. Our people are left to fight tribe against tribe" (P2b/12/07/ 2017). This participant emphasises how divisive ethno-political mindset led to the devolution of violence, thus making it difficult for the DDR due to intricate command-and-control.

Understanding these troubles requires reflection on the SPLM's power politics, a system that ran on one rule for us and another for everybody else. Such an assessment requires an understanding of the SPLM adherence to structures of subordination (Markell, 2003).

1.6 Inducting the Rebels to the Government in South Sudan

South Sudan is lacking is a functioning government; a state capable ensuring public protection (Moore, 2007; 2013). Thus, the security systems transformed into the unmanageable dynamic of political uncertainty. In this case, conflicts and violence are built upon an ever more intricate net of a fragmented socio-political system that supports continuity of disorder (Brown, 2011). As a new state with no developed institutions, the potential for the return to war accompanied South Sudan's independence from the beginning (Jok, 2013). South Sudan was built on the influence of the war-ridden past and the challenges of transforming warlords into bureaucrats. "When the SPLM assumed the power in 2005, we arrived in Juba the same way we used to enter the towns we had captured. There were no plans about governing. Most of us knew how to command the war. We used our power and rules to preserve control over the state" (P26/14/09/2017). This claim does not conform to the observations on the ground. The condition of South Sudan is the antithesis of a system capable of legitimately monopolising the use of force.

While South Sudan's leaders may not be as immoral as the system they were opposing, they have not been ideal bureaucrats. As an individualised state, South Sudan's socio-political institutions "have been deliberately weakened, subordinated or replaced by new regimented institutions used by the state or ruling party to control the society" (Kuajien, 2018, 3). My point is not to decry the ascendancy of ex-guerrilla leaders to the new governmental structures. It is to emphasise that they were the system during the war and the transition. Thus, what the secession replaced is the type of repressive agents; but the systems that were undermining the efforts to nurture a capable state in old Sudan remained. The SPLM instituted a system based on elite control; a structure in which impunity has taken precedence over the state. This situation has pulled apart various security institutions, which are not appendages of the state (Jok, 2017). Riding high on the pride of the liberation, the SPLM leaders duplicated the power of the state and the army without delivering the new basis for governing the state (Rolandsen, 2015).

This overlapping power, as Nyaba (2019) stated, has made South Sudan, not as a state with a military, but a military with the state. This assertion highlights issues with insurgents turned into parliamentarians. With that situation, there is a problem. When that is the case, it becomes challenging to understand how to establish criteria for peaceful power competition. According to the UNDP's capacity development report, South Sudan leaders "did not think directly about trust and legitimacy but concentrated on the overall goals of establishing themselves in power" (2010, p. 5). One can argue that the half-hearted attempts to restructure security fell to the wayside as soon as the CPA failed to address power configuration and distribution. Yet, South Sudan's case is more complicated than merely assessing the impact of ex-rebels dominating the government. Nyaba's analysis shows the SPLM is far worse than the former Northern regimes "which it used to despise and categorise as a one-man and no-system rule" (2019, p. 102). The SPLM/A, in Nyaba's belief, "could pass for a huge informality, which eventually became impossible to formalise" (2019, p. 102). Attention has focused on why and how a rebel movement takes power.

These studies raised that slight consideration has been placed on the downstream effects of rebel victory (Doyle and Sambanis, 2006). What state structures did rebel movements create when they inherited the state? How did they decide on policy priorities? These are vital questions because they link the violence to the problems of the DDR as well as presenting the implications of how rebel groups behave and act when they come into power. Knowing the types of state institutions ex-rebels are likely to build can help the international community to ensure an effective response when it comes to DDR. During the CPA, the IGAD preferred South Sudan to conduct the plebiscite, but paid slight attention to the perennial political crises in the SPLM, and how that can mutate into an ethnically charged political violence in South Sudan (Nyaba, 2019). This aspiration seemed indifferent about how the SPLM/A would distinguish itself from the government it opposes in the North. Will it build a stable state that delivers social services to the population? Despite the promise of liberation, the SPLM/A-led government is centred on the ruler and his core politico-military personals. This move is an opportunistic approach common among ex-rebel rulers, which obscures the rights of other minor ethnic and political communities.

As the state tore up in violence, the people who were supposed to respect its legitimacy resorted to the defence of their ethno-political homelands, properties, and political rights. The point here is not to argue that South Sudanese failed to govern themselves. Instead, the failure of the SPLM to meet South Sudanese aspirations stemmed from its elites' "refusal to organise and construct the democratic political institutions and instruments of power necessary for managing the liberation processes" (Nyaba, 2019, p. 16). As mentioned earlier, lack organisational legitimacy bowled into an explosive alloy, the domino effect of which transformed into the drivers of political violence. When ordinary men and women feared their state, doubted its capacity to protect them, or did not accept its legitimacy, its claim to a legitimate monopoly of force succumbed to violent dissidents. That practice prompts a complex militarisation that cannot be resolved without understanding the support networks of the armed groups.

The higher the stakes in the political competition, the more security became self-assured (Collier, 2010). It is impossible to purchase peace through DDR incentives where groups perceive an existential threat. Such concerns arrested South Sudan in its infancy. When war erupted in December 2013, it was "a signal that the centre can no longer hold" (Addai-Sebo, 2011, p. 16). The war took on an ethnic dimension, pitting President Kiir, a Dinka, against Riek Machar (ICG, 2014). One explanation for the civil war and proliferation of arms in South Sudan "became dominant; 'that this was a competition over political leadership fought out along ethnic lines" (De Vries and Schomerus, 2017, p. 334). The characterisation of the violence as tribal war makes it seem as if it was driven by the Dinka and Nuer competition for power. As this project argues prior, this explanation for the cause of war does not account for the complexity of what is occurring in South Sudan.

Interpreting ethnicity as the cause of war does not acknowledge the fact that all the leaders of the armed political factions, despite their ethnic identities, held government positions before they fell out with Kiir. Secondly, there are various rebel groups in South Sudan, led by other ethnic groups. One of the best examples is the South Sudan United Front/Army (SS-UF), under South Sudan's ex-army chief General Malong, a prominent Dinka. Instead of focusing on ethnic identity as the cause of war, this project emphasises that leaders use ethnic identity for militant mobilisation. In such a situation, ethno-political "nationalism can serve as an instrument for powerful groups that aim to retain power" (Snyder, 2000, p. 32). In this context, rebel leaders have a unique position for mobilising ethnic armies since they can use their networks to reinforce their power. The rebellion in South Sudan is "a negation of the established system of political exclusion", and the failure of governance (Nyaba, 2019, p. 16). By failure of governance, this thesis means the incapacity of the state to overcome internal conflicts. Thus, the proliferation of arms reflects how decentralisation of violence institutionalised the use of force.

1.7 Decentralisation of Violence

Given that state, according to the Hobbesian argument, was created as a response to violence and anarchy, what South Sudan's secession and state-based system of the DDR holds for peace and security is questionable. The existence of violent identity groups who have competing interests with the state is an indisputable fact (IDDRS, 2006). Because of the lack of collective security, there has been an expectation that a relative power of arms would be a more effective source of security. This feeling has proved to be fuelling the proliferation of arms in the sense that people depend on themselves. This self-defence mindset poses intractable policy dilemmas for the DDR. Whether to integrate or disband armed actors remained a puzzle. To dismiss them, as the CPA did, is a viable solution. The point here is not to suggest that the informal armies can fill the void left by the paucity of a functioning state. It is to argue that the groups' response to insecurity becomes an entry point for the proliferation of arms. Thus, the interplay between the lack of a functioning state and resistance to DDR enhances the decentralisation of violence.

These loaded guns wielded by hostile actors create a scenario where the state as the core peacekeeper with the role of pacifying violence became irrelevant (Broga, 2016; Mittelman, 2002; Hassner, 1995; Leander, 2004). Despite these concerns, the effort to link the spread of arms with the availability of the informal armies in South Sudan occupies a marginal place in the debate. Even though the theory of state-led control is valid, post-war processes need innovative statecraft to cater for inclusive strategies appropriate to the local actors, who need to be incorporated into the state-building processes. Essentially, this thesis argues that post-war processes in South Sudan need to consider hostile political plurality. This point is based on emerging patterns in security and conflict studies. As demonstrated above, perceptions of existential danger function as the core drivers of violence and resistance to the DDR. This is because, in anarchy, all aspects of lawfulness diminish. If, for instance, the factional wars and armed cattle raids continue, if people's well-being continues to be ignored by the state, armament becomes a necessity for those seeking to survive.

This contradiction between groups invited political thinkers to consider various forms of power and authorities instead of "all oversimplified representation of a state" (Chevallier, 2003, p. 336). South Sudan falls short of the capacity to address division. The reason, in this project's view, is that the new state did not become a shared belief; its practice does not differ from the pre-liberation era defined by unrepentant rent-seekers. Thus, the new political order allowed former insurgents to emerge from the bushes and swap their military gear for a place in public office. This situation needs an understanding of how competing actors make it hard for the state to provide a buffer against violent disintegration, mainly the dynamics of violent bargaining (Neiburg, 1969).

1.8 Conclusion

The legacy of civil war continues to be felt in the aftermath, given the challenges of trying to restore governance (Wallensteen *et al.*, 2001). The civil war and sectarian violence demolish political, economic institutions and uproot social fabric through displacement and famine. These challenges become entrenched when attempting to rebuild a post-war state into a competent sovereign political entity capable of guaranteeing peace and controlling its borders. The governments in most post-war states have fragile administrative capacity. They frequently suffer from institutional deficiencies, and that is the same case for South Sudan. This chapter has highlighted that the violence and weaknesses of South Sudan's institutions as not just due to the impact of civil war and various ethnic and violent identity struggles.

South Sudan is the newest state in the world, having gained its independence from Sudan on 9 July 2011. Thus, it did not just need to rebuild or reform the post-war state institutions but engage in building the entire new state from the makeshifts of war. Unlike other post-war states, South Sudan and its rulers were to transform from the rebellion political and security spheres, thereby changing their political stance and adopt or institute civil, political reforms based on the dominion of civil regulations and peaceful solutions to political disagreements.

These expectations challenge the traditional framework of top-down approaches as they fall short of addressing the mentality of violence or rectifying the political and economic system and inequalities faced by non-elites. This chapter emphasises the impact of violent competitors in South Sudan. This context is essential because disarmament of Ex-Combatants and disbanding of informal armies depend on cooperative relations and trust of the post-war system of government. The nature of politics in South Sudan made it challenging to build trust between the state and armed actors. This debacle arms make it easier for competing elite to mobilise with ease. I have presented in this chapter the causes conflict as well as the centrality of the challenges inherent in liberation, nation-state building and the impact of identity; highlighting these as the causes of the war that challenge the construction of an effective state and its institutions in South Sudan.

Chapter Two: Ethnicity and Political Discourse of Violence in South Sudan

The armed ethno-political factions in South Sudan are not just pilfering the state resources or each other's property, but they are slaughtering each other, burning villages and raping women. How did South Sudan get to this situation? Some scholars explained the cause of war in terms of "a relationship between the social construction of ethnic identities and the probability of ethnic war" (Fearon and Laitin, 2000, p. 845). Others explained that South Sudan only "fulfilled the declarative requirements of a state in international law" (Wassara, 2015, p. 639), but lacked control over the legitimate use of force. This chapter will argue that "the mere observation that ethnic identities are socially constructed does not by itself explain violence" in South Sudan (Fearon and Laitin, 2000, p. 845; also, Riehl, 2001). This project argued in Chapter Four that the weak and undemocratic system of government in South Sudan has created, or reintroduced, liberation era of dividing lines among the SPLM's leaders which have reignited violent power struggles among ethno-political elites. Moreover, the legacies of violent conflict among groups and individual leaders linger; institutions of governance are weak, arms proliferate, and "there is a violent political culture nurtured by the war" (Brosche and Höglund, 2016, p. 70).

This violent competition has resulted in a crisis of stability in South Sudan. Thus, this chapter will argue that the state monopoly of force, which is the core objective of the DDR in South Sudan, lacks political, economic and security incentives to entice the armed actors to lay down their arms. Achieving this goal requires an effective state and public compliance with the rules. Also, prevailing hostile relations between ethno-political identities mean that spoilers of the government have an accessible source of support, including arms. As mentioned by a participant: "DDR requires strong state institutions capable of building confidence. Weak institutions in South Sudan encourage citizens to take the law into their own hands" (P30/21/12/2018). The introduction of state-based DDR, from 2005- has bred a new wave of armed conflicts, with a significant proclivity for war. Jok Madut alluded to this argument, saying that:

> Independence alone is not enough if it is not accompanied by a programme of nation-building, something that must go beyond the material aspects of development. While services, and a sense of security would undoubtedly help citizens to identify with their country, it is also true that only national unity can produce an environment in which these services can be provided effectively. So, no matter what ventures the government of South Sudan embarks upon, it has to view nation and state as inseparable (Jok, 2012, p. 58).

While the CPA and secession silenced the guns between North and South, the battle for the South among protagonists was far from over. Sadly, three years after the referendum, secession proved to be a short-lived ceasefire. This situation arose from the state's lack of focus on "how to turn the young state into a nation all South Sudanese can embrace" (Jok, 2012, p. 58). This highlights the problem of nation-building. Thus, what is essential is for this chapter to recognise the variety of political, security and economic interests of armed groups, their norm of contestation and the means of imposing those interests explain the dismal results of DDR. The chapter will argue that multitudes of armed actors "leads to multiple patterns of violent contestation within reform programmes", and that this is underexplored in the DDR (Ansorg and Gordon, 2019, p. 2). While ethnic variety carries a dual potential to catalyse violence or become "a feature of diverse societies that celebrate their unity in diversity", the virtues of ethnic relationships are not entirely the subject of this chapter (Shulika and Okeke-Uzodike, 2016; Krause, 2019; Checchi *et al.*, 2018).

This chapter will discard the perceive premise that ethnicity or its social construction is the leading cause of war and adopt a functional or operational perspective of ethnicity. This mechanism is then used to argue that conflict in South Sudan is far from being unreasonable, but serves the political, economic and security objectives of the factions (Reno, 1998; Powell, 2002). In this case, the civil war in South Sudan may be down to "a decision problem and competitive situation, where the parties understand and take into account the fact that they influence each other payoffs perceptibly" (Stahl, 1972, p. 14). What is not known today in the DDR literature is how the power and resource competition transformed mere ethnic warriors into new forms of violent political groups. This chapter reflects on incidents of ethnic violence, some of which ended in a pogrom, and explains why scholars see ethnicity as the prominent issue in African studies.

This thesis argues that, while ethnicity is a contributing factor to war, the ethnic arguments are "clouded by incompatible interests, unfair access to political space, economic and other opportunities" (Shulika and Okeke-Uzodike, 2016, p. 25; also, De Waal, 2014b). Despite recognising that ethnicity has some impact, this argument does not offer an account of the mechanisms that link ethnic identities directly to the war. This gap occurs because those pushing the ethnic argument overlooked how the conflict in South Sudan related to political and economic marginalisation, resource competition and the public distrust in the state ability to ensure collective protection (Nyadera, 201). While DDR can be described as successful in some countries, as was the case in Burundi, it does "not encompass fully the tasks that must be carried out to reconstitute a viable and functioning state" (Ingram, 2010, p. 5). The "moment a state loses control over the use of force, be it through a rebellion or collapse, then the state is dead" (Adams, 2000, p. 5). Whether South Sudan is a dead country is a question of debate, but its political system is precarious and has no legitimacy outside the capital city of Juba. This situation unfolded because OAGs have taken control of several parts of the state since 2013. In the theoretical debate, a focus on ethnicity overlooked how the lack of consolidated statehood rendered the state assailable.

Hence, the selfish competition over power and resources gives life to a more commodified ethnic mobilisation and opportunistic violence. If ethnic identities are considered as the agents of elites, then the explanations for war in South Sudan would be based on the rationalist arguments, with emphasis on "elite manipulation of mass publics but also those that see violence stemming from ethnic interactions" (Fearon and Laitin, 2000, p. 846). This view refers to De Waal's argument that "South Sudan is an exemplar of a violent, fragmented, kleptocratic political marketplace" (2014 p. 347). Instead of mere ethnic division, South Sudan's public institutions are subsidiary to a competitive and "transactional politics pursued by a narrow group of elites" (De Waal, 2014 p.347). South Sudan is a state without the "capacity to implement and enforce central decisions" (Polese and Santini, 2018, p. 383). Thus, the multiple spheres of authorities hinder the regulation of arms (Krasner and Riss, 2014). Ethnic armies resisted the DDR because the state cannot wield control over the belligerents, ranging from armed cattle-herding youths and also over the armed factions involved in political mobilisation and coercion.

While these informal armies do not possess the unchecked right to self-defence, the fact that South Sudan is a fragmented state allows them to exercise this right, on behalf of a country failing to provide public security. This analysis reframes resistance to the DDR in terms of the cause of conflict and examines the systemic problems of governance in the SPLM. Reframing of the conflict is essential in analysing how post-war responses that were aimed at addressing violence failed to contextualise the structure of South Sudan's political system, and the socio-political and economic resources available to elites to promote the violence. Re-examining armed conflict in South

Sudan is vital in establishing that, while the war has been waged along ethno-political lines, ethnic identities are not the dole drivers that motivate armed conflicts. Instead, the war in South Sudan is motivated by an entrenched power struggle between the leading ethno-political opponents who engage in a self-negating power competition, using their ethnic identities as a tool for political violence (Berman, 1998).

As many states across the world are multiethnic, but stable, this provokes questions such as: Is ethnicity the leading cause of armed conflict in South Sudan? What role have these multiple conflicts played in the proliferation of arms? The response to these questions is that ethnicity has played a role, but that it does not comprehensively explain the intersection of ethno-politics and factional wars in South Sudan. Long-lasting competitive political relationships between elites can, over time, lead to the creation of socio-political fragmentation and that increase the risk for violent opportunism, insecurity and instability in the societal relationship (Broch-Due, 2005). Thus, the ethnicity of itself does not inspire people to engage in war. Academics have argued that ethnicity is prominent in Africa because it reflects ingrained allegiances to kin (Benhabib, 2004; Posner *et al.*, 2010). By this observation, the pattern of armed conflicts is seen as an ethnic war because it involved a clash of self-defined identities within the state (Rubin, 2006). Nevertheless, this project argues that ethnicity in South Sudan became the device used for waging war by political leaders for political control and extraction of wealth.

This is detrimental to the DDR because the use of force "bec[a]me divided between different warring parties" (Kalyvas, 2006, p. 87). This argument has historical backing. During the North-South war, the SPLM was able to mobilise Southerners using three charges. First, post-colonial Sudan was depicted as having illegal authority over the claimant territory; secondly, the Arab-Muslim doctrines of governance upset the Southern ideas around political freedom. Lastly, the South Sudanese suffered grave injustices and discrimination at the hands of the Northern Arabs. Thus, their struggle "was a reaction to the alienation of the peripheries by a small military ethnic-based group to achieve democracy and development across Sudan" (Clement, 2015, p. 2). For decades of civil war, ethnic identities played a role because they were used for the realisation of the group's interest. This brandishing of identities is attributed to the fact that Sudan has a limited political pluralism (Ekeh, 1975). In the past, ethnicity has served as a mechanism for marshalling disparate groups around a common purpose (Bates, 1983).

During the transition, South Sudan's leaders failed to implement lessons learned from the way they waged war. Nyaba argues that "the genesis of the war can be traced back to the formation, dynamics, and failure of the SPLM to become a national liberation movement. The political crises in the SPLM have mutated into an ethnically charged conflict pitting against each other the two largest ethnicities: Dinka and Nuer" (2019, p. 152). The fall of one dominant group [Arabs in the North] gives way to the perceived rise of the Dinka majority as the new dominant group. Nyaba (2019) perceived that there is a fear of exclusion by non-Dinka groups, and that this condition has led to varying rebellion. Most of these violent groups emerged during the inception of the SPLM and its many splinter factions that pitched elites against each other. Such conditions affected ethnic cohabitation and evolved into armed groups, which installed their structures of governance (De Soysa, 2000). This explanation alone does not connect the groups precisely to the war. It begs the questions: why has South Sudan descended to war swiftly, and why has a region that appeared cohesive during the war against the North disintegrated in a relatively short time?

The South Sudanese political system included the trading of rent-seeking for political loyalty. Such a condition emerged because at the national level, "the SPLM failed its mission by reproducing the bad trend of governance, it intended to combat" (Clement, 2015, p. 2). Armed groups entered a conflictual interaction that altered promises of economic gain and security demands into a procedure of political resources. Behind the facade of competition, ethnic groups have become a political tool wielded by elites. Reeves's work on South Sudan's militarisation had described how the elites become the "figures of intransigence" (1999, p. 147). When these groups disagreed, they amplified the slight existing socio-political grievances. Thus, armed conflict in South Sudan is a political war triggered by groups' failures to reconcile their narrow interests. The risk for the DDR is that each group responds to the strategic behaviour of their competitors. Before recruiting identities for a political war, they must be prepared emotionally. This interaction has given way to "politicised programs of ethnicised violence" (Jok and Patel, 2018, p. 5).

This argument is based on the political-economic theory inspired by Adam Smith and advanced by Fearon (2004; Grossman, 1999). Thus, the armed conflict is likely to occur "when individuals perceive that others are preventing them from attaining their goals" (Antonioni, 1998, p. 336). The contest of the variable interests via violent political contest can lead to armed conflict, mainly when significant ethno-political minorities are marginalised (Connor, 1994; Russett 1964). Much of the literature on the DDR that addresses this problem of fear is centred on researches, where the central system of authority has disintegrated (Donais, 2018; Sedra, 2010). In South Sudan, however, that approach is challenging due to the multiplicity of contending sources of authority (Deng, 2010). Thus, the role of ethnicity in resistance to the DDR requires demystification of ethnic militarisation. This emphasis requires a focus on "paradigms of military ethnicity, mechanisms of militarising civilian groups, the efficiency of the intervention in militarised societies" and emerging patterns of ethno-political militarisation in fragmented states (Owegi *et al.*, 2014, p. 3). This emphasis rejected an assertion that war is inevitable.

If war were inevitable, per se, there would be no point in attempting to end them. The war between political groups is not inevitable but derived from the conflict of interest (Yamokoski and Dubrow, 2008). Pareto (1935, n.p) describes elites as resembling lions whose strategy is "domination by force" as opposed to foxes, whose strategy is "domination by persuasion". In *Economy and Society*, Weber

([1922] 1968) expounded on the idea of domination and authority. Focused on the right to rule and the codes on which the rulers could exercise this right, Weber was less concern with the idea of power, which he saw as "an actor's position to carry out his own will despite resistance" (1968, p. 53). Instead, he focused on domination, which "constitutes a special case of power" (p. 941). To be precise, domination will, thus, mean the political setting in which "the manifested will of the ruler or rulers is meant to influence the conduct of one or more others and does influence it in such a way that their conduct occurs as if the ruled had made the content of the command the maxim of their conduct" (Weber, 1968, p. 946).

The project relates the above argument to the idea of power, "the capability of implementing one's will, even against the will of others" (Weber, 1968, p. 53). Power can be achieved through the accumulation of economic or symbolic resources, which in the case of South Sudan is the proliferation of arms and maximisation of the fighting forces (Gauba, 1995). In South Sudan, not only do ethno-political elites' power struggles reach different levels of violence, but new groups also use other violent political tactics to enter the game. At one end of this war lies fragmented South Sudanese state, which denotes the political situation where the central authority does not possess the legitimate means of violence, as well as the ability to impose decisions. The emphasis here lies on the elite's behaviours and interests. The link between war and self-interest in South Sudan lies with what Gramsci (1971, 320) refers to as a "war of position and manoeuvre". This situation requires the instrumentalist approach to understand ethnicity, as a device used by elites to organise and mobilise populaces to achieve broader aims.

2.1 Civil War in South Sudan: Is it an Ethnic Conflict?

On December 15, 2013, war erupted in the South Sudanese capital of Juba and spread across the country. Within weeks of violence, an estimate of over 20,000 civilians were killed, and it displaced two million (Amnesty International, 2014). Following a series of attacks and counterattacks between the SPLM/A forces loyal to either President Kiir or the Ex-Vice President Riek Machar, the war took on an ethnic dimension, pitting Dinka against Nuer (ICG, 2014). Why did the war assume an ethnic facet even though it was political, someone may ask? The war assumed an ethnic interpretation because of the extreme violent turn of the political crisis across the country. Despite evidence of ethnic hostilities, framing the war as an ethnic conflict served as a ready-made description for the war that external observers could easily deploy. For over four decades, South/ern Sudan has been characterised by violence and competing armed ethno-political and factional groups. The first phase of these factions emerged after the Addis Ababa Agreement. That crisis of violent power struggle worsened during the inception of the SPLM/A in 1983.

To some, ethno-political wars ensued because of the violent struggle over leadership of the SPLM/A, and its splinter ethno-political groups, which pitted ethno-political elites against one another. Although these groups never succeeded in ousting the mainstream Dinka-dominated SPLM/A from power, the armed groups continue to be critical players in the Southern military landscape (Leonardi *et al.*,

2010). Hence, the DDR that emerged from the CPA fell short of understanding internal dynamics and conflicts, which fuelled the proliferation of arms in South Sudan. The cases of successful DDR, cited in Chapter One, depended on the compliance of those designated for the DDR. There must be a perception by Ex-Combatants that the DDR is worthy of voluntary compliance, which is not the case in South Sudan. In post-secession South Sudan, these armed groups evolved into many other factions, including one of the leading splinter groups, the SPLM/A-in-Opposition. The process of the DDR ignores the participation of these ethno-political groups in public life, and their influence on the war and proliferation of arms.

Analysis of the political and local violence in South Sudan contributes to understanding the role of political leaders in building functional beliefs among their group through military networks. War names play a role in shaping perceptions of that war. For instance, America's 'war on terror' raises emotive feelings of fear and moral justification. The depiction of the war in South Sudan as 'ethnic' is misguided steps towards its resolution. Such framing is myopic in the sense that it disregards political grievances. This project seeks to enlighten, and to debunk, the perception of ethnicity as the leading cause of war in South Sudan by exploring the behaviour of ethno-political elites, arguing that the elites' selfish quest for power has significant implications for peace and security. In this case, the violence constitutes the culmination of a persistent crisis of governance in the SPLM/A since its inception. In particular, the calamity embodied an intensification of the violent competition between President Kiir and his ex-Deputy over who would become the SPLM's nominee for the presidential polls that were scheduled to be held in 2015.

The characterisation of war as "ethnic" is often consumed by a quick-fix solution, and that does not signal mediators understanding of the legitimacy of local wars or war-affected communities' grievances. An ethnic-based resolution risks failing, or has failed, in South Sudan because it did not address, nor de-politicise, contentious socio-political issues driving the conflict. Issues such as the historical impacts of civil war on society, and the warlords' instrumental role in instigating violence that would appear as an ethnic war, may not be solved through two parties' distribution of power. My thesis approaches South Sudan as a site of violent political struggle. This crisis does not require a simplistic context of ethnicity but needs to be analysed within a functional calculation between grievances and political-economic gains. Departing from the notion of violent politico-military aristocrats, Pinaud argues that "the politico-and military elite that found itself in power after the war established its hegemony through the capture of resources during the war itself. Through various predation strategies, it considerably expanded its kinship networks, and its political power, and constituted itself as a military aristocracy" (2014, p. 194).

The struggle for power drives the war, and ethnicity has become an accessible tool for elites. This issue of mobilising ethnic identities for political violence is not new among South Sudanese, but the current the rulers and challengers "feed the networks of their followers through the manipulation of state resources" (Pinaud, 2014,

p. 194). To analyse the ethnic paradigm, it is necessary to present a brief theoretical explanation about ethnicity and its perceived role in the South Sudanese war. This discussion will contribute to the debate about ethnic mobilisation through a focus on the role of framing. This emphasis will build on an approach that focuses on the links between leaders and types of political outcomes they seek (Rich, 2017). In doing so, this research stresses that security outcomes are essential in presenting how the measures taken by elites are connected to violence. First, the quest for political assurances provides armed actors with the opportunity of framing the securitisation of "identities of contentious actions and, second, they are instrumental in the implementation of violence" (Brosche and Höglund, 2017, p. 202).

This framework will show that political actors use ethnic recruitment as the strategy for the re-negotiation of power. The central thrust here is that the misery of war is not an unfortunate by-product of ethnic disputes (Ross, 2012; Barry, 2001). The war derived from President Kiir and his Ex-deputy's political motivation, but, primarily, their negative framing of each other led to the rapid disintegration of the country along ethno-political lines. The rulers and his challengers, in this case, resorted to mobilising armies based on ethno-political loyalty and interest. The phrase "ethnicity" is derived from the Greek word "ethnos", which means a grouping of people according to their shared beliefs, but its political use is relatively modern (Glazer and Moynihan, 1975; Bohannan, 1963). Ethnicity has permeated the socio-political debate. While the Greek context of 'ethnos' was meant to define specific forms of cultural variance, its usage as a tool has led to a different meaning. While these emphases of ethnicity lean away from "race", socio-political discourses have, to some extent, racialised the definition. One may talk about ethnolinguistic groupings (Smith, 1986), or racial appearance, and ethno-religious groups (Geertz, 1967).

Because of variations in what might be regarded as an ethnicity, Malesevic (2004, p. 2) contends that "institutionalised definitions, such as imposing the idea that an individual legally belongs to an ethnic minority are not only the strongest possible source of reification of the group and individual relations, but they also become a form of oppression by caging individuals into involuntary associations". A fixed definition means "cultural difference", which is flexible, is arbitrarily restrained, thus thwarting the process of social evolution. The popular idea of ethnicity defined based on indigeneity is "severely erroneous" when ethnicity is seen in terms of what the group stands for, whether political objective (Jenkins, 1997). This study has discussed the role of social capital in defining ethnicity and how it can be utilised as a tool to drive war. Woolcock (1999) defined social capital in terms of bonding, while political scientists, like Chandra (2004) see it as a "bridging". In South Sudan, social capital is a part of group "bonding and as the stock of reciprocal networks of trust and norms' that are rooted in each group" (Deng, 2010, p. 232).

Following Deng's conceptualisation of social capital, civil war might be said to hinder a groups' social capital, and war-affected states would be considered situations of social capital paucity. However, the empirical research criticises any notion that war corrodes social capital within ethnic groupings. During the war in Sudan, Southern identities "that were exposed to endogenous counter-insurgency warfare experienced a loss of social capital, but where exogenous violence dominated, there has been a strengthening of bonding social capital among and within communities" (Deng, 2010, p. 232). While war can erode certain kinds of social capital, the opposite is the case in South Sudan. To understand how ethnicity relates to war, academics have proposed varying definitions. According to Temitope (2014, p. 63), "an ethnic group is a people of similar cultural setting, and the historical context of shared a common heritage, ancestry and migration". Willigenburg, (1995, p. 13) defines "ethnic groups as cultural nations which are bound by a shared culture and which lack the internationally recognised organisation of a sovereign state".

These definitions are derived from the view that "group identities must always be defined by what which they are not" (Eriksen, 1993, p. 35). Thus, "ethnicity is an aspect of the social relationships between agents who consider themselves as culturally distinctive from members of other groups" (2002, p. 12). The idea of civil war as ethnic war has eschewed meaningful analysis and "has taken flight from the hard categories of social science to find refuge in deconstruction, relativism, and meta-narratives" (Singh, 2000, p. 22). The description of civil war in terms of ethnicity is concerned with international security as it allowed international analysts to "gladly lump together dissimilar cases, often in order to raise the gloomy spectre of civilisational clash or new security challenges" (Gilley, 2004, p.1158). If this project has a unique part to play in conceptualising the complex politics of South Sudan and the role politics played in the resistance to

DDR, it then needs to provide ideas "that enjoy both within-case and cross-case validity" (2004, p.1158). The basis of this argument is not only to criticise the concept of ethnic war, but to involved in what Weber described earlier as a "reconstruction" of ideas (Drysdale, 1994).

This approach requires wading into the messiness of South Sudanese politics with the view of finding what propelled the actors into violence. In doing so, I argue that ideas about the cause of civil war in South Sudan grasp only a partial segment of the full picture. Echoing of this ethnic excuse allowed researchers to peddle only one of many possible reasons that drove groups to resort to war. Ethnic identity is a group of people with a shared cohesive existence embedded in many socio-political affinities, conceived or actual shared history inspired by "common myths of origin" (Bates, 1983, p. 152). This affinity leads to a question of whether groups are politicised regarding self-definition or the groups politicised what they define as self. This politicisation of groups and groups' politicisation of their identity was evident during the North and South war, and in current South Sudanese war. The war in South Sudan weakens the country's social fabric by undermining elites' relationships as well as "communal group trust and values that underlie socio-political cooperation and collective action for the common good" (Colletta and Cullen, 2000, p. 1).

Turning these debacles into a notion of ethnic war/conflict is complicated. An ethnic war would make sense if the motivating factor of conflict mattered to a specific ethnic group. Yet the intrinsic complication of violence in South Sudan makes proving whether they are 'ethnic wars' problematic. Gilley emphasises that "constructed ethnicity is a moving and contested target and so explanations of political conflict with reference to such ethnicity are liable to be off the mark" (2004, p. 1158). Unlike disputes between socio-economic classes, which can be demonstrated or invalidated by using a matrix of measurements from individual's education to financial status, the "same cannot be said of ethnicity because prejudices against other ethnic groups that appear as essential wax and wane as conditions change" (Green and Seher, 2003, p. 509). Thus, the presence of conflict between the Dinka and the other ethnicities may alter the sense of ethnicity on all sides. Gilley argues that "ethnicity is found by the entrepreneurs to be a handy device with which to mobilise supporters in the face of some form of deprivation or repression" (2004, p. 1159). As such, ethnic identity provides an indispensable sense of unity within the political faction.

However, if ethnic identity is structurally drawn or can be made prominent, then the crucial causes of war are the structural problems. For Laitin and Fearon, (1996), ethnic conflict is "structural deprivation" conflict. The structural deprivation emerged in a political system where one or two groups dominate the means of production and distribution. In South Sudan, the Dinka ethnic group have produced high-ranking members of government institutions, and the army (Okojie, 2013). This ubiquitous deployment of the Dinka elites is seen as domination. That reality has prompted some scholars to argues that "the politics of domination the Dinka elite pursue in South

Sudan for the control of economic and political power is the main source of incessant conflicts among ethnic groups in the country" (Idowu *et al.*, 2019, p. 124). This assertion may not be entirely accurate, but this project acknowledged that the proportion in which ethnic groups in power have access to socio-political power stands in contrast to the proportion of those excluded, that may account for armed conflicts in South Sudan. This conflict leads to institutionalisation of ethnicity as a tool for access to political power, hence, corrupted the South Sudanese state.

From this point of view, deprivation and political uncertainty are perceived as the main culprits for armed conflict. Of course, rejecting the view that civil war that uses ethnicity instrumentally is an "ethnic war", does not mean this project seeks to label the armed groups in South Sudan as a criminal. Instead, it aims to focus on the vital elements and determinants of conflict. Sisk (2002) identifies that a determinant of ethnic conflict is the presence and "the role of ethnic entrepreneurs", elites who express conviction in ethnic ties and mutual benefit and who mobilise and organise a group to push for that mutual benefit. Hence, the notion of ethnic entrepreneurs may be observed as socio-political and economic "interest aggregators that serve a critical representative function, or as manipulative and exploitative power seekers that mobilise on ethnic themes for their aggrandisement" (Sisk, 2009, p. 19; also, 2002). One participant argued that "the war is caused by the interplay between people being seen as breadwinners by a portion of individuals attached to them in the political system" (P1/19/06/2017).

As a divided state, it is hard to dismiss an effort by one ethnic group to outbid another. Those who seek political offices have so far magnified ethnic differences to maintain or achieve political aims. Based on that intention, ethnicity and loyalty to identity have become a more valuable element of war as group politicises what they define as the self. The war and its relations to a mass mobilisation highlight that a divided populace does not discern manipulative propaganda from the truth. In the Dinka and Nuer example, the government is believed to be dominated by the Dinka. This argument highlights the ease with which elites can leverage ethnic differences into political conflict. While "the outbreak of a new civil war in South Sudan seemed to be centred on ethnic factors" we must also talk about leadership personalities to argue that hostile competition is "rooted in deep cleavages within the ruling party, the SPLM" (Rolandsen, 2014, p. 163). When the power struggle in the SPLM came to surface in 2013 "legacies of violence from the previous civil war allowed this to escalate into a full-scale armed conflict" (Rolandsen, 2014, p. 163).

In this situation, the disarmament faced three critical factors which will be described in the following paragraph. Having not ever existed as an independent state before DDR, "collective action among South Sudanese has historically been shaped in response to external pressures: in particular, the aggressive nation-building pursued by Khartoum-based regimes" (Frahm, 2012, p. 22). The perception of the North as the oppressive other' became instrumental in building the regional identity of the Southern groups, and politicisation of both aspirations and belongings. This politicisation of regional belongings built a makeshift nationalism not defined by "a language and symbolism, a socio-political movement and an ideology of the nation" (Smith, 2010, p. 6). This definition echoes Anderson's (1983) idea of nations as imagined communities where the members of a particular group express solidarity based on a socially constructed notion of belonging and affinity. For decades, scholars of Sudanese politics have presented the politics of belonging as the South versus the North (Johnson, 2003). This representation ignores the micro belonging, or how group express solidarity may be politicised.

Belonging represents emotional attachment and is about feeling safe (Ignatieff, 2001). In the South Sudanese war in 2013, belonging took a tragic meaning. The disintegration of Southern politics of belonging gave way to the politicisation of ethnic belonging. This is because Southern political unity "was not an exercise based on a fixed configuration of national identity" (P17/21/09/2017). This observer recognised that the politicisation of ethnicities against the North solicited a mass mobilisation, but also took tacit bānal forms. This view reflected on the ethnic diversity and suggested that the overlapping security subdivisions at the grassroots do not lend themselves to an easy categorisation of South Sudan as a nation-state. This view reflects the Primordiality emphasis that "ethnicity and ethnic identity may, in essence, be frozen in time, that once an ethnic collectivity has been formed, it remains so" (Ratcliffe, 2014, p. 2). What is lacking in South Sudan are strong ties that tightly knit all identities. When there are no trustable horizontal relations among ethnic groups, it becomes inevitable that the country will lie in ruins.

Without trust, the coordination of state actions becomes harder because that demands public cooperation. This emphasis implies that ethnicity can be operationalised. The armed conflict in former Sudan became a response to how the state functioned, and the same can be said of the nascent Republic of South Sudan (Denny, 2004; Gellner, 1997). While the literature offers insights into these elements, there is a gap to be explored, because ethnicity is interlaced with the territory, history, interest, and other dimensions (Haug, 2001; Nnoli, 1978). Thus, I suggest that the armed groups waged war and opposed the DDR because the perceived Dinka regime failed its mandate of public security. Moreover, some ethno-political elites rebelled because they were excluded from key positions in the government (Wimmer, 2004; Yeros, 1999; Geertz, 1996). This analysis presented two vital, but negative factors in South Sudan's politics: the challenges of guerrillas in government, and that the old Sudan, where most of the SPLM/A leaders learned their trade of governance, was an exclusionary system with a deep-seated political corruption (De Waal, 2014).

My thesis argues that the opposite of consolidated sovereign state in South Sudan lies in what I described in this Chapter One as limited statehood, a notion which manifests itself through different means of violent episodes, and armed groups. South Sudanese state's capacity to implement and enforce sovereign decisions, include who should use force, is lacking. Therefore, no one, not even the government, has a legitimate monopoly over the use of force. This restriction of South Sudanese statehood occurs on a sectoral, socio-political and security level. This decentralisation of violence and violent actors developed early because of fear, but it transformed into a protest over exclusion. The relevance of ethnicity, in this case, is that it is an intricate mechanism that can create frustration and competition (Lonsdale, 1994). In the state where arms are accessible, frustration and competition dwarfed the incentives for the DDR. When examining inequality in power and resource-sharing, the basis of socio-political cohesion perished, along with the state monopoly over the legitimate use of force. Having outlined this emphasis, the next section will assess the opposition to DDR as a rational decision where ethnicity is merely instrumental.

2.2 Instrumentalists on Conceptualisation of Violent Conflicts

The Instrumentalists' argument about ethnicity is different from the Primordialist emphasis presented by Geertz (1973). Geertz asserts that "humans have primordial attachments to what he labels the givens of social existence", whether those givens are immediate family or clan connections (Kataria, 2018, p. 133; citing Geertz, 1973). Conversely, "instrumentalism perceives ethnic identities in principally rational terms. There are two instrumentalist perspectives of particular value: the elite perspective and the social engineering perspective" (Kataria, 2018, p. 133). Brass (1979; 1991) presents a seminal contribution to the elite view. Brass highlights the responsibility of elites in the construction and relevance of ethnic identity. Brass argues that "elites and counter-elites within ethnic groups select aspects of the group's culture, attach new value and meaning to them, and use them as symbols to mobilise the group, to defend its interests, and to compete with other groups" (1979, p. 40).

This idea attributes the ethnic identity "to the machinations and calculations of its elite" (Brass, 1979, p. 41). Here, ethnicity is "neither inherent in human nature nor intrinsically valuable", but a tool (Varshney, 2009; Gellner, 1964; Berger, 1963). During the war in old Sudan, the SPLM adopted an elite perspective in its opposition to the authoritarian presidency in the North. The SPLM/A framing of the government in the North as corrupt and oppressive became a strategy in which the SPLM/A instrumentally manipulate and utilised evocative ethno-political and cultural symbols to garner societal support. While the mobilisation for war became an inevitable confrontation between the Africans-Christians against the Arab-Muslims in the North, the paradigm of framing the government in the North as oppressive sowed fear among the Southern Sudanese, enough reason for them to freeze their local ethnic differences for the collective good (Garang, 1987). When this fear is in place, the function of a leader in instigating violence becomes very important. A leader can construct a political message to galvanise ethnic groups and mobilise them to wage war on the platform of everyday political purposes. In this situation, mutual interest and threats can force the groups into a new socio-political grouping as a strategy (Lynch, 2011).

From this view, Southern elites could draw upon elements of groups' socio-cultural and political factors to mobilise disparate ethnic identities. During the war, the distinction between the Sudanese government and the rebels in the South as the illegitimate challengers of sovereign authority, was accurate from an international relations outlook. That distinction, however, was practically fictitious in Southern Sudan, based on how the rebel leaders run their movement. Moreover, while the SPLM/A leaders were framing the regime in the North as a coalition of Islamist generals, in a comparable manner, Southern politics was susceptible to the same exclusive and oppressive elements. Lacking a sense of public duty, a Dinka and Nuer dominated SPLM/A followed and defended ethnic leaders and looted properties of other groups. Having a sense of public duty does not mean that groups will give up their local symbols or norms and values. The symbols, norms and values held a deep and historical significance for the ethno-political group.

When the CPA was signed, it was a covenant between North and South, with little reflection on Southern Sudanese politics and the inter-ethnic relations. In particular, there was no real notion of how to address the simmering power struggles in the SPLM, and mobilisation around exclusionist identities. After independence, the SPLM ascended to power, an outcome that allowed the ex-guerrilla generals to award themselves with higher offices (Haile, 2012). As argued in Chapter Four, the independence of South Sudan transformed the SPLM/A from a rebel movement into the government, but not its mode of operation. Idowu *et al.*, (2019, 127) argue that the decades of war with the North prevented the SPLM/A "from looking into its soul to discover its own societal ills. The task of self-reflection had not been accomplished prior to the declaration of independence". War is likely in this situation if the excluded can ascertain the perpetrators of their suffering. Instead of moving away from the impression of ethno-political tribalism, the ruling political elites shaped the basis of government in their favour.

As shown in the introduction, the South Sudanese state derives its revenue from natural resources, mostly oil, however, the state is a subsistence economy. For peasants in the rural areas, "economic interaction within the informal sector is much more important than the formal government economy. If ordinary people benefit from the oil revenues, it is from the trickle-down effects of patronage networks" (Rolandsen, 2015, p. 166). This argument is derived from De Waal's emphasis on the devastating aspects of "neo-patrimonial governance in South Sudan", a condition that has been amplified by "the massive infusion of oil revenues into the state coffers" (2014, p. 347). Due to the fragility of the state institutions, South Sudan is considerably vested in violent patronage within bureaucratic and security systems. Therefore, controlling the state power and using it as a tool for coercion became the method for controlling state revenue, as well as the drives of violence and the proliferation of arms. The access to resource and power make a violent state capture by the SPLM elites and different armed factions attractive. As the threat from the North diminished, each group's contradictory political and economic interests surfaced.

"If you have political power nowadays, then you also have economic power" (P2/07/07/2017), expressed one participant. This argument suggested a linkage between the power, resource distribution and the civil war in South Sudan. Those who accused the government of exclusion from power resorted to war and found the nascent state unprepared for countering certain types of political framing, especially the mobilisation of identities influential in shaping a climate conducive for political violence. This violence echoes the Instrumentalists' argument that greed fuelled the war (Chandra, 2004). This context of war argues that despite the prominence of identity in war, unrestrained greed by the elites is the towering factor. The central thrust in this argument is that the bane of corruption is not merely an unfortunate by-product of the failed system, but the main gear is driving the institutional failure in South Sudan. In this case, South Sudan's problems are not confined to a dearth of political imagination. The state suffers because of the consecration of political power as the primary tool to acquire ill-gotten profits.

In this situation, ethnic unity is connected to socio-political and economic projects (Fenton, 2003; Blattman and Miguel, 2010). In South Sudan, each armed group may be particularistic in their socio-cultural setting, but their reason for war is self-interest (Tersoo and Ejue, 2015). Since the signing of the CPA in 2005, "South Sudan has experienced a combination of fragmentation of local government institutions and ethnic segmentation. These developments give subnational elites room for improvisation and shifting of alliances which exacerbate the unpredictability of South Sudanese politics" (Rolandsen, 2015, p. 166). To present why South Sudan unravelled, one needs to focus on factions' leadership personalities, ethno-political ambitions, and the grievances of the groups. Examination of personalities and ambitions is embedded in armed actors' histories, as people who have lived by the gun (ICRC, 1999). When political tensions arose in 2013, a lack of national cohesion allowed these tensions to escalate into a civil war in which rivals marshalled their ethnic identities into the war, worsening an already fragmented political system under fragile authoritarianism (Boswell *et al.*, 2019).

2.3 Ethno-Political Violence and Proliferation of Arms in South Sudan

South Sudan is not one cohesive nation; hence, any sort of violence can be mistaken as ethnically motivated (Yokwe, 1997). When the war erupted in 2013, the international media quickly labelled it as ethnic conflict. An ethnic conflict is "organised large-scale violent conflict among ethnic groups of which at least one has not achieved statehood or is not in possession of the state apparatus" (Angstrom, 2000, p. 25). The basis of such conflict lies in the existence of at least two different units, with the consensus that something differentiates them. These units may be individuals or identities, and the demarcating element may be territorial, ethnicity or a combination. Such demarcating elements are not far from the truth because of assaults along ethnically defined fault lines (ICG, 2014). The deep ethnic detachments within South Sudan "came to the surface after the liberation struggle had ended, and the South Sudanese were enticed to fight amongst themselves" (Rolandsen, 2014, p. 165). This assumption was deemed necessary because the war had taken on an ethnic dimension, but it missed the truth.

If left uncorrected, the ethnic idea can establish reasonable grounds for scholars to elevate such analyses without an insight into what led to the war. Before addressing what led to the war, let us first understand whether ethnicity matters in the South Sudanese war. Ethnicity emerged in South Sudan as an influential aspect in the politics of violence against the North, as well as during the SPLM split in the 1990s. The basis of this lies in the literature cited previously, as well as within the reflections of those interviewed. "When there are deeply felt grievances in society, it leads to the mobilisation alongside ethno-political parties" (P19/28/09/2017), explained one participant. This argument attributes the war to grievances deriving from unfair access to power. Thus, the conflict, in this case, is 'a situation of interaction involving two or more parties, in which actions in pursuit of incompatible objectives, or interest result in varying degrees of discord" (Alao, 2007, p. 20; citing Deng, 1996). The dichotomy in Deng's emphasis is between peaceful and cooperative relations and disruptive adversarial hostility, culminating at its worst in high-intensity conflict.

Thus, armed conflict occurs as "these groups become involved in mutually opposing and violent interactions aimed at destroying, injuring, or controlling their opponent" (Alao, 2007, p. 20). The most challenging question is, "if all behaviour in conflict is explained at the individual level as dominated by the desire for individualistic material gains of a few elites, how do the atrocities, of the members of these ethnic groups, genocide, torture contribute to these gains?" (Williams, 2015; citing Weitsman, 2008, p. 114). The fact that ethnic identities are mobilised does not explain the eruption of war in South Sudan. The cause of war is "the fallout of a political crisis within the SPLM; a crisis exacerbated by the lack of cohesion and central control within the SPLA" (Rolandsen, 2014, p. 165). Thus, there is mistrust among fighting forces because they belong to different ethnic groups. If all interested parties belonged to the same ethnic group, would we have a similar conflict or not? While the war in old Sudan was seen as occurring between North-South, bickering among Southern elites almost destroyed their bid for statehood, as leaders of the SPLM strove for power and mobilised along ethnic lines (SAS, 2012).

Despite these violent struggles, most SPLM/A political leaders shelved their political differences, choosing to focus instead on presenting a unified front against the North. Yet, after secession in 2011, the simmering tensions and rivalries among the high-ranking generals continued to exist and intensify during the disquieting process of establishing functional institutions and development responsibilities (Kuajien, 2018). De Waal's (2017) argument denotes the crisis in South Sudan as an escalation of political competition rather than ethnic conflict. Hence, the reason why ethnicity is an integral part of this project's analysis lies in the political framing used by competing leaders to mobilise support for the political war. For that reason, focusing on political rivals is meant to highlight how specific leaders are influential in instigating violence. An interpretation of this argument symbolises the militarisation of every aspect of life in South Sudan, including cattle camps (UNSC, 2016; Wudu and Muchler, 2014). Inasmuch as the civil war is concerned, the puzzle is why the conflict endured, who is fighting who, and what are the motives?

The easiest supposition that permeates the international media, and echoed by some groups of academics, is that the war was born from inherent tensions between the Dinka and the Nuer (Hutton, 2014). In short, the war of 2013 started when South Sudan's President Kiir, a Dinka, accused his ex-Deputy, Machar, of inciting a coup. I agree that ethnicity is a central issue in political life in South Sudan but insist that the political competition has created a siege mentality that perpetuates a defensive paranoid attitude predicated on the belief of self-defence. This argument contradicted the assumption of ethnicity as "deeply ingrained in human history and experience" (Wolff, 2006, p. 33). Ethnicity is primal, in this context, meaning "one that stems from the givens as a culture is inevitably involved in such matters, the assumed givens of social existence: immediate contiguity and kin connection" (Geertz, 1973, p. 259). Despite the merits of this argument, it does not scratch the surface in relation to the war in South Sudan because it does not include the impact of the frictions that arise from an imbalanced distribution of power.

When individuals identify with a particular group, "they form a potential interest group that can be manipulated by political leaders, who often choose to mobilise support by singling out some groups for persecution or exclusion" (Kimemia, 2016, p.16). Ethnicity in South Sudan "remains functional, providing ethnic identity, a sense of belonging and a link to the broader community based on salient features" (2016, p. 92). In response to why the conflict endured in South Sudan, and who is fighting who, this project identified two types of warring parties. The first is the dozens of armed political factions fighting the government for power. These groups are often aligned with ethnic groups, but their members do not always belong to a single ethnicity. The second set of groups are informal armies, most of which are ethnic youths running a commercialised cattle-raiding network (Walton, 2010). Before proceeding with the argument about ethnicity and its role in South Sudanese conflict, it is worth stating that these groups affected the DDR in different ways. First, these tiers of violent groups use arms to engage in conflict. That in itself is a hindrance to the DDR.

Battlegrounds became multidimensional; hence, the arms and those wielding them proliferate along manifold lines of alliance and aggression. Thus, the gap in DDR is related to how it focused on formal Ex-Combatants with the exclusion of OAGs. This pays little attention to the armed ethnic youths and their motivations for arms. I emphasise how the DDR failed to concentrate on the context and the reasons for war among groups, particularly noting the exclusion of resistance to the DDR among informal armies. The costs of this myopic approach are presented in Chapter One. It is argued that every aspect of the CPA and the DDR was designed as to put an end to the war between North and South and to re-allocate the power and resources to the two dominant parties within each region, North and South (Munive, 2014). As a result, the SA favoured the SPLM's politico-military hierarchy dominated by the Dinka ethnicity. As per the CPA's arrangements, Garang became the president of the GoSS, deputised by General Salva. After Garang's demise, Kiir assumed the presidential role of his fellow Dinka.

Even before the war started, it was apparent that South Sudan was going to have severe political problems based on the issues of power and domination. Real or perceived disproportionate distribution of power and resources are a recipe for violent confrontations even in moderate democracies like Kenya, let alone in South Sudan; a country that emerged without functioning state institutions to check the power of the rulers (Elkins, 2005; Moseley, 2012). The SPLM's leadership that ascended to power brought along their exclusive politico-military systems from the bush. That political system created a quasi-tyranny government where political and economic organisations departed from societal norms and descended into an abyss of quasi-authoritarianism. The outbreak of war 2013 regressed this quasi-tyranny, thus transforming South Sudan into a violent vampire state. As a result, the government, as a collective institution, ceased to exist, hijacked by unrepentant ex-SPLM/A politico-military opportunists who pillaged the state to the advantage of themselves and their ethno-political group (Copnall, 2014). The adamant refusal of the SPLM elites to share political power fuelled the violence that erupted in 2010.

The violent mayhem created a situation inimical to the DDR. It became difficult to ensure sustainable peace through the demilitarisation of politics (Lyons, 2006). When South Sudan conducted their elections in 2010, a year before the referendum, the process failed to move the "competition from the battlefield to the ballot box" (Hoddie *et al.*, 2010, p. 9). The aftermath of the elections triggered armed conflict between those who were already dissatisfied with the power distribution born out of the CPA, a discontent compounded by the election outcomes. To some, the overwhelming win by the SPLM was deemed as a renewal of the licence of Dinka dominance of political and security system (Brosché and Höglund, 2016). It was not easy for a democratic process to succeed in South Sudan because it depended on security stability and a mature political system (Behn, 1998). The fact that South Sudan lacks these elements of stable public administration highlights the difficulties of organising transition to an effective electoral process without prior groundwork (Arnold, 2007).

Five years after signing the CPA, and a year from the historic referendum, South Sudan was plunged into a savage round of violence, which has continued persistently (Jok, 2013). After losing his bid for the seat of the governor of Jonglei State, General Athor, a Dinka, formed the South Sudan Democratic Movement (SSDM), accusing the system of fostering authoritarianism (Marc-Andre, 2010). David Yau Yau, an ethnic Murle who also lost an election, joined him. The same scenario extended to Upper Nile State when General Olony, a Shilluk, assumed command of the local SSDM branch. Unlike Athor, Olony's rebellions transpired from a land dispute between his native Shilluks and the subsection of the Dinka he accused of occupying an ancestral land (Arensen, 2012). This grievance shifted conflict from a mere ethnic dispute to issues of consolidating land rights through customary communal land ownership. The basis of Olony's rebellions reflects "the increasing levels of social inequality and conflict resulting from the private ownership of land" (Hakim and van Dijk, 2017, p. 6). This grievance consists of political and economic interest grounded in strategic behaviour by armed ethno-political groups.

If ethnicity is the sole factor for war, one will find it difficult to explain why Athor rebelled. Perhaps several factors may have fuelled the desires for those engaging in armed conflicts. That is to say, if South Sudan is a state "where power and resources are still concentrated at the centre" (Kovac and Bungura, 2017; citing Höglund, 2009, p. 415), the attraction to get involved in competitive politics and the potential to be frustrated when the results are not in favour of some contenders is high. In this case, the dissenting leaders under the SSDM umbrella had grievances related to politics. Their resort to the violence resulted from an effort to (re)establish their political and economic positioning (Douglas, 2015). This scenario of rebellion requires a critical exploration of South Sudan's socio-political dynamics by asking questions about the problems of political evolution, to infer how a divided society's system of government arises and disintegrates.

While the violence waged by General Athor did not interrupt the referendum, independence changed a little to offset the violent political setting. All that was wrong with the SPLM/A during the war of liberation overlapped with the fragility of the new state (Jok, 2015). To some, continuing waves of war were inevitable unless the government could "move to establish effective systems of administration and respond to widespread grievances" (Young, 2006, p. 37). Instead of addressing the concerns arising from the structure and state formation, the SPLM doubled down by engaging in a vicious power struggle and political negation. After months of uncertainty, President Kiir appointed a leaner cabinet. Among his notable appointments were the elevations of the dominant liberation era Dinka generals to the positions of the defence and interior minister. Departing from the fact that the SPLM, since its inception, has been viewed as nothing but a political vehicle of a selected few, the elevation of the two most senior Dinka generals caused immediate concerns. The frustration of the leaders excluded from the new formation added to existing tensions in the SPLM/A, resulting in a civil war. While Riek Machar resumed the position as a leader of the armed rebellion, the SPLM-in-Opposition (SPLM-IO), it is appropriate to characterise the civil war as a war, rather than as mere ethnic violence.

This condition is inevitable when there is a prize attached to holding state power. South Sudan has no other economic resources except for oil. This resource became a prime means for military and political leaders to achieve private fortune and to secure advantages for their important communities. Thus, the parties to the war are elites in defence of their political positions and those in pursuit of the same power to access resources. The stakes to be a minister or a general are high, since politico-military power is the easiest way to political and economic influence in South Sudan (Pinaud, 2014). The actors involved in the South Sudan political system are politico-military leaders who held ranks within the armed factions, which heightens the probability of a political discrepancy turning deadly. This condition suggests that weak political institutions create a condition where dissenting political elites are susceptible to engaging in violent ethnic mobilisation. While I am aware of Collier's identification of natural resources, he focuses away from ethno-political justifications for war. To understand the impact of this situation, one needs to identify conditions that explain why armed actors have engaged in violent tactics.

It means looking at resistance to the DDR based on the hostile ethno-political framing and the security (Kaufman, 1996). The security dilemma justifies why armed structures sought to control or compete. The idea of a security dilemma offers an understanding of the resistance to the DDR in a civil war when armed actors are seeking to increase their productivity, or predation, through maximisation of force. This problem culminates in the practice of a group's self-help. While the mobilisation of factional armies represents a politicisation of ethnic belonging, such practice is driven by the failure of elites to reconcile their narrow interests with the public concerns (Nichols, 2011). Factional leaders in South Sudan performed an essential task in framing the socio-political scene in a context that securitised ethnic identities. Although these emphases are reasonable, the question is why it is easy to mobilise armies along ethnic lines. The debate in earlier chapters recognises that elites do not fabricate every ethnic grievance; they only need to understand, appeal, sometimes accentuate or exaggerate the grievance (Cordell and Wolf, 2010).

This art of tapping into a grievance makes it easy for leaders to assume a negative framing function. After his rebellion in 2013, Machar accused the government of excluding non-Dinka ethnic groups (ICG, 2019). This accusation was intended to justify organised violence. "A phone call informed me on the night of December 2013 that the government soldiers had killed my family. From there, I resolved to take revenge, starting with Dinka colleagues. I later find out that my family was not hurt" (P3/08/07/2017). The caller to this participant intended to render him vulnerable for manipulation through false messaging. Although not all the calls on that day were false, the caller achieved their aim: to infuriate recruits. The subterfuge allowed leaders to assume a position that could be perceived as standing for something apart from selfish reasons (Kane, 2001). This outlook gave the leaders the "capacity to persuade and perhaps inspire others" about the justness of their course (Whitehead, 2002, p. 11). When looking at all the militias in South Sudan, "the rationale upon which they were mobilised is formulated in symbolic frames which provide the link between the leaders' interest and the mass level, or group" (Pappas, 2008, p. 1223).

When the basis of civil war became 'us' and 'them', not necessarily in terms of ethnic identity, such an outlook creates political opposition aimed at the legitimacy of those in power. To use the lexis of collective action, opposing leaders appeal to in-group solidarity, be it political or ethnic, and emphasise how the group in question will benefit from such actions. That is to say, the interaction among hostile groups tends to get out of hand, to make a mockery of deliberate political strategy, and to result in havoc immensely out of proportion to rationally conceived purposes. Thus, the militarisation of public life in South Sudan lies in an understanding of why civilians supported the networks of armed groups. It is not about the prevailing circumstances necessary for a state to be overwhelmed by violence, but about how the group's interests have inspired violent structure. Thus, ethnic participation in violence can be seen as a decision problem, "a competitive situation, and a conflict situation where the parties understand and take into account the fact that they influence each other payoffs perceptibly" (Stahl, 1972, p. 14).

This practice has created a chaotic system in which "patron-client relations are unstable" and subject to constant violent renegotiation (De Waal, 2016, p. 2; and 207). Here, the conceptualisation of a power struggle in South Sudan as a strategy for political and resource bargaining applies to my earlier argument that disarmament and disbanding of other informal armies fall short of meeting the strategic interests of the armed factions, where a defensive position taken by one group threatens others (Ganguly and Taras, 2002). Hence, the persistence of violence and accumulations of arms lies in the fact that South Sudanese ethno-political actors decided to engage in a purposeful militarisation of their group to outbid each other in the race to grab the state power and resource therein. The idea of ethno-political actors outbidding each other is not entirely based on ethnic tendencies. It is instead a "mass responsiveness to playing the ethnic card" (Sisk, 2009, p. 19). That mindset has entrenched in South Sudan as ethno-political chauvinists unleashed heated rhetoric for political reason. My thesis emphasises that elite exploitation of their ethnic group has been a fundamental cause of extreme violence in South Sudan.

What this project will emphasise in the next section is the fact that South Sudan has become a contested state. This argument may appear as if this thesis suggests the struggle over the ownership of the state. However, that is not the case. It instead, implies the war over whose power belongs. Although it appeared between the Dinka that Nuer that they targeted each other, these groups grievances are often aimed at the system in place or state. Esman contends that:

> The territorial state has everywhere become the arena in which competing ethnic groups' claims are asserted, contested, and regulated...Rules established and enforced by the state determine the goals that ethnic communities may legitimately pursue and the strategies and tactics they may employ...The state, then, is a party to most contemporary ethnic conflicts (Esman 1994: 18, 19)

This highlights that the challenges facing South Sudan are based on the armed actors' quest for self-defence, acquisition of power and resource. A crisis unfolds when the state lacks the political capacity to address the group's grievances, or at the very least, limit the escalation of dissent.

2.4 Ethno-Political Factionalism and the Proliferation of Arms in South Sudan

It is apparent in the literature that the domination of old Sudan's politics by ethnic Arabs, to some extent, 'heighten[ed] the cultural identity and solidarity of subordinate groups' in the South (Markakis, 1999, p. 75). After 2011, the influence of these constructs weathered, and the new state disintegrated. This disaster prompted a search for answers that led to differing conclusions. For years, the war between North and South has obscured hostile relationships between ethno-political factions in the SPLM/A (Laudati, 2011). This division creates the "conditions of political conflict where fighting and defending one's family, and the property is a major preoccupation" (Jok, 2005, p. 145). Thus, the war of 2013 hinge on a historical power struggle. As noted by a participant in this study: "Instead of complying with constitutionalism, the SPLM elites transcended rebel hierarchy, seized power, and excluded others. They personalised the decision about who will access power and have favoured the Dinka ethnic group" (P1/19/06/2017). This emphasis saw the rebellion as a desperate search for security, recognition, and inclusion.

This argument is counter-productive to the DDR due to the objectives of the leaders driving the conflict. After independence, South Sudan descended into deadly prospects. First, the SPLM/A leader, John Garang used to enthuse South Sudanese by telling them he is fighting for freedom, justice and prosperity, but his death in 2005 robbed the South Sudanese of his charismatic leadership (Deng, 2012). When the SPLM came to power in 2005, Garang's promises were not kept, partly because the CPA and independence failed to coax SPLM elites out of their jungle mentality, vested with self-interest. Hence, the first significant hurdle facing the disarmament in South Sudan was the nature of the country's security forces. A participant clarifies that the "SPLA is a traumatised rogue militia, with experience and skills completely unsuited for security provision. All they want is cash, weapons, and a licence to rampage" (P3/21/07/2017). Those who were excluded rose in violent protest. This socio-political system created laissez-faire security, allowing each group to operate according to the context of self-interest.

Based on earlier emphases, political or economic frustrations caused war driven by a sense of fear and injustice. It is worth exploring how this violence became a critical incentive for militarisation. Some analysts assumed that this accumulation of arms was because of a lack of command-and-control in old Sudan as well as in the SPLM (Gordon, 2014). This claim is valid, but the optimal account surrounds how different armed actors have become fraudulent enterprises propagating fear. Many of those who live in fear seek arms, and suspicions among groups urge them to invest in self-security. This mindset propagates decentralised use of force and heightens complex grievances at the local level. This situation requires rethinking the approach to the DDR and the continuing proliferation of arms in accordance with the challenge of convincing armed factions that the DDR is not a threat to their power. Focusing on the motivations of the groups, could miss half of the conceptual puzzle. It can ignore the opportunity of armed criminal to act as the spoilers. One vital issue that affects the opportunity of spoilers is the capability of the state.

Capable countries can address the demands of their populations in ways that diminish the incentives and motivations of political war, which curbs the capability of groups to incite violence. However, the absence of state capability in South Sudan has led to pervasive militarisation throughout the society, and a complicated informal arms race, as each group develop rigid, state-like systems of governance with different security systems tasked with defence and protection of ethnic territorial integrity. In most cases of the DDR in other countries, ethnic militarisation was not seen as a challenge. The reintegration model used in South Sudan focuses on giving skills training for SPLA as the main strategies of achieving peace and preventing war (Dradiga, 2010). As such, armed structures have been empowered by the ruling elites and the South Sudan DDR commission attempting to carry out the DDR have been disempowered in a way that appears self-defeating for security reform institutions. The literature on the civil war, political competition, the proliferation of arms and the balance of power cited before, hints that the probability of civil war is high when the power and resource distribution between groups is inequitable.

The effort of bargaining for power can require groups to resort to an arms race to "retain an advantage in such power-relations" (Okodolor, 2005, p. 3). This is main problem in South Sudan, where the rationale for violence revolved around groups' interests. In this context, there is a way to incorporate ethnicity as a grand strategy for both survival and security (Walt, 1990). Johnson, (2012, p. 32) asserts that "the problem of political control has more to do with weapon development and transfers than with theft or unauthorised access". Thus, arms spread across South Sudan through an internal supply line, but it is the demand from groups that fostered militarisation. Building on this scenario, the supply and demand for arms are not accidental steps, but considered choices aimed to provoke a war (Lake and

Rothschild, 1996). This precarious situation allowed the elites to overstate slight grievances for political purposes. This deliberate aggravation was evident in an interview with one official. While he was once one of the most highly ranking military officials in South Sudan, he attributed his grievances to what he described as "the tribal clique", accusing the ruling Dinka majority of looting "all our resources" (P2/16/07/2017).

To him, the rebellion was a result of post-secession governance characterised by a corrupt political practice, discounting his own role in those practices. Resisting such a system became a duty for the oppressed, based on this assessment (Olzak, 2006). While he claimed that he is fighting "to rescue the people of South Sudan", his politics are not as impartial as he implies. Many rebel factions accused the government of marginalisation for strategic reasons. They sow fears by exaggerating threats to incubate insecurity among their political groups. Thus, resisting the DDR became a necessity for protection (Tomchak, 2017). While scholars tout the irrationality and hatred, those analysing the impact of political and security uncertainty treat irrationality and hatred as strategic reactions for war (Cederman and Min, 2010). When the state is fragmented, armed conflict is a rational response because each group foresees the danger in terms of self-interest. Some simplistic analyses of the challenges facing post-war states suggest that there is no struggle for loyalty in South Sudan because the hereditary nature of identities fixes groups (Fahmi, 2012).

Hence, armament is an outcome of security as a zero-sum game (Kaufmann, 1996). This project does not want to overstate the strength of ethnic mobilisation in a refusal to disarm, but it argues that, under the conditions of uncertainty, the opposing groups compete to ensure survival (Zambakari, 2013). This analysis recognises the role of ethnic affiliations in organised violence as interlaced with how identities are mobilised as a strategy for political struggle. Such a conflictual situation forced the opposing groups to rely on perpetual defence strategies, described by this project as violent political tribalism. This system altered the actor's behaviours, thus, opening a floodgate for arms racing. This argument leans on the emphasis that "saw the lack of governing capacity as the critical factor in the rise of political violence in the developing world", but that does not emphasise the impact of armed vulnerability (Sobek, 2010, p. 270; citing Huntington, 1968).

2.5 An Impact of Armed Group's Insecurity Surrounding the DDR

South Sudan is ungoverned space, an anarchist situation impossible to police, control, and manage, given the power of the actors wielding violence. Although a bulk of Gurr's (1970) study focused on the motives for political violence, he demonstrates "it clear that the (in)actions of the state in question affect how the potential for political violence becomes actual political violence" (Sobek, 2010, p. 270; citing Gurr's 1970). In specific, armed conflict "is most likely to manifest in societies that rely on coercion to maintain order in lieu of providing adequate patterns of value-satisfying action" (Gurr, 1970, p. 317). From this angle, South Sudan has not satisfied the demands of its populations to co-opt political violence. Empirically, this suggests that armed conflict emerges from the fact that "weak states invite collective dissent" (Lichbach, 1995, p. 68). When South Sudan disintegrated in 2013, every corner became a shelter for growing bands of ethno-political armies. In this case, the DDR is hindered by groups' need for self-protection. As argued earlier, fears allow groups to maximise arms and armies and interpret their security along lines that pre-suppose an unavoidable necessity of self-defence. Accordingly, groups living in fear behave like states in international politics.

The suspicion, political and economic interests and security preferences are enough in this case for the competing armed factions to amass arms are armies. In a report by the Arms Trade Treaty (ATT) monitor in 2015, South Sudan is ranked highly among many countries as being filled with millions of small arms. The report indicates that every corner of the country is experiencing violence because of mounting accessibility to arms. Some observers argue that South Sudan's informal armies possess twice the number of arms than those of state law enforcement agents (Kimenju et al., 2003; Muthike, 2015; Cheruiyot and Kizito, 2008). The Human Security Baseline Assessment asserts that the accessibility of guns among ethnic youths in South Sudan is having permanent consequences for the DDR (Cheserek, 2007). Here, local militias' reservation towards the disarmament and the fear of an attack diminishes the status of the DDR.

While these armed actors undermine and impede state security, their communities consider them as protectors. This situation reflects the normative view of why many countries in Africa fail to establish a monopoly on the lawful exercise of violence (Herbst, 2000; Acemoglu *et al.*, 2006; Besley and Persson, 2009). This uncertainty rubber stamps ethnic armies as genuine protectors of their communities (Muchai, 2005). Despite the well-intended purpose of the DDR, the lack of political will among the armed actors created a stalemate in the disarmament arena.   What this project emphasises, and perhaps answered in previous chapters, is when does the fragility or the collapse of the post-war states embodies with informal armies make the agenda of the conceptual idea of the DDR? This debacle is exacerbated by poorly managed arms and ammunition that make existing ethno-political violence much more deadly. In South Sudan, ill-conceived security measures such as selective and forcible disarmament, as well as the arming of local ethnic militias further destabilise the situation, thus, making resistance against the DDR inevitable (Jok, 2017).

2.6 Self-Defence and the Militarisation of Identities in South Sudan

Whether they are political factions or pastoralist communities, armed groups in South Sudan share a common propensity to violence. As such, the DDR faced power struggles and communal armed conflicts. It might be possible to address "the structural problems of governance, through post-war institutions enhancing programmes" (Weilenmann, 2014, p. 16). However, the effectiveness of DDR via Security Sector Reform SSR is challenged in South Sudan by various types of armed conflicts, and by military structures created over time through the war with the North and local conflicts. The literature on DDR concentrating on the capability of emerging states to organise the DDR and the role of the international community's funding. These strategies failed to emphasise the politics of the groups opposing the monopoly on violence. What is essential in the failure of the disarmament in South Sudan is the militarisation of identities based on the ideas ingrained during decades of war. It worth noting that the ethno-political armies in South Sudan became "total institutions that mould the beliefs of their members for life" (Cohen, 2004, p. 98).

Because military activism theory is not relevant to violent situations, each ethno-political groups in South Sudan are indoctrinated to believe that they have to fight for survival. The readiness to defend oneself or community emphasises the focus on security and survival while ushering in a belief-system that cherishes the status-quo of a militarised mindset rather than the DDR. The armed pastoralist communities, for instance, defined themselves based on "community defence forces", a sentiment derived from the existing security gap or absence of collective security (Burnett, 2012; Hatcher, 2014). Each group has subscribed to a mutual feeling: "we will disarm, but only if all the other communities disarm as well" (Saferworld, 2012, p. 6). The irony of seeking arms for self-defence is a stalemate of the DDR and insecurity that underwrites the proliferation of arms. These debacles make it difficult for the post-war state to police the use of force (Cheserek *et al.*, 2012; Brewer, 2009). South Sudan, as a result, is saturated with arms, and the demand for arms increases surplus circulation (Gobinet, 2011).

Surplus refers to "small arms that are deemed unnecessary for a state's national defence" (Bevan and Wilkinson, 2008, p. 30). Such accumulation becomes dangerous to peace because these guns are illegitimately diverted from national defence and used to provoke ethno-political conflict (Karp, 2010). While a tiny section of the population feels that the government provided the necessary security, South Sudanese from minor ethnic groups live in fear and resorted to self-defence (Murphy, 2017). The basis of this argument is not an effort to negate the extraordinary devotion of individuals, government and international organisations scattered across South Sudan who offer peripheral communities' degrees of safety. Nevertheless, in the end, those efforts are not enough, and many people are left with no other option but to mobilise their armed youth for community defence. If there were to be effective disarmament in South Sudan, it necessary to have an understanding of the ways ethno-political armies seek to protect their livelihood in a situation where state either cease to exist or can no longer be depended upon (Patinkin, 2017).

The sentiment of fear fuelled expanding bands of armed groups inspired to defend themselves. The key conclusion is that the militarisation of South Sudan is a by-product of decades of civil war and ethno-political division that the nascent state cannot control. These conditions allowed elites to mobilise their ethno-political groups for self-interest, which increases the risk of opting for a violent path. The lack of security management systems worsened such a situation. This deficiency encourages manipulation of the DDR for partisan interests. This existence of arms in the hands of those who have no trust in the state's capacity to ensure essential security was apparent, only to be ignored by the CPA and post-secession DDR. Thus, this project is critical of the state-based DDR as nothing more than further proof that peacebuilders are insincere. If the violence in South Sudan inferred heightened scale for armed struggle and scope for manoeuvre by political leaders, it also meant that the DDR had to rely on, or at least emit an understanding of, this situation. Most destructive violence in South Sudan comes to rest on a foundation built on "opposing tenets and legitimacies" (Di Maggio and Powell, 1991, p. 267).

This study does not reject the supremacy of the state but argues that violent fragmentation of South Sudan exists as a historical reality as well as the demise of the post-secession state system. Hence, resistance to the DDR is caused, not just by the lack of the outward manifestations of a state capability, but also a lack of the 'new codes of conduct and new social standards of self-restraint' that can pacify hostile actors and society as a whole (Linklater, 2011). In Chapter Six, the project will analyse how the CPA, as a mediated peace, pay little attention to the internal problems of the South Sudan that would later make DDR undesirable. Thus, South Sudan's post-war transition was going to be characterised by calamity and a bizarre form of political cannibalism where a state-society would be its own prey. This research has alluded to the layering of authority, legitimacy and agency of violence to argue that state-driven DDR cannot address groups' resistance by enhancing the state's ability to maximise the use of power/violence.

2.7 Conclusion

South Sudan experiences armed conflicts that set state against some ethno-political groups and ethno-political groups against other groups: thus, resulting in political turbulence, insecurity and human tragedy. This relates to the inability of the post-war South Sudanese state to pursue inclusive policies that promote social cohesion. Government and armed political movements induce ethnic groups to become accomplices of inter-elites' political wars. This conversion of civilian populaces into the competing groups' militaries and paramilitary groups became a common feature of South Sudan. Within this context, every ethno-political group takes advantage of the proliferation of small arms to arm themselves for protection, cattle rustling, banditry, and revenge attacks (Assefa, 1999). Even before the CPA, Sudanese civilians participated in various security-like activities in areas affected by armed violence. Prospects for disarming ex-fighters after the CPA did not include the strategy of containing civilian militarisation. This deficit will form the core of the discussion and examination in Chapter Three of this book.

The criticism towards the CPA's SA is its inability to design the DDR within the military mindset of South Sudan, primarily noting the importance of addressing the fear that armed groups hold about the role of the factional armies. The theoretical debate on ethnicity and its role in South Sudanese conflict and arms proliferation need to be considered in the process of the DDR. This chapter has discussed ethnic division and politicisation as a well-used and useful tool for mobilisation. Still, the critical point that emerges from the analysis of

South Sudan's violence is the difficulty in balancing strong ethnic gravitation with allegiance to the state. In this sense, marginalisation, competition and fears of domination cause conflict that counters appeal for the state monopoly of violence. Because of these problems, this project examines the structural conditions and presents how they heighten polarisation of socio-political assertiveness, which increases the risk of armed conflict, and affects perceptions towards DDR (Wood, 2008).

Chapter Three: The Autopsy of the Sudan Comprehensive Peace Agreement (CPA): Its Shortcomings and Their Effects on the DDR in South Sudan

This thesis argued that, while ethnicity is a contributing factor to war, the characterisation of the violence in South Sudan as an ethnic war is inadequate. Chapter Five stressed that inter-ethnic relationships in South Sudan are "clouded by incompatible interests, unfair access to political space, economic and other opportunities; and inter-group identity competition" (Shulika and Okeke-Uzodike, 2016, p. 25). Each of these issues needs to be addressed to avoid the recurrence of civil wars and resistance to the DDR because of the commitment problem (Powell, 2006; Fearon, 1998; 2004; 2005; Mattes and Savun, 2009). The commitment issues leave the warring parties "with fear of future uncertainties concerning both their physical security and their abilities to pursue the interests of the constituency they claim to represent" (Chen, 2015; citing Joshi and Mason, 2011, p. 390). In the CPA, the focus was on provisions and implementation of power and resource sharing (Arnault, 2006). When it comes to the CPA-DDR, the SA outlook prefers the victory of the SAF and SPLA "than the inclusion of other veto players" (Barreau, 2016, p. 16).

Cunningham contends that "the exception to the inclusion of all veto players at the negotiation table is the will to forcibly disarm groups that blocked the peace" (2013, p. 45). While Cunningham prescribes this type of DDR, I argue that this is the nature of the DDR adopted by South Sudan. This realist argument of preferring the victory of one dominant group form the basis of Ottaway's argument, that a collapsed state "carries too much animosity to engage in a negotiated peace process and that raw power generated by superior force is the only solution" (2002, p. 1013). While she was focusing on outright victory in a civil war, her points are met in the design of the CPA-DDR, but at the detriment of the following. First, the realist approach to conflict and security often ignores the fact that the quality of the design and implementation of both political and security measures in the post-civil war context are not separate. Sometimes, even a well-designed accord may not be implemented and thus lead to the renewal of war. The condition in old Sudan was unable to allow only the SAF or SPLA to reign supreme because there were many armed groups in the North and South, respectively. This situation highlights the problem of how IGAD distinguishes those groups that must be included and those that could be excluded from the CPA.

To answer this question, this chapter discusses the bumpy road to the CPA. It will highlight how every aspect of building a lasting peace in South Sudan was near impossible when the war ended. This chapter will argue that the way the civil war ended and the terms of the power-and-wealth sharing between the GoS and Southern rebels hurt the DDR. This argument requires critical reflection on IGAD mediation, and thus, this chapter will assess how its peacemaking processes influenced the CPA-DDR. The accord ignored the rules of the game by which North and South, and OAGs, pursue their interests.

I use the informal armies to argue that the DDR excluded armed groups that should have been included for required changes in security policy to occur (Tsebelis, 2002). An informal armed actor's political "interests must divert from the other players' interests, and it must be sufficiently organised to exercise a veto, meaning continuing the war independently even if the other actors find an agreement" (Cunningham, 2006, p. 878).

In this case, veto actors in South Sudan were not mere spoilers per se, who believe the DDR would impede their power and hence refuse all settlement attempts (Cunningham, 2013). This project recognises that there were multiple informal armed actors in Southern Sudan during the CPA's negotiation and that the more there were, the more problematic it would be to include all of them in any peace settlement. Yet, if it involved all armed actors, the post-war arrangements would have been inclusive. The contradiction between the DDR and the South Sudanese political dynamic is the fact that not all armed actors agreed on the dominant group/state's legitimacy to monopolise the use of force. Thus, the nexus between design and implementation is essential to understanding why the DDR was resisted. While the CPA ended the war, it did not address the legacy of war and the inherent commitment problem towards the demilitarisation of politics. The intermittent civil war in Sudan since 1955 has killed millions of people through violence and famine, and millions of refugees. This breakdown of social fabrics ushers in a political space where a transitional government is unable to prevent violent scuffles between groups (Deng, 2017).

Besides, the war "has led to the emergence of warlords and tribal militias, which operate to derive political and economic benefits and to defend their ethno-political territories from the regime in the North or the SPLM/A" (Babiker and Özerdem, 2010, p. 213), both of which were incapable of discharging legitimacy to warrant absolute monopoly of violence (Schomerus and Taban, 2010). This fragile warlordism hinted that the emerging state was not only susceptible to violence but also unable to constrain parochial violence. The armed groups securitised the world of their own making, where socio-political and economic issues are conceived and approached as threats to group survival. Despite the war with the North, conflicts among the South Sudanese were intractable because of the power struggle within the SPLM and among ethnic groups. These conflicts were securitised, thus, elevated into a struggle for survival. In efforts to end the war between North and South, several peace initiatives were launched. Still, none were successful, given that decades of civil war made violent actors more authoritative than putative state leaders.

In the early 2000s, however, the IGAD convinced the Sudanese government and the SPLM/A to pursue peaceful conflict resolution to transcend the common theme in Africa of coming to power as a direct result of sustained armed conflict (Babiker and Ozerdem, 2003). When the war finally ended in 2005, it was a step in the right direction. However, that hope quickly dissipated. Southern Sudanese reservations about the security motivated the SPLA to approach the DDR on the precipice of spoiler behaviour. Instead of productive meetings with other armed stakeholders, the SAF and

SPLM continued their arbitrary control. Academics concluded that the SA in the CPA was designed to the detriment of long-term peace in South Sudan (Ahmed, 2009). This chapter analyses how the CPA has led to a vital political transformation in the whole territory of Sudan, but not in power relations between the SPLM. The implications for the DDR have shown a surprising lack of critical enquiry on how this mode of settlement shapes the political strategies chosen by peace partners and those excluded.

This observation prompted an open question on what the SPLM's dominance in the South means for the outcome of the DDR. This question problematised how the CPA was approached and its impact as a vital precursor to the DDR. The point here is to link the flaws of the CPA processes to the failure of the DDR in South Sudan. This analysis requires a review of the strategic conflict management approach applied by the IGAD and the incentives model that was loaded with political and security potential to hinder the DDR. The awkward truth about the CPA is that it did not bring about a lasting end to the conflict in South Sudan. One of the blunders that affected the DDR in South Sudan was the IGAD's dichotomisation of war as between the North and South, whereby the resolution and post-war intervention was tailored in a manner contrary to the violent South Sudanese heterarchical political order. A heterarchical order refers "to systems with multiple, and often "tangled" hierarchies, where units are variously related, generating multiple rankings according to authority" (Polese and Santini, 2018, p. 383).

The IGAD's focus on the North-South conflict dimension reflected a strategic logic of peacemaking, that had proven itself to be a successful mediator with the capacity to end the wars in the region. "The CPA might not have been perfect, but we ended decades of war", argues an IGAD official (P2/14/11/2017). While IGAD was right to approach the peace in the North-South dichotomy, that approach excludes other political structures that were fighting the dominant groups in both North and South Sudan. The flaw is a failure to recognise the presence of armed veto actors and the effects of the violent fragmentation of local authority. These flaws affected the DDR because of unresolved tensions between and within political systems over authority, security and resources. De Waal (2017) sensed that such a piecemeal approach was unsuitable for tackling the Sudanese violent political order. The basis of this criticism lies in the fact that "the CPA came about in the context of a balance of power between the two warring factions, and the agreement lays down the principles for a possible independent South Sudan" (Baas, 2012, p. 177).

Thus, the CPA's SA sets the stage for transforming the SPLA into a conventional army in case of Southern secession. Despite this condition, the IGAD failed to speculate on the possibility that the end of the war between North and South would not grant the SPLM sufficient power or definitive institutions in South Sudan (Gates and Strøm, 2008). This situation rendered the DDR vulnerable to manipulation and instrumentalisation by violent groups in pursuit of selfish goals (Eriksson and Wallensteen, 2004). Denying the legitimacy of these groups ignored their influence on the potential benefits of calibrating the DDR according to these dynamics of violence. The CPA failed to lay a suitable basis for a contractual DDR. Without those arrangements, a costly (politically or socially) military option remained relevant for those who were living in fear, especially those subjected to varying degrees of exclusion. This strategic thinking is akin to Mao Zedong's famous remark that "power grows out of the barrel of a gun" (cited in Jervis, 2001, n.p). Cox and Sisk supported this argument that "historical dominance of single or blocs of larger ethnic coalitions create deeply entrenched forms of marginalisation that are volatile" (2017, p. 6).

An enquiry into the link between fear of domination and violence in South Sudan yielded a blunt response from one elite participant: "we have poured our blood for this state. When our people were dying, they did not say Dinka dominate death" (P4/22/07/2017). This view confirmed how "the post-liberation states are also subject to contestation when the state-building becomes too exclusivist or predatory" (Dorman, 2006, p. 1087). While the CPA addressed the issue of the dominant between North and South, it failed to read the same script to the SPLM's leadership dominated by the Dinka ethnic majority governing South Sudan (Badiey, 2010). The transfer of power to the dominant group in South Sudan was a recipe for disaster because the "institutions and instruments of public power and authority were weak or non-existent, save in the person of the leader during the war of national liberation" (Nyaba, 2019, p.152). By adopting the exclusivity over inclusivity, the CPA excluded the whole gamut of warring parties. Such exclusives approach ignored "the correlation between identities and interests" (Wendt, 1999, p. 258).

Wendt refers to interests as "needs or functional imperatives" (p. 258). Individual interests are "beliefs that actors have about how to meet their identified needs, which are the proximate motivation for behaviour, and what rationalists refer to as preferences or tastes" (Wendt, 1994, p. 385). Some may find inclusivity unnecessary in the CPA because it was an effort to end the secessionist conflict, but the success of the DDR requires a collective engagement aimed at addressing subjective interests of the armed group (Torjesen, 2013; Muggah 2005). This project agrees with critics who decry the CPA as incomplete, or who argue that it has created the conditions for untenable peace. The basis of this argument lies in the hybridised nature of the conflict that existed before the CPA. The motives for this violence make it extremely improbable that purely political solutions could support the DDR. This deficiency requires a brief survey of internationally driven conflict management and an analysis of how the mediation strategies of the CPA, and its post-war responses did more harm than good to the DDR in South Sudan.

3.1 A Bumpy Road to the Negotiated Settlement of Sudanese's Civil War

The pacifist response to internal armed in the post-Cold War era has been adequate, but rarely resulted in unparalleled success (Deng, 2010). Although the incidence of intra-state warfare has decreased substantially since the end of the Cold War, sustainable solutions to the menace of civil war remain elusive. Building peace after a protracted armed conflict is not difficult, but it is challenging to bring ex-foes together. It is even more challenging to disarm Ex-Combatants and control arms surplus (Quinn *et al.*, 2007). The debacle in South Sudan is evidence of that challenge. To find a way to resolve armed conflicts, an array of contradictory explanations emerged to unpack motives for participation in civil wars. To date, not all competing conflict resolution concepts have been grounded in determinants of conflict resolution. Filling this gap requires an analysis of the international peacemaking processes that culminated in Sudan's CPA. The following analysis emphasises the deficiencies of the external logic of peacemaking towards the DDR in South Sudan, as a state beleaguered by warlords (Duffield, 2001; Reno, 1999; 2000).

Although signing an agreement to end a civil war is often an emotional demonstration of intentions towards a peaceful future, its implementation is another process altogether. The CPA was a cause of celebration in South Sudan. It was expected that the elation of the masses emerging from the harsh realities of war would translate into peaceful co-existence and collaborative action towards political and economic development. That has not been the case in South Sudan, where ex-rebels divided the state into personal fiefdoms and engaged in a power struggle, which propelled an outright militarisation of the competing groups (Brosché and Höglund, 2016). Thus, the peace agreement failed to create a situation where the groups co-exist with one another within the agreed political framework. By focusing on the North-South dichotomy of war, the IGAD focused its efforts in pursuit of an exclusive political agreement to end the civil war without emphasising how the extent of power-sharing institutions would lead to stable post-civil conflict peace. In an empirical context, South/ern Sudan did not enjoy a durable peace.

The cause of instability is not just because there are many guns in the hands of civilians who can be readily mobilised by their tribal elites. It is because the IGAD failed to contextualise the modality of the CPA-DDR according to the fact that "politics in South Sudan is tribal in nature"; thus, exclusion of one group would lead to the use of one's tribal masses as a tool to ascend to power (P23/21/11/2017). This participant stressed that "some of our politicians do not have a clear political agenda, and that is why they resort to what is readily available, which is the guns possessed by their tribesmen". Thus, several OAGs, from minor ethnic militias to armed rebel faction, continued to fight the SPLM/A and loot rival communities' resources (Barreau, 2016). Because OAGs actions obstructed the peacebuilding, they should have been considered as veto actors. Mostly the CPA was a political commitment between North and South but lacked the inclusive political and security procedures to make it compatible with the interests of OAGs (Isike and Okeke-Uzodike, 2010). This approach raised questions of how the DDR would solve the abundance of arms when the peace process did not consider the insecurity of armed actors.

While it was fair for the IGAD to presume that the political allegiances of the Southerners lay with the SPLM due to its political reach, the CPA did not provide clear channels to address the competing demands among the groups. While the CPA mandated the right to self-determination and a separate army, it failed to explore how the extreme levels of violence among South Sudanese were going to derail the DDR. Viewing the South Sudanese as a unified group of peoples based on their war with North disregarded the fact that the use of force in the region is dominated by the actors who oscillate between the main SPLM/A, and militias fighting local wars. Also, the institutions required for a legitimate monopoly of force were weak or non-existent. Besides, the CPA did not address the concerns of OAGs regarding the dominant group. This situation arose, in part, because each group sought military power for its political strategies. Secondly, the post-war situations alone can affect the outcomes of the DDR (Brosché, 2014). Countries emerging from the civil war lacks socio-political and economic institutions to support peace.

The lack of functioning public institutions is often exploited by dissenting armed groups, thus, pushing the emerging states to further crises. First, the obsolescence of security and weak institutions of governance have a negative influence on an emerging state. Security failure also creates unrests that give ways to some extremes conditions that actively solicit violence capable of propelling the states to perilous trails of failure. Such debacles are evident in South Sudan. When there is no functioning political and economic system, the short-term incentives provided by the DDR cannot ensure Ex-Combatants' socio-economic reintegration into society, thus reducing the ability to divert them away from a violent path. I am aware that "violence and the deprivations of people caught in conflict compel negotiators to focus on ending the war" (Zartman, 2008, p. 56). Under this imperative,

IGAD paid less attention to the localised wars in the remote areas where ethno-political factions engage in an informal arms race. When armed conflict is between the local armed group, as it is in South Sudan, such types of violence are entrenched in the socio-political dynamics of the society (Jarstad and Sisk, 2012). Peace agreements need to interpret potential threats that can spark an increase in violence, and that was not the case in the CPA.

An ending of the war in Sudan was an essential prerequisite for peace. However, the CPA programmes in Southern Sudan lacked any measures to entice informal armed groups to dismantle their security measures. Post-colonial Sudan was a fragile state, defined by enduring armed conflicts between the regime and the peripheries in Southern Sudan (Sørbø, 2010; Daly, 2007). Since independence in 1956, state capacity in former Sudan was eroded through deliberate policies of military rule, where the state lacked the legitimacy to rule (Deng, 2012). As a result, intensified violent competition emerged between contending authorities. The SPLM/A, for instance, assumed the role of public authority in Southern Sudan. This projection of capability to defend the interest of Southern Sudanese was meant to appeal to peripheries burdened by oppression and marginalisation (Garang, 1986). This effort to liberate the oppressed resonates with the rationale expounded in the literature on development in weak states.

The state's political system is precisely referred to "the exogenous introduction of state institutions, which instilled in the citizens an enduring sense of resistance to "decentralised despotism" (Lange, 2004; citing Mamdani, 1996, p. 37). For years, academics who analysed the state of Sudanese wars have projected varying views, with some arguing that the state has been irrelevant outside of major cities, or even suggesting that there is no such thing as the Republic of Sudan (O'Fahey, 1996). Others, like De Waal (2014), argued that deficiency of state order, but that the existing system is predatory. According to this argument, focusing on ending the war and ensuring the state monopoly of force is a mistake because economies and informal security structures can function in the absence of the state where state authorities are ineffective. One of the controversies in the pursuit of a military solution in Sudan was the mass armament of civilians through the creation of the Popular Defence Forces (PDF) through a Paramilitary Act in 1989 (Fluehr-Lobban *et al.*, 2001). This order allowed the Northern elites to mobilise their tribal youths for three critical reasons. First, the President desired and demanded the formation of such force.

Second, it became a source of employment for youth. Third, the armed youth was required as a backup against the SPLA. In response, the SPLA countered this by forming its tribal militias (Hutchinson, 2000; 2001). The proliferation of arms that accompanied this tit-for-tat recruitment was barely anticipated or mentioned in the CPA's DDR. These informal armies became proxies of the SAF and the SPLA, as well as defenders of their ethnic groups. One would expect that any peace accord must have mechanisms for delegitimising these groups before preparing to disarm them. Although these armies were visible during the CPA, mediators ignored them, a mistake that cost South Sudan deeply (Brewer, 2010). The SPLA attempted to disarm some of the armed groups forcefully ended with catastrophic consequences. A 2006 campaign to disarm the Nuer While Army (NWA) for instance, led to the death of over 1600-armed youths and SPLA soldiers (O'Brien, 2009). This encounter led to an outcry from the international community who accused the SPLA of commit massacres in the process forcefully disarmament (De Waal, 2014).

A participant recounts when giving an interview to this research that "DDR was tried in 2006-2012, but the process turned bloody. Some communities refused to give up their arms for fear of the government. You can recall that some communities were not in good terms with the SPLA" (P19/11/09/2017). Knowing that the underlying discontent within the Sudanese political spectrum could no longer be politically expedient, IGAD moved to resolve the question of North-South war (Simmons and Dixon, 2016). Launched in the late 1990s, discussions leading to the CPA achieved "a breakthrough in 1994 with an agreed Declaration of Principles" followed by several inconclusive rounds of peace talks until 2000s (Deng and Morrison, 2001). In the meantime, while these intermittent talks were happening, the South Sudanese were engaged in perpetual inter-groups wars. It appears this situation would make it impossible to foresee a unified political front working towards a substantive negotiated settlement. What was evident in the IGAD's effort, however, was the creation of a peacemaking model with a manifold of socio-economic and political equilibria, an institutional re-setting and self-determination.

These aspirations missed the point as "the end of the war does not signal a return to security" (Richmond, 2010, p. 172; citing

Muggaha, 2005). When there is no security, the DDR is in immediate jeopardy, as well as when political attitudes of armed actors are endogenous to exposure to forms of collective security and governance. The predicaments facing DDR success were distinct. The disputants in the Sudanese armed conflict forcefully defended their socio-political and economic interests during the initial peace process. Both GoS and the SPLM/A took what some described as profoundly entrenched positions on political, cultural and economic disputes, with slight inclination or unwillingness to compromise, but with the obvious intention of addressing these issues militarily (Honoroff *et al.*, 1990). As the war persisted, the severity of socio-political division, economic crisis, and disabled political institutions fuelled a protracted conflict that makes instability inevitable, and the violence becomes the "means of political advocacy and social change" in Sudan (Rowayheb, 2011, p. 424).

In this context, war aggravates the views of warring parties that political outcomes are zero-sum. Changing this mindset proved extremely difficult in the post-CPA-DDR era because of the historical lack of a state's control over the means of violence and the existence of armed parallel actors in South Sudan. Sceptical that GoS and the SPLM would reach a compromise over their stance, some researchers were convinced that the rulers in the North would not yield to Southern demands (Arnold, 2007; Johnson, 2014). Representatives of both camps were playing an intricate political game, each expecting the worst of the other (Young, 2005; Lyons, 2002a; 2002b). However, to the surprise of observers, and even some political players in both

North and South, in 2002 a momentous breakthrough was achieved, prompting a hope that the end of the Sudanese war was in sight. The negotiators of both camps began to soften their rigid stance and to comply with some essential solutions proposed by the IGAD, as will be examined in the following section.

3.2 The Breakthrough: 2001 - 2002 Momentum for Negotiated Settlement

Due to the immense political gap between North and South, the end of war optimism was not without its risks. While the National Congress Party (NCP) appeared as a united force during its execution of the war in the South, it had been preoccupied with internal power struggles and international isolation due to the carnage in Darfur (Carney, 2007). A power struggle pitted a potent Islamic cleric and academic; Dr Hassan al-Turabi, against President Omar Bashir, whom he helped to seize power in 1989 (ICG, 2011). This internal discord led to the creation of a governing system controlled by military elites and militias, as Bashir feared losing power (Rogier, 2005). On the economic front, uncertain oil revenue could only mitigate rising foreign debt and sanctions. To counter the threat, the government approached peace talks aware of the history of unconstitutional power transfer. Hence, President Bashir did not trust his adversaries nor his lieutenants (De Waal, 2016). It is evident that, beneath the commitment to peace, each group would preserve a fall-back option. The SPLM/A emerged cohesive from its internal division. Yet, such a temporary unity was not an antidote for absent of formal governance mechanisms.

Nothing would enable South Sudan to construct stable political order amidst the chronic dysfunctionalities of the post-war situation, fomented by an antagonistic relationship between the SPLM's leaders (Høigilt *et al.*, 2010). In these conditions of indefinitely extended political ambiguity, both North and South, and factions, "established competing governance mechanisms, which has, as a result, created a duplicate set of state-like violent institutions in the same territory" (Thakur and Venugopal, 2018, p. 2). Prompted by these uncertainties, the IGAD seized the opportunity to mediate an end to the war, but not to build sustainable peace, because each member was pursuing its interests through mediation (Ahmed, 2009). The IGAD bloc, at the time, comprised of Djibouti, Ethiopia and Uganda. These states had different political and security interests for ending the war in Sudan. For example, Mkutu (2008) emphasised how the war in Sudan led to unregulated borders, enhancing the flow of arms into Kenya and Uganda. While there could be other political and economic reasons, one could argue that both Kenya and Uganda were meditating on a blend of both defensive and offensive goals.

Although the ending of the Sudanese civil war showed IGAD's influence and the triumph of negotiation, such an approach lacked an appropriate strategy to control arms and reneging groups. Previous cases showed that if spoilers succeeded, they could counter the quest for peace as they did when Jonas Savimbi snubbed the U.N. supervised elections in 1992 and forced Angola back into civil war (Anstee, 1996). Moreover, the casualties of disastrous peace in Rwanda 1994 were higher than the cost of pursuing inclusive peace. However, not all spoilers succeed in their efforts to thwart peace. The Mozambique National Resistance (RENAMO) stalled in meeting its obligation and threatened to return to war, but the presence of an international force with a clear mandate compelled RENAMO to join the democratic political process, accept losing an election and disarm (Berman, 1998; Hall, 2009). The distinction between the effectiveness and insignificancy of spoilers is the mandate accorded to the guardians/protectors of peace and their ability to create practical approaches for managing armed spoilers.

Adedokun (2019, p. 1) argues that critical "components' of Mozambique's success in negotiating peace and creating conditions for political stability were the provision of demobilisation before democratisation, and relief efforts to district levels, financial support directly for the development of political parties and budget support to sectors relevant to peacebuilding". These procedures involved power-sharing, but what is vital are critical transitions: "from war to peace; from a one-party state to formal liberal democracy; and from state-based economy to market-based economy" (Adedokun, 2019, p. 2). With the presence of these elements in Mozambique, Rwanda and Burundi, ex-fighters were disarmed (Jones and Olken, 2005). In contrast, post-war South Sudan lacks all the desirable pre-conditions conducive to peace (Nicols, 2011). While refraining from dismissing the CPA as an absolute failure, this project contends that the cause of war in South Sudan during and after the CPA is due to IGAD's exclusion of three interrelated factors. The first is the paucity of local ownership/input in the peace process.

Second, the lack of an exclusive elite bargain, and finally, the lack of credible external actors' support through the U.N. By credible external actors' support through the U.N., I mean an external force with a mandate to enforce the contract of the DDR. The key to comprehending these challenges lies in understanding how violent actor assumes authority. It was evident that the decades of war in Sudan, which challenges any attempt to establish a state (Hall and Biersteker, 2002). In that case, peacemakers could have stipulated that violent actors in South Sudan institutionalise governance in three ways: monopoly on violence, political legitimation and economic security. Despite these situations, the CPA state that: "no armed group allied to either party shall be allowed to operate outside the two forces" (The CPA, 2005, p. 87). This mandate underestimated the mode of factional hierarchical steering and their ability to cast a consolidated shadow of hierarchy over a societal division, a point echoed by a participant below (Risse, 2010). "We assumed the power without functioning branches of government. We were able to put senior commanders to higher positions to continue where we were in the bush" (P27/12/09/2017).

Apart from an inevitable reaction from OAGs, there was no emphasis on the SPLM's lack of the capacity to govern. In the North-South relationship, the GoS standpoint was that "any secession in Africa challenges the long-held norm of accepting borders drawn by colonial powers as illogical" (Dowden, 2003, n.p). This fear was genuine. Eritrea has seceded from Ethiopia, but both states went back to war over disputed borders. Regardless of these fears, the stalemate and recurring internal discords in the North and South forged a conundrum, thus exhibiting a necessity to negotiate, although the SPLM/A came to the negotiation table on the stronger position. "When the CPA started, we were controlling 80% of Southern Sudan. Our next target was Juba, the capital of now South Sudan; once it falls, we were going to declare our independence through a military victory" (P23/21/11/2017). This participant reputed the idea that war-fatigue had reached a stage of despair, where the SPLM/A would agree to a deal selling its interest cheap.

So, what changed in leading to agreement on some protocols? The above interviewees claimed that the SPLA was ready for "any ceasefire"; an accord that would pause the war. Also, external involvements beyond IGAD added pressure (Cockett, 2010). Following the September 11 terrorist attacks in America, the Bush administration showed a readiness to use force on countries suspected of supporting the terrorists, and the government of Sudan was one of them. In response, members of the U.S. Congress followed this threat through with the *Sudan Peace Act*, aiming to pass further punitive measures against peace obstructionists (Rogier, 2005). In the words of a National Congress Party's official, "the U.S. looked like a wounded lion. It was difficult to predict what kind of action they would take tomorrow" (Johnson, 2011, p. 19). Among the leaders in the North, peace talks become a matter of survival (Justice Africa, 2001). By early 2002, peace talks appeared to be moving towards compromise. Perhaps the limited objective of ending the war was more vital in the determination of IGAD's approach irrespective of what might occur after.

3.3 IGAD Mediation: An Assessment of Peacemaking and its Effect on DDR

The first round of peace talks started in the early 2000s with little optimism. It was astonishing when a significant agreement was reached (Justice Africa, 2001). Despite the parties' consent on the roadmap for ending the war, they were still far apart on overarching issues. What needed to be addressed was Southern Sudan's demand for a semi-autonomous government, based on a power-sharing formula that would ensure the SPLA's capacity to deter the North from dishonouring any future peace accord. A participant in this study recalled that: "despite agreeing to the DDR, the SPLA was silently opposed to it because it was not useful for the interest of secession" (P19/08/11/2017). Until this 2002, the National Congress Party and the SPLM/A were not committed to a peaceful resolution. First, the unwinnable war in the South, an uprising in Darfur, and pressure from the West were seen to have overwhelmed the GoS. In preceding rounds of talks, gestures of a conciliation started, but the parties shied away from the commitment to peace.

Observers recognise that the SPLM/A was not willing to settle for anything less than a deal that would assure proper security for a referendum (Justice Africa, 2002a). The South Sudanese were demanding, not just their separate army, but also a fully equipped force. When this demand came to fruition after the finalisation of the CPA, the DDR was faced with a military debacle, as no one was willing to disarm a portion of its army. Academics stressed that "if a negotiated settlement to a civil war is to succeed, the rebellious group(s) must relinquish its arms and permit its soldiers to be integrated into the government army or returned to civilian life" (Downes, 2004, p. 240). This demand was not going to materialise in Southern Sudan for many reasons. First, the SPLM was unenthusiastic about the DDR. They argued that to "do so removes both their ability to defend themselves and their ability to threaten or use violence to enforce the agreement should the other side cheat" (Downes, 2004, p. 240). To understand the issues underlying acceptance of the CPA, it is necessary to revisit its predecessor and analyse the collapse of the AAA Brokered by Emperor Selassie, the AAA was the first pact to end the war in Sudan.

However, when the AAA was signed, there were no mechanisms to discourage future war, or reneging from the agreement, a point this project discussed at length in the introduction chapter. The Vice President of Sudan during the AAA-era, Abel Alier, emphasised how the government was not committed to full implementation of the AAA, citing how the Northern economic concerns reigned over Southern political demands and grievances. He described the AAA as "quite satisfactory on paper and could have gone a long way to meet some complaints of the South...but none of the parties believed they would be implemented!" (Alier, 1992, p. 61). Malwal argues that AAA unravelling began almost immediately (1985; 2014). Conversely, Sylvester argued that there was "nothing on the horizon that could seriously upset the AAA" (1977, p. 184). Sylvester was criticised for placing stock in President Nimeiry's power to ensure the success of the AAA. While Sylvester recognised that Southern elites were expressing reservations about the AAA, he failed to appreciate that the government was not funding the South sufficiently.

Additional challenges like the "problems experienced by returning Southern Sudanese refugees and displaced persons and efforts by the North to impose the use of Arabic in the South" exacerbated issues with upholding AAA (Shinn, 2004, p. 6). Sylvester's unbridled enthusiasm in the early stages of the AAA came crashing down when President Nimeiry abrogated the accord and imposed Islamic law across the country, triggering the return to war. In the context of the CPA, SPLM leaders had sufficient justification for caution. The previous experiences with the AAA were enough to cause concerns among the Southern Sudanese. One of their crucial concerns was based on what happened when the first guerrilla forces were disarmed as per the AAA. From the SPLM leaders' view, through this act South Sudan forfeited their military advantage to enforce the contract and, in doing so, made themselves vulnerable to the North. In the view of SPLM's leaders, the AAA was abrogated due to the lack of security to enforce the contract (Collins, 2008). Reviewing the failure of the AAA, Alier stated, "security was where the fight for effective power centred during the peace talks" (1992, p. 196).

In the lead up to the CPA, those experiences caused the SPLM to approach negotiations with care, remembering the destructive consequences of past cooperation. The effort that the SPLM/A has invested in addressing security issues during the CPA negotiations hints that the Southern Sudanese have learned from the past and understand the importance of getting security matters right. When this war ended in 2005, there remained a more major challenge awaiting the DDR. First, SAF and SPLA were far apart on the Southern secession. Secondly, the SAF and the SPLA were poised to turn their attention inward to confront credible internal security issues ranging from power struggles to new rebellions. Here, strained North-South relations and the SPLM/A and OAGs conflicts in the South gave heightened importance to the maximisation of armies by groups seeking to survive. The South Sudanese understood that, even if the payoff for maximisation of force can be counter-productive, it appears a more attractive option. For the DDR to be successful, mediators must have a formula acceptable to warring parties.

The creation of the two armies was a death knell for the DDR, as it created a precarious situation whereby any political disagreement could lead to the resumption of hostilities. Second, "military units retain their ethnic or regional loyalties even years after they have supposedly been integrated into the government army and can form the nucleus of a renewed rebel force" (Downes, 2004, p. 240). This is similar to what happened at the outbreak of the second armed conflict in Sudan when Southern units in the SAF mutinied in 1983. The mutiny came when President Nimeiry's government attempted to transfer the units of Southern ex-rebels to the North in response to tensions between the North and Southern Sudanese (Kasfir, 1977). The context of the Sudanese civil war proved that conflict interest between North-South could be solved by negotiation; the experience of AAA proved that certain forms of interest remain outside the power-sharing model. Given the hostile political interaction between the government in North and Southern Sudanese, the negotiation was conducted in accordance with the SAF and the SPLM/A's bargaining power, but neither party was subject to the commands of others.

This condition affected the DDR because security parallelism "prevent[ed] the central government from exercising any real authority in parts of the country controlled by different ethnic groups" (Downes, 2004, p. 240). When the use of force is not centralised, it is not only the DDR that is affected, but the situation can easily drift towards re-ignition of war. Rather than a mere flaw of DDR design or lack of substantial economic incentives, it was evident in South Sudan that other critical factors guided Ex-Combatants and groups' sentiments towards the maximisation of the military. Anyone seeking to conduct DDR needs to have both political and security procedures to reassure armed actors about each group's intentions. Instead of learning from history, IGAD misinterpreted the position taken by the SPLM as a bargaining ploy. It assumed it could pressure the SPLM into accepting Southern autonomy within the confines of a united Sudan to ensure the country's territorial integrity (Knox, 2012). Such contemplation derived from mediation aims, but not from a consideration of how to maintain peace (Wagner, 1993). To some extent, IGAD was right to assume that bargaining is a suitable starting point in Sudan's conflict resolution.

The main grievance emphasised by the SPLM/A against GoS was bad governance, which marginalised South Sudanese. Even though the war later transmuted into a secessionist conflict, the point of depart lies in disproportional "distribution of power" and access to resources (Wagner, 1994, p. 593). In that case, bargaining implies the procedures of determining the way to split the political or economic benefits from the collective action, which in this case. It is this instinct that Powell referred to as a "coordinated action to increase the size of the pie" (2002, p. 3). With that interpretation, IGAD was able to direct attention to the strategic nature of the civil war, adopting the negotiated approach as the strategy for ending the war. In contrast to a military victory, a negotiation is meant to "lead to an expansion in the size of the governing coalition in the post-war state" (Joshi and Mason, 2009, p. 6). The process of compromise or negotiated resolution resulted from a military stalemate where competing groups cannot mount a decisive military victory (Brandt *et al.*, 2008). This approach can be an alternative in situations of protracted civil war.

Proponents of the settlement approach describe it as "seeking to balance, divide, or share power among competing groups" (Downes, 2004, p. 240). To arrive at a settlement solution, IGAD persuaded the GoS and the Southern rebels to commit to peace through several incentives. These incentives included "security guarantees against defections from the agreement and power-sharing institutions to resolve the credible commitment problems that otherwise would make the parties reluctant to agree to a settlement" (Joshi and Mason, 2009, p. 6). This approach is a conflict transformation process focusing on equitable power relationships robust enough to prevent a further war among competing structures. Negotiating peace involves the establishment of the means for agreeing on ethical decisions within the state or among groups that had engaged in armed conflict (Fearon, 2004; Auerbach, 2009). When applied in a protracted armed conflict, the settlement approach is implemented under war termination theory (Zartman, 1983). Civil war termination is not regarded as an independent puzzle in need of exhaustive explanation.

Most academics either have overlooked the entire topic of civil war resolution or have argued that civil war is mostly irreconcilable and thus uninteresting to study from a war termination perspective (Lake, 2009). Thus, a political concession between the warring parties has been almost impossible (Jervis, 1976a; 1976b; 1978). This lack of compromise became more acute and precarious in Sudan in the early 2000s, where warlords and militias, such as the Janjaweed, have become powerful and pose more authority than that country's putative leaders. When the genocide started in the Darfur in late 2003, Sudan had what this project describes as an imaginary central government institution, causing war to stall without a military solution. That signal emboldened the IGAD to initiate the negotiated settlements. Like any other peace in Africa, the negotiation between North and South Sudanese was based on finding an equitable solution through a recalibration of power. The settlement approach appeared to be unconcerned about how best to enhance the prospects of stable peace and good governance. Also, the settlement approach does not question rebel motivations in-depth.

At the beginning of the peace process in Sudan, the IGAD did not engage in a lively conversation on whether Southern rebels were motivated by 'grievance or greed', or whether their aim was a public good, private gains or both. After settling on the motive of war as a 'grievance' of exclusion, the IGAD applied a power and resource sharing model to end the war (LeRiche and Arnold, 2012). "We did not think the North-South could go back to war again; the stakes were high", argued an IGAD official (P26/08/11/2017). This view was partly right, given the fact that the North and South did not go back to war. However, that could also mean that the war between North and South was not solely based on power grievances. Anchoring the peace settlement in the North-South context might have been done with the right intentions, but that led to a misreading of Sudanese politics where the GoS and SPLM/A were just other actors among various groups fighting over public authority. Despite these concerns, the IGAD devised a politically sensitive approach, shifting the peace strategy to the consensus between the principal actors.

The IGAD Secretariats used this tactic while seeking to utilise their authority to legitimise regional policies (Waihenya, 2006). That bargaining approach led to a failure to understand that the interests of the parties do not end with power-sharing. South Sudan holds vast deposits of Sudan's natural resources. The prospect of its secession meant the North should concede a significant source of national revenue. Despite these concerns, some voices within the GoS appeared happy to allow Southern Sudan to secede to help the North maintain the purity of the Islamic State (Sharkey, 2008). When they arrived at Machakos for peace talks in 2002, discussions started in much the same way as previous encounters. As they were placed under immense pressure, both parties agreed the plebiscite would occur within six years of the ratification of a peace accord. A month following the ratification of the Machakos Protocol, Garang and Bashir met as peace partners in Kampala (ICG, 2002b). The perceived intention of the meeting was to thrush out the rhetoric of war and hostility among the two leaders who have an ultimate influence on whether or not the negotiations would be a success.

That consensus soon vanished when the SPLA seized Torit town in late 2002. This violent action showed the effects of behavioural interference in the peace process. A behavioural interference is a "presence of random shocks that might make the remote possibility of outright military victory a more attractive option to compromise and peace" (Addison and Murshed, 2002, p. 487). To some, the "commitment problem is essential to understanding civil war recurrence because during the DDR phase each side knows that it would be better off with a sucker outcome: induce your rival to disarm while you covertly retain enough military capability to annihilate them once they are disarmed" (Chen, 2015, p. 3). Since the North and South "have this motivation and both sides know their rival has the same incentive, neither can trust their rival's commitment to disarm and demobilise under the terms of the settlement" (Walter, 2002, p. 34). When the Sudanese government and its Southern antagonists returned for the peace talks, it was encumbered upon IGAD to ask how psychological characteristics of warring parties could affect the civil war.

How does the psychology of Southern military-political elites would affect behaviour towards the disarmament? That view was also prevalent among OAGs in Southern Sudan who did not trust the SPLM/A nor accepted its political legitimacy over them. Instead, the commitment problem "can arise or continue into the implementation stage based on armed groups' fear of government reneging and government apprehension to cede power" (DeRouen and Chowdhury, 2013, p. 2). As argued earlier, the presence of an impartial, external intermediary can ease this commitment issue by "providing private information about warring parties' strength, resolve, and preferences to the opponent, and thus diminishing fear and security uncertainty in the subsequent implementation stage" ((DeRouen and Chowdhury, 2013, p. 2; citing Fearon, 1998; 2005). After a month of intense intercession and diplomacy, the IGAD managed to convince the parties to return to the negotiation table (Pendle, 2014). Despite convincing the parties to return to the talks, IGAD failed to interpreted back-and-forth confrontation between the SPLA and SAF as the other side of parts' commitment to a military solution.

3.4 Shifting the Peacemaking Strategy to the Principals' Haggling

A failure to prevent the SPLA's hostile action indicated that the CPA's implementation would be unstable. When parties are motivated by total political and security goals, they define the stakes as all or nothing. That situation creates an impasse that can be addressed through matching solutions to problems (Sisk, 1996; 2003). Despite these concerns, the IGAD persisted in reaching settled peace devoid of local needs. These types of peace accords are effectively prescriptive contracts intended to end or transform armed conflicts. "1) the major parties in the conflict are involved in the negotiation process and (2) substantive issues underlying the dispute are included in negotiations' (Muggah and Rieger, 2012, p. 3). This approach supports the claims of those who accused the IGAD of advancing Troika's (United States, United Kingdom and Norway) interests. Aleu Garang (2015, p. 11), not the SPLM/A leader Garang, argues that 'IGAD-led process on Sudan had a specific distinct style of management of external actors' roles and interventions', arguing that IGAD was not calculative about when to apply pressure and when to minimise push.

If peace is derived from external actors, "the process runs the risk of being driven unilaterally by external actors while the mediator should remain in full control" (Garang, 2015c, p. 19). It became apparent that IGAD worked to mobilise disputants but failed to check whether actors outside of the dichotomy of the SAF and SPLA were included in the talks. It can be argued that the CPA and its DDR were not inclusive, thus, susceptible to resistance. The main challenge for South Sudan was that, despite fighting the north in the name of a common enemy, the ethno-political groups united in a different format of ethnic armies such as the Nuer White Army only composed of Nuer. Concentrating on national politics as the means of ending the war and ensuring a successful DDR led the IGAD to miss the point or misconstrue the political and security concerns of OAGs. As demonstrated in Burundi, the challenges of working through a peace accord "tend to be manageable by states when there is a high degree of economic interdependence, formal democratic politics and lively Civil Society" (Stedman, 2000, p. 105).

Observers stated that the IGAD secretariat should disengage from active participation and allowed Garang, and Sudan's Vice-President, Taha, take control of the process. While procedures adopted by mediators are crucial to a negotiated settlement, interest-driven formulas may not overcome or minimise the threat of spoilers (Zartman and Touval, 1996, p. 454). To some, the IGAD provides mediation process from an 'interest-driven' approach (Young, 2012). The procedures at IGAD's disposal, including choosing the conveying site and formulate the protocols (Abrahms, 2013). This approach reduced the cause of war Sudan to the context of egoistic actors using force as the way of soliciting power-sharing. Such a perception was accurate in twofold competitions. Force boosts credibility via two arguments familiar to international relations scholars. Actors' use of force "imposes costs on the challenger, credibly signalling resolve to fight for his given preferences. Second, violence imposes costs on the defender, credibly signalling pain to him for non-compliance" (Schelling, 1966, p.75).

This process might be suitable to the position of the main protagonists, but it was a detriment to the DDR in South Sudan because that logic of power-sharing could not address the strategic dilemma, and political calculus of OAGs excluded from the CPA. It became clear that IGAD has worked to mobilise disputants but failed to check whether SAF and SPLA proxies were included in the negotiations (Morrison, 2004). Garang and Taha/Bashir's meeting was performed on a formula provided by IGAD (Young, 2006; 2007a; 2007b). Undeterred by the fact that long-running civil war has created the structural nature of violence, the IGAD pre-ordained the CPA's agenda and muscled it through via the principals. According to Zartman (2009, p. 4), a "mediator with muscle has been called coercive if force is used; directive if a particular solution is sought or manipulative if the input or outcome needs to be sweetened". Strategy at the IGAD's disposal differs from "taking responsibility for concessions, making substantive suggestions and proposals, making parties aware of non-agreement...[p]ressing parties to show flexibility, promising resources or threatening withdrawal" (Bercovitch and DeRouen, 2005, p. 115).

The above strategies echoed liberal peacemaking assumptions driven from above by external actors parading as apolitical institutions. In IGAD's view, the Sudanese problem was internal, but the solution must come from outside. However, a peace between the GoS and SPLM/A would not be a panacea to decentralised use of force in Southern Sudan. Achieving peace requires understanding the dynamics that motivated and governed OAGs. Instead, the core topic of Security Arrangements was the future status of the SPLA and SAF. This approach ignored "sub-national and community supportive perceptions and attitudes in addressing the security dilemmas and increased the potential for stabilisation of the post-conflict environment" (Molloy, 2013, p. 19). "...Over the past decade, the evolution of DDR theory has gone some way to recognising the criticality of these qualitative elements of perception and attitudes as appropriate indicators of achievement. This is reflected in consensus regarding the moves towards conflict sensitivity in addressing the multiple dilemmas" (Molloy, 2013, p. 19). Like the AAA, the GoS called for a default solution: to absorb the SPLA, while Garang preferred parallel armies.

One issue that would later affect the DDR was the absence of a pre-negotiation stage, which some academics refer to as characterised by a turning point. At its most potent political and military power, Jok Madut emphasises how IGAD induced the SPLM/A into what it reconsiders viable, peaceful alternatives, thus making the settlement approach more relevant. It worth arguing that the initial stage of the CPA led to a discussion of pertinent issues, which led to a de-escalation of war. Concisely, the CPA negotiation was defined by many techniques such as warring parties' calculation, identification of critical negotiators and sorting out the preferences and issues (Lax and Sebenius, 1991). In DDR, the CPA made the grave mistake of not recognising separate armies within South/ern Sudan. Within these confines, the SPLM/A worked to avoid confrontation with the North and to desist from using force against local dissidents for fear of upsetting unstable politics in the South that might lead OAGs to eschew an internal order. This approach culminated into a dialogue and the incorporation of OAGs into the SPLA.

As stated earlier, both armies had their interests to defend. Without committed, watchful eyes, they engaged in an outright arms race. What happens when South Sudanese vote in favour of secession and the North rejects such an outcome, asked one political leader interviewed for this research. She argued that none of them would initially compromise on secession. "We strengthen SPLA's capability in anticipation of war" (P20/13/09/2017). After achieving separation of the armies, Garang appeared to have scored a political point. For SPLA, self-interest, vested in Southern quest for statehood is reflected in Garang's effort to achieve SA that will increase internal stability in the South and deny the North chances for reneging without a cost. This situation was the backdrop against which the formula for the DDR was designed. One lens for studying the effects of the CPA on the DDR in South Sudan is that it was a contract between the SAF and SPLA for each to consolidate power. De Waal (2017) admitted that SPLA's consolidation of power presents no tangible solutions for the DDR in South/ern Sudan.

Drawing upon analogies of military readiness, De Waal (2017) sensed that the CPA failed to elaborate upon a framework for the two parties that would explain their decision to enter negotiations. Inasmuch as the theory of bargaining is concerned, the next issue on the agenda was wealth sharing. Because they deferred the problematic topics, wealth-sharing did not become a tiebreaker. Instead, the disputed regions and power-sharing became the last significant obstacles. After signing the wealth-sharing protocol on 7 January 2004, the end of the civil war seemed imminent, and both parties shifted their attention to haggling over the power-sharing quotas. Contented with these accords, the SPLM watered down its demand for secular North, and thus failed its armed allies in the Northern regions of Southern Blue Nile and Nuba Mountains (Willis *et al.*, 2009). One could only imagine how difficult it turns out to be to disarm these groups. Regardless of these concerns, "an extraordinary U.N. Security Council meeting in Nairobi gave the GoS and SPLM/A an ultimatum: reach an agreement by 31 December 2005 or severe consequences would ensue" (Rolandsen, 2011, p. 559; citing Rogier, 2005).

Bringing in the main political leaders from the North and South ensured that a peace accord was reached. These principals haggling shaped the contents of the peace between the GoS and the SPLM/A and affected the way the CPA was later implemented (Young, 2007). Nonetheless, it was a precarious procedure because "there was no higher authority to fall back on if the talks failed, in which case a resumption of the war would be the likely outcome" (Rolandsen, 2011, p. 559). One the other hand, the pressure exerted by the U.N. implies a multilateral centralisation of peacemaking (Jones *et al.*, 2011). While it would be challenging to implement such peace, especially the DDR in a country with multiple armies, the CPA was signed on 9 January 2005 without an effective political strategy on how to address political and security autonomy and distinct local grievances of the informal armies in South Sudan.

3.5 Implementing Exclusive CPA and the Impasses of the DDR in South Sudan

The most concise protocol of the CPA is its Chapter VI on (SA). Signed on 25 September 2003; it covers a little over three pages. Nowhere in this section is the Security Sector Reform (SSR) mentioned by name. As argued in Chapter One, the (SA) provision in the CPA mandated the SAF, and the SPLA should deal with OAGs in whatever way they felt necessary (De Waal, 2017). This approach hindered the implementation of DDR by ignoring the legitimacy of

OAGs, by providing SPLA with scope to manipulate the DDR for political purposes. The core demand of the SPLM/A was the secession of Southern Sudan. Aware of Northern efforts to thwart that aspiration, as happened to the AAA, the SPLA resorted to absolute militarism in disregard of the DDR (Schlee and Watson, 2009). To boost its military capability, the SPLA approached a dominant armed faction, the South Sudan Defence Forces (SSDF) led by General Matip, a Nuer warlord and proxy of the North (Arnold and LeRiche, 2008). After a brief negotiation, Matip re-joined the SPLA with his army, allowing the Southern leaders to bloat the SPLA (McEvoy and LeBrun, 2010). Without adequate external security to check potential violations of peace, there cannot be "deep implementation of a post-war peace settlement" (Spear, 2002, p. 130; 1996).

While a large contributor to DDR failure in South Sudan surrounds design flaws, some blamed the inefficiency of U.N. peacekeeping troops deployed after the CPA. While the protection of civilians was part of the mandate of the United Nations Mission in Sudan (UNMIS), the mission was only intended to monitor ceasefire provisions (UN OCHA, 2008). Observers have argued that substantial attention was dedicated to planning post-war international assistance without understanding the South Sudanese quest to fulfil their political interest, and their fear of the North. Preoccupied with defending their rights to self-determination, Southern leaders paid less attention to implementing defence transformation related projects, such as converting the SPLA from a guerrilla mindset into a national army and political institutions (AllAfrica.com, 2011). As the SPLA amassed force, the post-war procedures remain unfledged vis-à-vis the complex political challenges facing sustainable peace in South Sudan. Regardless of these concerns, the IGAD pushed through the post-CPA interventions, followed by the bulky World Bank managed MDTF, as mentioned before, accompanied by the rushed Joint Donor Office in Juba (Baas, 2011; 2012).

This approach meant that the MDTF was instituted on a liberal rigid reporting regime and a conservative mindset of the DDR (Ghobarah *et al.*, 2003; Murdoch and Sandler, 2002). A practical problem for the conservative DDR was the politics of the CPA's partners. However, some had argued that the failure of disarmament could partly be traced to the late disbursement of the MDTF budgets toward the DDR (Bennett *et al.*, 2010). It is problematic to predict the extent to which any approach toward the CPA's DDR could have succeeded. An insecure political environment after the war, makes nascent political and economic institutions weak. Snyder and Jervis argue that "institutions do not bind by magic; they normally do so by creating a pattern of behaviour around which expectations converge" (1999, p. 19). They further emphasise, however, "that new political institutions of the type that emerge out of civil war settlements have no track record on which patterns of good behaviour can be observed" (Spears, 2002, p. 131).

In contrast, having been engaging in armed conflict, the SPLM/A build a political and security outlook from nothing but destructive behaviour and distrust of its adversary. There was little in the CPA to keep armed disputants in South Sudan together after 2011.

As the SAF, SPLA and OAGs cannot trust each other; the security provision in the CPA does not settle security uncertainty, nor the parties' preferences. The SAF was rightly worried because reduced revenue and relinquishing its battle frontier in the South limited its ability to enforce the status-quo of unity and to counter the rebellion in Darfur. The SPLA also worked tirelessly to avoid the DDR because a smaller army would limit its chances of enforcing Southerners' demands and defending its domestic dominance. What became an issue in implementing the DDR is the fact the SPLA became battle-anxious based on the expectation of a probable war with the North, or internally. This mindset reflects prevailing attitudes of insecurity. While the SPLM knew that power-sharing denotes an "institution dividing or sharing political, economic, territorial and military power" (Jarstad, 2009, p. 41), it focused on military power-sharing.

The parties' preferences in the CPA worsened this problem. While IGAD was continuing to engage the parties, Troika settled for prevention of war and pushed for timely execution of a Southern referendum. To ensure this happened as planned, the International Criminal Court indicted President Bashir for war crimes in Darfur (Borger, 2008). The impact of this indictment in softening the regime's stance is debatable, but one thing was clear: the uncertainty provoked added to the complex political and security challenges, which included everything from the DDR to the looming partition of Sudan. Here, the GoS could not influence the outcome in its favour. What affected the DDR in South Sudan was not all about the relations with the North, but also domestic strategic interactions. The armed conflict in

South Sudan represents a remarkable turnaround from the previous assumption that North is the source of all problems, to a new claim of oppression by the Dinka. This challenge derived from a lack of institutional capability to dispossess elites of their guerrilla mindset and reconcile them with various other political factions.

Branch and Mampilly relayed some causes of war using a real scenario to explain why groups resorted to war: A Madi man (small ethnic groups) "returning from Uganda goes to the land he farmed before being displaced and finds a Dinka living in his house. He demands that the Dinka return his home. In response, the Dinka points to a date inscribed above the doorway. "On this date, I liberated this house from the Arabs. Where were you?" (2005, p. 1). The effects of this story on the DDR are many. Perhaps a Dinka man, who is refusing to relinquish the house, has not benefited from the DDR. Thus, the impact for DDR on the macro-level of South Sudan reflected both how the CPA was achieved in disregards of other factors that would later lead to war. As the CPA-DDR programmes were based on the forces of the SAF and the SPLA, its context of reintegration became exclusive, without procedures on how to resettle returning refugees and settled land disputes. Perhaps the CPA-DDR failed because its "normative process of change has not altered the identity of combatant to a civilian, from individual dependency on military structures to civilian self-resilience" (Munive, 2014, p. 334; 2013a).

The story of the Madi versus the Dinka man encapsulates the lack of social integration. This backdrop serves as an additional point for re-thinking ways to enhance the prospects of successful disarmament. It would require DDR promotors to include factors that would enhance peaceful co-existence among the groups, hence turning their minds to what is occurring at the local level. The DDR needs to emphasise political dimensions and their importance in the prevention of war through the highlighting process in which community members could resettle after the war. When those like the Madi man are left without a means for re-establishing themselves, it became apparent that DDR does not consider how individuals or groups can internalise socio-political grievances: "No one will listen to you when you are not armed, or have the support of powerful ethno-political military elites", argued one participant (P33/21/01/2018). This interviewee explains that those blocked from access to power because of ethno-political reasons had few reasons to be loyal to a government that imposes an exclusive ethnic rule.

As discussed before, DDR is conceived as "vital to stabilising a post-war situation, to reducing the likelihood of renewed violence and to facilitating a society's transition from conflict to normality" (UNSC, 2000, p.1). This perception is myopic because it lacks an understanding of the internal dimension, especially how group relationships may lead to new grievances and rebellion. My thesis contends that successful DDR requires managing macro and local grievances by dressing groups' perception and attitudes, towards the government and each other, instead of rushing for a quick-fix solution by focusing directly on SPLA. The CPA-DDR focus on the armies of GoS and SPLM/A constitutes a deficit that diminishes the sustainability of outcomes as it lacks factors that contribute to positive socio-political attitudes. The greater the intensity of the dilemma facing citizens, like the Madi man, the higher the negative impact of that deficit on the DDR. This project talks about the "curse of the liberation" and shows how the "limited capacity of the state is a critical element in the strategic interactions between collectivities" (Hartzell *et al.*, 2001, p. 185).

The cumulative effects of civil war "act as constraints on the state's capacity to regulate and oversee individual and group compliance with social rule" (2001, p. 185). Further, "a society with weak political institutions lacks the ability to curb the excesses of personal and parochial desires" (Huntington, 1996, p. 24). South Sudan emerged as a weak state; thus, "a society with weak state institutions is unable to contain predatory behaviour by elites" (Hartzell *et al.*, 2001, p. 185). In Chapter Five, this research observes that the weakness of the South Sudanese state has created two interconnected conditions, both of which are destabilising. First, when a single ethnic group dominates the state political system and acts aggressively towards smaller groups' interests, it can combine the inflexibility of the military with the softness of political illegitimacy. Under these conditions, it is not just the concept of the irresponsible state that is foregrounded; the South Sudanese state itself becomes the basis of manifest grievances. As stated earlier, the SPLM elites' self-interested behaviour contributed directly to the emergence of a coalition of ethnically based armed factions who negated the DDR.

These conditions related to the CPA in the sense that its processes made the SPLM the only legitimate political and military power in South Sudan. According to analysts, the current situation in South Sudan is reminiscent of a similar one in which the SPLM found itself in the early years of its formation (Munive, 2013a; 2013b; Richard, 2005). Several lessons could have been learned from the SPLM/A's formative inter-elite conflicts and their resolution, which could have informed and resolved the tensions that were simmering after signing the CPA. Here, the extent to which the CPA could have resulted in a successful DDR depends on whether its policies were products of ideological fantasy or a realistic response to experiences of the situation. It worth arguing that IGAD overlooks the uncharted South Sudanese politics by focusing on the settlement approach and ambitious top-down DDR. Scholars have argued that the SPLM's elites consented to the DDR mindful of their domestic history of politics as well as being concerned about their long-term political objectives (Baas, 2012). The violent political competitions that ensued after the CPA attempted to shape security governance but failed because of the zero-sum nature of politics.

3.6 Conclusion

Despite its inadequacies, the CPA had ended the war in Sudan. The negotiations allowed the parties to confront their differences and forge political readjustments. While it was driven externally, the pressure to explore new ideas and feelings challenged the parties to move from stringency to flexibility. The Machakos Protocol in 2002, for instance, on self-determination, was ground-breaking for the peace process. In comparison with other peace processes, the CPA precisely echoed the priorities of the GoS and SPLM/A. When pressed by the IGAD to make "a compromise, maintaining a firm political grasp in the North was more important to the NCP than securing the South" (Rolandsen, 2011, p. 562). For the SPLM/A, presiding over its separate forces was an outright victory, especially to those who favoured secession. This compromise provided the opportunity to negotiate the end of the war and ensured some political and SA to prevent war relapse until the Southern referendum was conducted.

Despite these successes, some issues were left unattended, whether wilfully or due to the flaws in the design of the CPA (De Waal and Mohammed, 2014). These concerns add to a known fact that the CPA did not include OAGs even though the political climate in both halves of Sudan was troubled by internal conflicts. The fact that factional violence persisted in the sub-regions increased the complexity of insecurity and caused greater difficulty in managing the DDR. The lessons from the negotiation and implementation of Sudan's CPA show that ambitious peacebuilding procedures might be doomed when multiple sovereignties are at war with each other. In line with Cramer's (2006) emphasis, this thesis may raise similar questions of the literature on external intervention: are external actors, especially IGAD, neutral in Sudan's peace? Are their interests benevolent? With the above problems, how do we strike a balance between a need for pragmatic commitment to end a war and the goal of building a lasting peace? It became considerably probable that Southerners would opt for secession during the CPA interim period.

However, the reality that the CPA committed the NCP and the SPLM/A to making continued unity 'attractive' was pretentious on the part of mediators. This double-standard approach hindered positive discussion about making separation bearable to the North and assessing the credibility of South Sudan to function on its own as a sovereign state (Rolandsen, 2011a; 2011b; 2005; 2015). With Ethiopia and Eritrea as examples, the IGAD knew that division of the state would solve, at least in the abstract, the North-South conflict. Still, it would not eradicate the possibility of future inter-state war given the issues cited earlier, nor does it ensure internal cohesion and security within the two states. The framework instilled in the final phase of the CPA, signed on January 9th, 2005, enabled a relatively quick end to the war and allowed some critical issues to be deferred. In contrast, South Sudan's secession on July 9th, 2011, brought an abrupt ending to compromise. The independent promulgation installs the SPLM/A as a sovereign government without capacity and legitimacy to govern, or the diplomatic strength to engage neighbouring states and the wider international community.

4: Conclusive Summary

The peace accord heralding the end of the war between North and South in 2005, and the secession of South Sudan on July 9th, 2011, marks a substantial step in the peace procedure. Yet, neither the ending of overt conflict via a peace agreement nor the formation of the new state achieves sustainable peace, as the nascent republic descended back into war shortly after independence. This project gives many reasons why the nascent state disintegrated, but what I emphasise is the existence of conflictual exclusionary and violent identity politics. The armed groups waging war are driven by competition for political hegemony and resources. Thus, a precondition for overcoming the destructive dynamics of conflict and arms is the repudiation of exclusionary and violent politics in South Sudan. Until then, dreams of transforming South Sudan into a peaceful nation remain an illusion. The state emerged from decades of war without active institutions of governance to provide collective security, justice, and accountability for civil war crimes.

Thus, this lack of state systems that could effectively control the use of force and conduct DDR created a political vacuum where individual and groups' seizure of the use force becomes inevitable. This thesis argues that while South Sudan existed as a sovereign state, the lack of functioning government institutions impeded incentives for governing the behaviour of political groups, particularly Ex-Combatants and ethnic identities that the state sought to disarm. Therefore, weak, or absent institutions drives the persistence of armed conflict and the proliferation of arms in South Sudan. The key to understanding the cause of this perennial violence is that South Sudan lacks consolidated institutions. I further argue that warfare experienced by South Sudanese ethno-political identities provides armed factions with sufficient evidence of their rival's malign intentions. Such suspicions pushed the armed actors into increasingly militaristic political and security positions, culminating in a highly decentralised arms race. This violent and adversarial attitude condemned security governance and other forms of socio-political pluralism.

Since the signing of the CPA, and after the secession in 2011, nascent South Sudan had followed the trend of emerging states relapsing back to deadly civil war and inter-communal violence. This prompted difficult research questions: What are the significant factors affecting the operationalisation of the DDR in South Sudan (2005-11)? What was realistically expected from new efforts of DDR after the secession of South Sudan from Sudan in 2011, given security imperatives on the ground? The finding is clear. The country whose socio-political, security and economic organisations are in some form of transition are more likely to descend to war. This condition emerges due to frustrated expectations amongst a populace previously yearning for good governance (Ball and Fayemi, 2004; Collier, 2009). While the disarmament in South Sudan was designed as a strategy to redress security instability and transform the former rebel army into a national army capable of reducing the risk of violence, the procedure failed, and the nascent state relapsed to civil war in 2013. This project argues that the passion with which the secessionist war and ethnic conflicts were fought in Southern Sudan created many hurdles.

After the secession in 2011, the international organisations responsible for DDR have openly linked the re-creation of peace and security to state-building. The medium of the state, and specifically the liberal democratic state, with an open market, has been perceived as providing the essential basis for the achievement of sustainable war prevention (Brown and Patrick, 2007). The IGAD sees the state fragility in South Sudan as ensconcing conditions for armed conflict and widespread destitution within, but also beyond, the borders of

South Sudan. However, throughout this thesis, I have illustrated how the groups' reliance on the use of violence, rather than just the fragility of the state, has influenced the shortcomings of the DDR. As South Sudan remained in perpetual armed conflicts, it became apparent that the mainstream conflict resolution approaches and the post-war interventions programmes failed because they were not designed to resolve protracted local conflicts. I argue that violence can affect the peace process, and the nature of the peace process can affect the DDR (Muggah, 2015a).

This project makes these observations linked to the argument in Chapter Six that the IGAD mediators falsely assumed that the SPLM/A best represented the political, security and economic interests of OAGs in South Sudan. Such an assumption overlooks the socio-political processes through which informal armies were formed. Given the fragile security situation in South/ern Sudan during, and after the CPA, I argued that the risk of violent fragmentation was inevitable because the DDR was not linked more closely to broader efforts in community security and trust-building. One of the main issues emphasised in this project as the challenge to the DDR, surrounds ethno-political factionalism and links between armed identities and security. My thesis has criticised the phases of the DDR in South Sudan for not scrutinising the effects of political factionalism and the securitised world in which they operate (Waever, 1995). These intermeshing trends and the proliferation of arms have come to be regarded as a central response to insecurity.

The South Sudanese have lived under a weak authoritarian government in the form of various Khartoum-based regimes, and exclusive and predatory SPLM/A leadership. Thus, ethno-political groups who raised armies, and mounted resistance to the DDR, approached their political issues from threats to their survival that merit emergency and exceptional security measures. It became impracticable to integrate ethno-political procedures of competition and securitisation within the dynamics of the post-war DDR in South Sudan. This project has argued that socio-political identity and security among South Sudanese armed agents remain interwoven. Deriving from this conflictual situation, I stated that the DDR vision for South Sudan prompts ontological insecurity, which sets in motion political dynamics that led to what this project described as the re-mobilisation, re-armament and re-securitisation of post-war political issues. This situation created a reflexive, self-driven process of violent securitisation coupled with a re-configuration of violent competition. The crux of South Sudan's DDR woes rests on the original failure of the CPA to include all structures of violence in the peacemaking process.

An official ending of the war between North and South was not an indication that all problems facing armed structures and unarmed civilians, especially women and children, will vanish, as they continued to live under a real threat of violence. This condition is not addressed even when the DDR is defined as successful. Issues like violence against women or a broken economy cannot be easily fixed through successful DDR (Hartzell and Hoddie, 2007). Like any other conflict situation, civil war onset, actors and political interests involved, stipulate a set of national attributes that render a DDR in South Sudan more susceptible to resistance. In the absence of a centralised use of force, armed actors were dependent on violence governed by the antics of belligerents. The effects of the complexity of violent actors and security structures were not adequately explored under the CPA. Even before the CPA, the situation in Southern Sudan was fragmented because of the consequences of "a multiplicity of actors with a stake in violence and the provision of security" (Bryden *et al.*, 2014, p. 3).

When the war ended in 2005, the DDR was implemented amidst uncertainty and power struggle driven by the violent behaviour of ex-rebel leaders who divided South Sudan's political system into fiefdoms (Wassara, 2007; 2015). Hence, the DDR in South Sudan was "aim[ed] at neutralising Ex-Combatants in the short-term, by ensuring their socioeconomic reintegration into society, diverting them away from a criminal path, or continued armed rebellion" (Baas, 2012, p. 177). The DDR in South Sudan was approached as a war prevention strategy. Giving ex-fighters another means of livelihood may encourage them to forsake war, a perception that better economic opportunities will raise the opportunity cost of war (Ball and van de Goor, 2006). The expected effects of DDR "are considered to be twofold: first, a direct positive effect of DDR on the security situation is assumed. Besides, successful DDR is thought to help create a conducive environment during the few years after the signing of the peace agreement, which is considered crucial for achieving full implementation and sustainable peace" (Baas, 2012, p. 177). While the North and South did not go back to war with each other, both regions suffered a great deal of civil war.

The reasons influencing such outcomes are many, as articulated throughout this thesis. Another issue not considered by the DDR was how the civil war has impoverished South Sudan, and how even after secession, the nascent state suffered from aftershocks. Because of this uncertainty, South Sudan remains in a state of war, where inhabitants live in an insecure future. This instability created unstable inter-group relationships. The designers of the DDR do not understand why individuals join armed groups in South Sudan, where one or more armed groups opposed the authority of the state. For Tilly (1973), as cited in Chapter Five, multiple sovereignty creates a structural condition that makes civil war possible and challenging to solve because of the causes and actors. It became even harder to achieve a successful DDR because the "war hardens ethnic identities to the point that cross-ethnic political appeals became futile" (Kauffman, 1996, p. 137). This thesis agrees with the argument that "the extent to which multiple sovereignty this preserved in the post-civil war environment varies according to whether the civil war ended in a rebel victory, a government victory, or a negotiated settlement" (Mason *et al.*, 2011, p. 173).

Thus, the criticism of the traditional DDR is that it does not take into consideration how the shifting political landscape can cause violent political dramas. While the importance attached to the DDR is evident, the same cannot be said about South Sudan. One of the main shortfalls emphasised is a wilful assumption that any DDR will "deal with the post-conflict security problem that results from Ex-Combatants being left unprotected or without livelihoods or support networks" (Knight, 2008, p. 25). There are considerable mistakes in this argument. Even when such a version of the DDR thrived, it is devoid of an evaluation of the political and security stakes involved in possessing arms. The traditional DDR lacks a broad understanding of the actors in violent political life. Additionally, DDR focuses little attention on institutions and their prominence in the legitimisation of violence (Kieh, 2011). The CPA was signed when Southern Sudan had eighteen armed groups (Munive, 2013). Some of these armed groups were dormant rebel groups from previous conflicts, or coalitions from new and former groups.

Either way, they were not part of the CPA. The ability of these groups to mount a violent assault against the state is captured by Tilly's (1978) early notion of multiple sovereignty, introduced in Chapter One. If the distance between the institutions seeking to monopolise the means of force is unbridgeable, as is the case in South Sudan, the state's claim to the legitimate use of force becomes contested and takes on an inherent irony. This decentralisation of violence shows that power and the legitimacy to use force in South Sudan is not a monolithic construct in favour of the state (Gleditsch *et al.*, 2002). The essence of this analysis is the dynamics of power and behaviours. Thus, what is essential in the failure of the DDR in South Sudan is not a mere weakness of the state, but also the existence of violent actors with no political line to align with their divide. As such, a suitable starting point in analysing the shortfalls of the DDR is to emphasise the significant political and economic trade-off that allowed armed actors to frame the causes of their resistance. A few interpretations of the causes of resistance stand out: Armed actors in South Sudan shape the narrative of what leads to war and why they should have their arms.

By giving in to these simplified or actual versions of security demands, they obstruct, rather than construct, the road towards successful DDR. As the war raged uncontrollably, the use of force came in many guises. When no supreme front of power exists, it becomes impossible for a top-down approach to ensure the success of the DDR. This argument is susceptible to criticism from those who have not learned lessons about how the experience of the South Sudanese dwarfs the cost of conventional DDR. I argue that the legacy of violence and the absence of centralised security systems in South Sudan produced rigid and adversarial behaviour designed to meet some individuals' or groups' political and security objectives. The security behaviour among the groups affected the DDR because it encompasses the full range of political and security activities in which individuals and groups engage, such as violence and the proliferation of arms. Both phases of the CPA and post-secession DDR in South Sudan failed to study these behaviours and the effects of decision-making attached to those behaviours.

Interpreting armed conflict through the lens of state failure fails to recognise the less visible forms of war in South Sudan. Despite these contradictions, the DDR policies in South Sudan do not question whether resistance and further re-armament occurs as a function of the

Ex-Combatants having incentives to act violently. This failure to contextualise these types of violence hindered the DDR in South Sudan, where the difference between the state as the legitimate authority and non-state actors as the unlawful challengers is virtually fictitious. Thus, the DDR falls short of presenting armed groups with choices built on their valuation of the costs of resistance and benefits for disarmament. Every success or failure of DDR hinge on decisions made by armed actors when they weighed the cost of disarmament. South Sudan, on the other hand, faces "a strikingly difficult balance between reforming the security sector in line with best practice and dealing with a political situation that remains deeply construed in terms of potential for armed force and the threat of destabilisation" (Le Riche and Arnold, 2013, p. 160).

This project has criticised strategic conflict management's inability to incorporate agency of violence. This failure allowed the warring parties to freelance disarmament and institutionalised the conditions that preserve multiple sovereignties. The CPA did not focus on these dynamics, in part because it was based on the North-South context of war, thus creating the CPA's "negotiation myopia" (Antrim and Sebenius, 1992, p. 97). No one questioned whether the mutual gain of power-sharing between the GoS and SPLM would produce an integrative solution for all parties' concerns (Albin, 2001). Besides, while the GoS and SPLM built mutual trust by adjusting their positions in reaching the CPA, they did not give up their main political aims nor disarm their forces. This rigid distrust furthered the accumulation of arms. An accumulation of arms can occur for a range of reasons. The decades of civil war in Sudan have increased the desire for arms. This desire is brought about by the push factor for armament. The fact that GoS wanted to maintain the unity of Sudan, while SPLM/A sought to tear the state apart, was recorded as a push factor for arms accumulation because those two contradictions are internal to the competing group.

As such, this inspires both armed actors seeking change and those who want the status-quo to arms. What prevented successful disarmament of local groups in South Sudan was a pull factor, often based on fear. The CPA was loaded with various pull motives that fractured attempts to downsize SPLA and convince OAGs it is safe to disarm. The SA in the CPA make it appear as if there was a broad consensus on solutions to fix a fragmented society and to convince the armed groups to accept the DDR. I argue that the CPA-DDR in South Sudan was approached from the prism of external agents striving to prevent the relapse to war. This context enforces the security-development nexus that does not have an inside perspective of why groups resorted to war, and what is at stake when there are no security assemblages. Such concerns played a significant role in the collapse of the DDR and war in South Sudan, where the menace of arms dwarfs any surplus management policy. Although no amount of surplus management policy would have prevented the collapse of the DDR in South Sudan, inadequate involvement of armed groups in DDR planning is another factor hindering the process of the DDR.

My thesis has argued that the situation in South Sudan required a tailored response, and perhaps a second-generation DDR (Munive and Stepputat, 2015). A second-generation DDR strategy is suitable because the armed groups in South Sudan have outpaced efforts to ensure traditional compliance with the state. In correlation with the suitability of second-generation DDR, I used the notion of the armed groups' disposition of power to emphasise the impact of political and security psychology on the DDR. In criticism of both phases of the DDR in South Sudan, I depict the South Sudanese as people sitting in a burning building. Imagine that someone set the house on fire, and the flammable furniture will soon catch fire. Predictably, everyone would rush for an exit, or the occupants will perish because of fire and smoke inhalation. In the political context, the group's awareness of the danger, such as state violence against the groups, informed their behaviours. These challenges require the DDR to be rethought, and to concentrate instead on what prompted the emergence of contesting authorities that magnified militarisation.

This study pays attention to the role of informal armies and argues that the South Sudanese state is present, either "in its hurtful presence or in its painful absence" (Smith, 2015, p. 17). In this case, groups live by the gun as an essential companion for security. The dynamics of violent actors indicate that conceptual boundaries of who should use force is transgressed. The SPLA Ex-Combatants fight for statehood, and different motives drive armed ethnic youths acting as the defenders of their communities. These dissimilarities are not necessarily precise, but this study determined them empirically rather than merely assuming them. Besides, even if there are distinctions between ex-liberators in SPLA and the cattle-raiding bandits, the policy interventions that South Sudan had adopted have substantial similarities. The choice by beneficiary states and those helping them is not just between top-down impositions of a liberal model of state-building. It is also a choice between accepting direct and indirect forms of authority that makes the dilemma actual for liberal-based DDR (Mamdani, 1996). While I am not pretending to offer a solution to the dilemma, I emphasise how this dilemma led to the failure of the DDR in South Sudan.

Thus, part of the way forward to ensure successful DDR requires a move away from the state-based fixation. This argument is a call to re-think the Hobbesian notion of the liberal state: "the essence of stateness is enforcement: the ultimate ability to send someone with a gun to force people to comply with the state's laws" (Fukuyama, 2004, p. 8). I argued that "for the liberal state to provide security and protection to its citizens, the state must demand a force superior to what others may have at their disposal" (Andersen, 2011, p. 12). From this view, establishing a state monopoly over the means of force in South Sudan includes, not just the taming of the Hobbesian Leviathan, but creating the Leviathan itself. This view reflected the view that "stable and legitimate governance structures must be built on the actual institutions that function in the specific context, rather than on generic blueprints provided by outsiders" (Andersen, 2011, p. 12). This argument recognises that South Sudan "has hardly had a monopoly of legitimate force at any point in time" (Ebo, 2007, p. 37).

Thus, the central authority is exercised by "twilight institutions" whose connection to the public authority or state waxes and wanes (Lund, 2007). As an alternative of insisting that fragile states should dominate all legitimate means of force, DDR needs to be "more in tune with the realities on the ground to work with multiple authorities to maximise their strengths and minimise their weaknesses" (Baker, 2011, p. 217). The DDR lacked an understanding of these dynamics and failed to provide a coherent strategy and shared vision towards a more entry-oriented mode that recognises DDR's role in establishing a space for security. The security perceptions and how to react to those threats are different, based on the groups, which promotes the necessity of engaging with violent actors. As civil war and inter-communal conflicts become intricate, it is essential to link the DDR with arms-wielding actors to avoid "the pitfalls posed by strengthening one actor at the expense of others, or removing a single group from an interconnected landscape, for the maintenance of long-term security" (Tatiana and Pangburn, 2018, p. 2). As argued in Chapter One, incentives in DDR did not address the fears and other defined objectives of armed groups.

In its place, those incentives became a spike in violence when disarmament is applied as an interim step in any project to extend irresponsible state authority. As is the case in South Sudan, the ethnic territories within which these groups operate have become more complicated because of the arms they use. This research argues that a vital factor affecting the DDR is that policy response derived from the CPA-DDR did not target the local drivers of conflict because they were not designed to engage with local contexts of armament (Snowden, 2012). While the international organisations' promotion of democracy and institution building involves measures aimed at strengthening fragile governments, I argue that such procedures failed in South Sudan. This is because they did not promote interaction between war-affected communities. Instead of conceiving interactions in the DDR as between donors and recipients, I argue that interaction in a hybrid context, if taken seriously, has a vital socio-political dimension.

The scope of such socio-political dimension in South Sudan, may involve considerable (re)negotiation with armed groups about the appropriate conception of the DDR with their set of political norms. This interaction is at least partially about grassroots or localised justice. Instead of seeing the challenges to the DDR "either as a contest among elite patrons who command hordes of tribal clients" (Pinaud, 2014, p. 211) or as "the financial collapse of a state held together by ethnic patronage alone" (De Waal, 2014, p. 347), my thesis argues that conventional DDR peddled the idea of elite-led agencies. The challenge of the state's fragility to DDR alone neglects locally powerful rulers and youth leaders charged with defending the ethnic territories, recruitment, and commanding informal ethnic armies. I am cautious that an overemphasis on local conflict risks romanticising informal armed authorities. Nevertheless, paying attention to the role of these networks is necessary to understand the political processes of violent securitisation, which held groups back from the DDR. An inclusive approach would mean establishing DDR with the capacity of including all structures unwilling to cooperate with the conventional process.

The violent securitisation by OAGs is even more astonishing considering De Waal's reflections whereby he describes the whole of Sudan as an interpretational point of all informal authorities' realities. De Waal argued that "Kiir's principal method for controlling South Sudan was patronage, not military power" (2017, p. 187). This notion of patronage led to an offshoot of the private Dinka army known as Duoot Beny, meaning 'rescue the leader' in Dinka. Duoot Beny, militia fashioned itself into "an efficient strike force loyal to its creators" (De Waal 2017, p.188; citing Pendle, 2016). The situation that arose after its formation is a typical trajectory for real security governance where there are both political and inter-ethnic threats to the power of the state. When I interviewed a senior officer of Duoot Bany about the DDR, they baulked at my question and claimed that what we (researchers) have missed is that they already enjoy legitimacy. The critical issue here is that several armed groups became part of the structures competing for public authority, a role that endowed them with practical legitimacy.

Since then, other types of armed groups have influenced the stability and security of ethno-political groups by establishing a high degree of flexibility and "adaptability to shifting circumstances" (Paudel, 2016, p. 550). After signing the CPA, the shifting anatomy of violent armed groups has not been addressed. In criticising the DDR, this project argues that the changing contexts of legitimacy to use force hinder a temporary gained in ending the civil war (Boege *et al.*, 2009). While the types of warfare waged by various armed groups are "asymmetrical", some of them possess sophisticated arms, which pose considerable threats to systems and institutions that seek to mitigate the impact of those arms. Thus, the literature revives (chapter one) reconstructed each of the conventional arguments about DDR, concluding that the main challenge in South Sudan is the need to surpass institutional category of blame games/victim-perpetrator and look at practices on the ground instead. The critical questions examine the actors taking part in this violence and assess why they should take centre stage. It is crucial to address these questions instead of remaining inflexibly fixed to the blueprints of the DDR.

De Waal was adamant about the lack of reflection in the CPA, arguing that "a mystery lies at the heart of the CPA SA. Part of it is that, contrary to expectation and prior experience; the SA was the simplest and most rapidly agreed" (2017, p. 185). For hybrid scholars, many of the DDR processes are "akin to rearranging the deck chairs on the Titanic" (Mac Ginty, 2014, p. 3). Supporters of the settlement approach counter-argue that they must play the cards were given rather than waste time wishing for a better hand. They cannot change the meta-picture overnight and instead are forced to engage in piecemeal activities that will at least alleviate suffering or allow people to make a change. There is no doubt that the power and wealth sharing paradigm is dominant in terms of both peacemaking and peacebuilding practices. Most research on peacebuilding can be placed in the negotiated settlement paradigm, without offering 'solutions' to the problems faced by armed groups who are fearful of the state or other groups. This literature on peacemaking is apolitical in the sense that it shuns the central questions of where power lies.

In applying a hybrid theory, this project questions the underlying basis of conflict mechanisms and dominant approaches to peacebuilding. It has developed a critique of the liberal peace model favoured by leading democracies and international organisations. In South Sudan, violence matters to ethno-political groups and national political constituencies across South Sudan while DDR matters for the state elites. The current context of the DDR centred on efforts to ensure the state monopoly of force is a constant element of public discourse in South Sudan, even if concerns about the threats of OAGs is rising. Rather than discussing the emergence of DDR templates, we should talk about the emergency of templates in the context of the proliferation of armies and arms. Policymakers in IGAD are interested in work from the war-ending and state-building paradigm. Again, there are exceptions to the rule, but formal and external actors are interested in policy-relevant information and operational models that will suit pressing needs. The negotiated approach camp is not in the business of challenging accepted norms.

Proponents of settlement approach had fallen in love with the notion that functioning states operate perfectly. South Sudan, however, had turned out to be more intricate. The outbreak of war in its nascent stage is a wake-up call, and the latest warning sign about state-based DDR and peacebuilding (Berdal and Achim, 2010). Massacres and other human rights abuses have landed a debilitating blow to mainstream DDR in South Sudan, where a public authority is fragmented. The emphasis of "institutionalisation before liberalisation" (Paris, 2004, p. 179) called for the provision of exit options for at-risk groups and development of alternative approaches to control unregulated arms where transactions are more comfortable with little or no state control in areas of informal armies. The civil war in Sudan has brought much of its political cohesion, public authority and security to the brink of collapse, creating an unregulated crisis of armed violence. For decades, conflicts and civil strife crippled Sudan in which armed violence and relentless killings were ubiquitous (Annan, 2014). These challenges prompted interventions by the international community to end the war and build peace to prevent future conflicts.

Ending the protracted civil war in Sudan was a predicament because of complex factors, actors and the nature of the conflict. This project identified that ethno-political war and related violence tend to be difficult to resolve because they are often based on ethno-political grouping contesting authorities and inadequate governance. The effective tactic applied to end the war was a negotiated settlement, which resulted in power and resource equity among the warring parties. Adhering to this agreement, the CPA shared power and wealth between the GoS and the Southern dominant rebel group, the SPLM/A (The CPA, 2005). To prevent relapse to war, the CPA mandated that both the GoS and the SPLM/A should "create DDR commissions with the stated aim of implementing the agreed downsizing of their armies, as stipulated in the CPA" (De Waal, 2017, p. 187). With the help of the U.N. Mission in Sudan (UNMIS), the SPLM created the interim DDR to demobilise non-essential combatants, including child soldiers, women associated with OAGs, and disabled veterans. Three years after signing the CPA, the GoS and South intended to disarm and demobilise 400,000 Ex-Combatants from both sides (NDDRCC, 2007).

This total DDR caseload figure seemed impossible, but donors pushed for the launching of IDDRP to "set up and build the capacity of DDR institutions and Civil Society while initiating basic DDR processes for selected priority target groups" (IDDRP, 2005, p. 20). Despite these proposals, the DDR failed to meet its defined target. Second, it did not prevent the proliferation of arms and force. As mentioned throughout this thesis, the primary source of contention throughout the implementation of the DDR was security. Nichols argues that "genuine security motives remain for the DDR in both Northern and Southern Sudan" (2014, p. 12). This project argues that the CPA was reached while North-South Sudanese continued to live in situations of uncertainty. In this view, the SPLM signed the CPA to "balance the opportunity costs of fighting with the fear of being attacked" (Chassang and Miquel, 2008, p. 4). Here, the perception of danger and the possibility of future harm from the North were born out of history. This research argues that the South Sudanese perceived the North as presenting some danger to their political interest.

While the anxiety of inter-elite conflict remained the cause of uncertainty in the South, fear of the North was a response specifically to an existential. In this case, the opportunity costs of the DDR change with the political situation which determines the risk of attack. The same could be said of the OAG's opposition to the SPLM in the South. While anxiety between North and South may have resulted from propositional fear about the resumption of war, the localised conflicts in South Sudan were based on the fact that SPLM/A was a guerrilla dictatorship. De Waal (2017, 182) argues that the SPLM was a dictatorship and had no effective control over its hinterlands. This project posits that groups' fear and suspicion drove armament among the South Sudanese. If the SPLM was a guerrilla dictatorship as De Waal had argued, minor groups outside the SPLM/A's channels of power and resource distribution might be afraid to dissolve their armed structures and leave themselves unprotected. To be afraid is to experience fear of possible danger, and this thesis emphasises how most minor groups had come face to face with threats from the SPLA.

To be afraid is an experience common to non-Dinka groups. When these fearful groups were targeted for the DDR, they already had reasons for fearing that the DDR could endanger their life. This project has explained that the South Sudanese refused to disarm because they experience existential fear from the North. The CPA-DDR poorly understands these fears. While peacemakers and state-building projects seek to channel state formation along the liberal route, the hybridity of armed actors and violence becomes part of domestic strategies for arms proliferation, gaining legitimacy, securitising the transition, and consolidating power (Gellner, 1983). The hybridity of armed conflict and actors demonstrates that adaptation, opposition to the state or resistance to the disarmament are not part of a zero-sum game; instead, an intricate interaction among diverse nature of authorities in transition. Instead of including these structures and actors who exercise control over ethnic territories and populations in post-war contexts, DDR's response is akin to asserting the supremacy of the state.

If the disarmament of Ex-Combatants and OAGs is understood as a political procedure, inasmuch as it is recognised that DDR policy process, interventions in South Sudan, indeed, other post-war countries should not always persist in treating the disarmament as a technical exercise. This state-centric view has led to a paucity of political organisation in areas under the control of informal armies. While attention has been paid to how informal armies recruit their fighters and finance their operations, little has been said about how rebels' governance or other informal authority such as armed cattle herders, in the case of South Sudan, could affect the DDR. In South Sudan, the possession of arms is an indispensable part of vulnerable civilians and an insurgent force. While these armed actors may harbour socio-political ambitions, their activities are often a chaotic mix of armed struggle, illegitimate commerce, intimidation and security (Guibernau, 2000). Thus, the DDR should be robust enough for all groups to feel included to reduce the grievances of potential spoilers. That approach would require the DDR operators to reflect the socio-political and security complexities they are addressing.

References

All the interviewees are cited anonymously throughout this project. This application of anonymity is in line with the requirements of this project's ethic approval. I was born and raised in the Republic of South Sudan. Hence, I have both ethnic and political labels. I am also aware of the political and security sensitivity of the information collected during the field trip. The majority of interviews were conducted in Nairobi, Kenya, where I was confined due to the travelling restriction. Therefore, the anonymous nature of research allowed me to cite all the participants as P1 or P2, for instance, to protect their anonymity. All interviews were conducted by the author.

1.   A senior member of the ruling SPLM/A, (P3a/08/07/2017)

2.   A senior member of the ruling SPLM/A, (P3b/08/07/2017)

3.   A senior member of the ruling SPLM/A, (P3c/08/07/2017)

4.   A senior member of the ruling SPLM/A, (P3d/20/07/2017)

5.   A senior member of the United Nations in South Sudan, (P21/17/11/2017)

6.   A Senior SPLA Military Official, (P33/03/01/2018)

7.   Confidential document on the SPLA's Arms Shipment (P27/12/09/2017)

8.   Confidential insight about the SPLA's behaviour toward the DDR, (P20/13/09/2017)

9.   Discussion with senior with international advisers (P19/11/09/2017)

10.   Discussions with former IGAD official and international adviser (P26/08/11/2017)

11.   Discussions with international advisers on South Sudan DDR (P19/17/11/2017)

12.   Ex-SPLA General, (P26/23/10/2017)

13.   High-Ranking Rebel General, (P5/04/08/2017)

14.   High-ranking officer of the SPLA-in opposition, (P30/21/12/2018)

15.   Informal, but confidential discussion with senior U.N. SSR adviser, (P23/21/11/2017)

16.   Interview with a confidential source (P17/21/09/2017)

17.   Interview with a confidential source (P26/14/09/2017)

18.   Interview with a confidential source (P4/22/07/2017)

19.   Interview with a confidential source, [Senior UN SSR adviser] (P26/23/10/2017)

20.   Interview with confidential source [Academic] (P17/04/09/2017)

21.   Interview with confidential source [One of the senior rebel generals] (P17/10/01/2018)

22.   Leader of a local NGO, (P16/03/08/2017)

23.   Leader of a rebel faction, (P21/21/07/2017)

24.   Member of foreign mission, (P27/21/12/2017)

25.   Member   of   South   Sudanese   Informal   Army, (P16/19/09/2017)

26.   Member   of   the   Dinka   Informal   Armed   Youth, (P23/21/09/2017)

27.   Member   of   the   Dinka   Informal   Armed   Youth, (P26b/23/09/2017)

28.   Member of the foreign mission, (P12/04/09/2017)

29.   Member of the foreign mission, (P17/04/09/2017)

30.   Member of the foreign mission, (P17a: /14/09/2017)

31.   Member   of   the   Nuer   Informal   Armed   Youth, (P19/28/09/2017)

32.   Member   of   the   Nuer   Informal   Armed   Youth, (P26a/23/09/2017)

33.   Member   of   the   SPLA   ex-intelligence   community, (P23b/12/2017)

34.   Political/military leader (P14/03/08/2017)

35.   Senior   Clergy   of   South   Sudanese   Anglican   Church, (P2b/07/07/2017)

36.   South Sudan's Government Official, (P6/24/08/2017)

37.   South Sudanese's expert, (P1/19/06/2017)

38.   South Sudanese's Member of Parliament Security Committee, (P17b/21/09/2017)

39.   South Sudanese's Political Leader (P26a/14/09/2017)

40.   The United Nation Member of Peacebuilding, (P19/17/11/2017)

41.   Youth leader and activist (P2a/07/07/2017)

Abbott, A. (2001) *Chaos of Disciplines'*, Chicago: University of Chicago Press.

Abbott, A. (2004) Methods of Discovery: Heuristics for the Social Sciences', In: W. Norton. Aiken, Scott, F., and Robert B Talisse, (Ed.), Pragmatism and pluralism, (pp. 17–26). *Revisited Political Studies Review*, New York.

Abdel Salam, A.H. and De Waal, A. (2001) *The Phoenix State: Civil Society and the Future of Sudan'*, Asmara: Justice Africa and the Committee of the Civil Project', Lawrenceville NJ: Red Sea Press.

Abrahamsen, R. (2001) *Development Policy and the Democratic Peace in Sub-Saharan Africa'*, Conflict, Security and Development, Vol. 1, No. 3, pp. 79-103.

Abrams, P. (1988) Notes on the Difficulty of Studying the State', *Journal of Historical Sociology*, Vol. 1, No.1, pp. 58–89.

Acemoglu, D. and Robinson, J.A. (2012) *Why Nations Fail: The Origins of Power, Prosperity, and Poverty*', Crown Business, New York.

Acemoglu, D. *et al.* (2001) The Colonial Origins of Comparative Development: An Empirical Investigation', *American Economic Review*, Vol 91, pp. 1369-1401.

Adams, K.R. (2000) *State Survival and State Death: International and Technological Contexts*', PhD dissertation, University of California, Berkeley.

Addai-Sebo, A. (2011) How the U.N. Failed Côte d'lvoire', New African, No. 503, pp. 16–19.

Addison, T. and Murshed, S.M. (2002) Credibility and Reputation in Peacemaking', *Journal of Peace Research*, Vol. 39, No. 4, pp. 487–501.

Adeba, B. (2015) *Making Sense of the White Army's Return in South Sudan*', CSG Paper No. 1, Centre for Security Governance.

Adeba, B. (2019) A Hijacked State: Violent Kleptocracy in South Sudan', *The Enough Project*, https://enoughproject.org/reports/a-hijacked-state, [Accessed: 29/03/2019].

Adedokun, A. (2019) Transition from Civil War to Peace: The Role of the United Nations and International Community in Mozambique', *Peace and Conflict Studies*, Vol. 26, No.1, pp.2-25.

Adekanye, J.B. (1995) *Structural Adjustment, Democratisation and Rising Ethnic Tensions in Africa'*, Development and Change, Vol. 26, No. 2, pp. 355–74.

Aeberli, A. (2012) Decentralisation Hybridised', The Graduate Institute', *Graduate Institute ePapers*, Geneva, https://repository.graduateinstitute.ch/record/13629 [Accessed: 23/12/2019].

Afisi, O. T. (2009) Tracing Contemporary Africa's Conflict Situation to Colonialism: A breakdown of Communication among Natives', *Academic Journals, Philosophy Papers and Reviews*, Vol.1, No. 4, pp. 59–66.

Afolabi, B.T. (2009) *Peacemaking in the ECOWAS Region: Challenges and Prospects'*, In Conflict Trends. Durban: Accord, Vol. 2, p. 24.

Ahmed, E. (2009) *The Comprehensive Peace Agreement and the Dynamics of Post-Conflict Political Partnership in Sudan'*, Africa Spectrum, Vol.44, No. 3, pp.133-147.

Ake, C. (1993) *The Unique Case of African Democracy'*, International Affairs, Vol. 69, No, 2, pp. 239-244.

Albin, C. (2001) *Justice and Fairness in International Negotiation'*, Cambridge University Press, Cambridge.

Albrecht, P. (2015) *Building on what Works: Local Actors and Service Delivery in Fragile Situations'*, In: P. Jackson (Ed.). Handbook of International Security and Development, pp. 279-93. Danish Institute for International Studies, DIIS, Copenhagen.

Albrecht, P. and Buur, L. (2009) *An Uneasy Marriage: Non-State Actors and Police Reform'*, Policing and Society, Vol. 19, No. 4, pp. 390–405.

Alden, C., Thakur, M., and Arnold, M., (2011) *Militias and the Challenges of Post-Conflict Peace: Silencing the Guns'*, London: Zed Books

Alesina, A., Özler, S., Roubini, N. and Swagel, P. (1996) Political Instability and Economic Growth', *Journal of Economic Growth*, Vol. 1, pp. 189-211.

Alexander, J. (2006) *The Unsettled Land: State-making and the Politics of Land in Zimbabwe 1893-2003'*, Oxford: James Currey.

Ali, A. and Albadawi, I. (2002) Explaining Sudan's Economic Growth Performance', *AERC Collaborative Research Project on Explaining Africa's Growth Performance*, https://media.africaportal.org/documents/Sudan.pdf.

Ali, M. (2011) *Gender and State-building in South Sudan'*, Special Report, Washington: United States Institute for Peace.

Alier, A. (1990) *South Sudan: Too Many Agreements Dishonoured'*, Ithaca Press, Exeter, UK.

Alkire, S. (2004) *A Vital Core that must be Treated with the Same Gravitas as Traditional Security Threats, Security Dialogue'*, Vol. 35, No. 3, pp. 359-360.

AllAfrica.com, (2011) *Sudan: Joint Donors warn South government over Corruption'*, http://allafrica.com/stories/201104130175 html [Accessed 26/07/2018].

Allen, T. and Vlassenroot, K. (2010) Introduction: in Allen, Tim and Vlassenroot, Koen (Eds.), *The Lord's Resistance Army: Myth and Reality'*, London: Zed Books, London, UK.

Altbach, P. and Knight, J. (2007) The Internationalisation of Higher Education: Motivations and Realities', *Journal of Studies in International Education*, Vol.11, No.3/4, pp. 290-305.

Altheide, D.L. and Schneider, C. (2012) *Qualitative Media Analysis'*, 2nd (Ed.), Thousand Oaks, CA: Sage.

Altschuld, J.W. AND Witkin, B. R. (2000) *From Needs Assessment to Action'*, Thousand Oaks, CA: Sage.

Alusala, N., Gasana, J-M., Lamb, G. and Francis, G. (2012) *Rumours of peace, Whispers of War: Assessment of the reintegration of Ex-combatants into Civilian Life in North Kivu, South Kivu and Ituri Democratic Republic of Congo'*, Washington, DC: World Bank.

Andersen, L. (2011) *SSR and the Dilemmas of Liberal Peacebuilding'*, DIIS Working Paper, No. 31. Copenhagen: Danish Institute for International Studies.

Anderson, B. (1983) *Imagined Communities: Reflections on Origin and Spread of Nationalism'*, London: Verso.

Anderson, D.M. (2002) *Vigilantes, Violence and the Politics of Public Order in Kenya'*, African Affairs, Vol. 101, No.405, pp. 531-55.

Anderson, D.M. and Rolandsen, Ø. H. (2014) Violence as Politics in Eastern Africa, 1940–1990: Legacy, Agency, Contingency', *Journal of Eastern African Studies*, Vol. 8, No. 4, pp. 539–557.

Andeweg, R.B. (2000) Consociational Democracy', *Annual Review of Political Science*, Vol. 3, pp. 509–36.

Andreski, S. (1968) *The African Predicament: A study in the Pathology of Modernisation*', Atherton Press, New York, pp. 108-9.

Andrews *et al.* (2008) *Doing Narrative Research*', London: Sage.

Andrews, M. (2007*) Exploring Cross-cultural Boundaries'*, In D. Jean Clandinin (Ed.), Handbook of Narrative Inquiry: Mapping a Methodology (pp. 489-511). Thousand Oaks, CA: Sage.

Andrews, M., Pritchett, L. and Woolcock, M. (2012) *Escaping Capability Traps Through Problem-Driven Iterative Adaptation* (PDIA)', UNU-WIDER Working Paper.

Annan, K. (1999) *Preventing War and Disaster: A Growing Global Challenge'*, Annual Report on the work of the Organisation, (A/54/1, United Nations.

Annan, K. (2000) *The Question of Intervention: Statements by the Secretary-General'*, New York: United Nations Publications, We the Peoples: The Role of the United Nations in the 21st Century (A/54).

Annan, K. (2006) *Towards a New Definition of Sovereignty'*, In G.M. Reichberg, H. Syse, & E. Begby (ed.), The Ethics of War, (pp. 683-693). Malden, MA: Blackwell Publishing

Annan, K. (2014) Violent Conflicts and Civil Strife in West Africa: Causes, Challenges and Prospects, Stability', *International Journal of Security and Development*, Vol. 3, No. 1, pp. 1-16.

Ansorg, N. (2017) SSR in Africa: Donor Approaches versus Local Needs', *Contemporary Security Policy*, Vol. 38, No.1, pp. 129-144.

Ansorg, N. and Gordon, E. (2019) Co-operation, Contestation and Complexity in Post-Conflict SSR', *Journal of Intervention and Statebuilding*, Vol. 13, No.1, pp. 2-24.

Ansorg, N. and Strasheim, J. (2019) Veto Players in Post-Conflict DDR Programs: Evidence from Nepal and the DRC', *Journal of Intervention and Statebuilding*, Vol. 13, No, 1, pp. 112-130.

Anstee, M. J. (1996) *Orphan of the Cold War: The Inside Story of the Collapse of the Angolan Peace Process 1992–93*', London: Macmillan.

Antonioni, D. (1998) Relationship between the Big Five Personality Factors and Conflict management styles', *International Journal of Conflict Management*, Vol. 9, No.4, pp. 336-355.

Antrim, L.N., and Sebenius, J. K. (1992) *Formal Individual Mediation and the Negotiators' Dilemma: Tommy Koh at the Law of the Sea Conference*', Mediation in International Relations: Multiple Approaches to Conflict Management, (Eds), Jacob Bercovitch and Jeffrey Z. Rubin. New York: St. Martin's Press.

Arjona, A. (2009) Social Orders in Warring Times: Armed Groups' Strategies and Civilian Agency in Civil War', *Paper Presented at the*

Workshop Mobilisation for Political Violence: What Do We Know? Oxford University Press.

Arjona, A. (2016) *Rebelocracy: Social order in the Colombian Civil War'*, New York, New York: Cambridge University Press.

Arjona, A., Kasfir, N. and Mampilly, Z. (2015) *Rebel governance in Civil War'*, New York: Cambridge University Press.

Arnold, M. (2007) The South Sudan Defence Force: Patriots, Collaborators or Spoilers? *Journal of Modern African Studies*, Vol 45, pp. 489–516.

Arnold, M. and Alden, C. (2007) This Gun is Our Food: Demilitarising the White Army militias of South Sudan', *Norwegian Institute of International Affairs,* (NUPI) Working Papers, Oslo.

Arnold, M. and LeRiche, M. (2008) *Allies and Defectors: An Update on Armed Group Integration and Proxy Force Activity',* Geneva: The Sudan Human Security Baseline Assessment (HSBA).

Arrow, K. (1985) *The Economics of Agency'*, In: J. Pratt, R. Zeckhauser (Eds.), Principals and Agents: The Structure of Business, Harvard Business School Press, Boston.

Arthur, P. (2012) Reintegration and Reconstruction in Post-War South Sudan', *International Peace Support Training Centre.*

Arthy, S. (2003) *Ex-Combatant Reintegration: Key Issues for Policy Makers and Practitioners, Based on Lessons from Sierra Leone'*, Department for International Development, United Kingdom.

Asghar, J. (2013) Critical Paradigm: A Preamble for Novice Researchers', *Life Science Journal*, Vol.10, No. 4, pp. 3121-3127.

Assael, H. and Keon, J. (1992) Non-sampling Vs. Sampling Errors in Survey Research', *Journal of Marketing*, Vol. 46, No.2, pp. 114-123.

Assefa, H. (1999) *A Lack of Visionary Statesmanship and Democratic Leadership'*, In: Searching for Peace in Africa, Utrecht: European Platform on Conflict Prevention and Transformation.

Atkinson, P. and Coffey, A. (2003) *Revisiting the Relationship between Participant Observation and Interviewing'*, In Jaber F. Gubrium & James A. Holstein (Eds.), Postmodern is Interviewing, (pp. 109-122). Thousand Oaks, CA. Sage.

Atkinson, P. and Delamont, S. (2006) *Rescuing Narrative from Qualitative Research'*, Narrative Inquiry, Vol.16, No.1, pp. 164-172.

Atkinson, R. (2010) *The Realists in Juba?' An Analysis of the Juba Peace Talks'*, In A. Tim and K. Vlassenroot (eds.) The Lord's Resistance Army: Myth and Reality, (pp. 205-223). London: Zed Books.

Atkinson, R. and Flint, J. (2001) Accessing Hidden and Hard-to-reach Populations: Snowball Research Strategies', *Social Research Update*, Vol. 33. Retrieved from http://sru.soc.surrey.ac.uk/SRU33pdf, [Accessed: 25/06/2019].

Auerbach, Y. (2009) *The Reconciliation Pyramid—A Narrative-Based Framework for Analysing Identity Conflicts'*, Political Psychology, Vol. 30, No. 2, pp. 291-318.

Awolich, A. (2014) *The Unwarranted Carnage in South Sudan'*, The Sudd Institute, Policy Brief, Juba.

Ayoob, M. (2007) State Making, State Breaking, and State Failure', In Crocker, C., F. Hampson, & P. Aall (eds.), *Leashing the Dogs of War – Conflict Management in a Divided World*, (pp. 95-114). Washington, DC: United States Institute of Peace Press.

Baas, S. (2012) *From Civilians to Soldiers and From Soldiers to Civilians: Mobilisation and Demobilisation in Sudan'*, Amsterdam University Press, Amsterdam.

Baaz, E. M. and Verweijen, J. (2013) *Between Integration and Disintegration: The Erratic Trajectory of the Congolese Army, Social Science Research Council: DR Congo Affinity Group'*, New York, USA: Social Science Research Council, Conflict Prevention and Peace Forum.

Babiker, M. and Ozerdem, A. (2003) A Future Disarmament, Demobilisation and Reintegration process in Sudan: Lessons learned from Ethiopia, Mozambique and Uganda', *Conflict, Security and Development*, Vol. 3, No. 2, pp. 211-232.

Badiey, N. (2013) The Strategic Institutionalisation of Land Tenure in State-building: The case of Juba, South Sudan', *Journal of the International African Institute*, Vol. 83, No. 1, pp. 57-77.

Baholzer, L. (2014) *When Do Disarmament, Demobilisation and Reintegration Programmes Succeed? Discussion Paper'*, German Development Institute, No. 8, pp. 597-8. Deutsches Institut für Entwicklungspolitik (DIE), Bonn.

Bailey, P.H. and Tilley, S. (2002) Storytelling and The Interpretation of Meaning in Qualitative Research', *Journal of Advanced Nursing*, Vol. 38, No. 5, pp. 74-583.

Baker, B. (2008) *Multi-choice policing in Africa'*, Uppsala: Nordiska Afrikainstitutet.

Baker, B. and Scheye, B. (2007) *Multi-layered Justice and Security Delivery in Post-Conflict and Fragile States'*, Conflict, Security and Development, Vol. 7, No. 4, pp.503-528.

Baker, C.L. (2011) *South Sudan's enduring Secession Issues: is Peace Possible*? The Applied Anthropologist, Vol.31, No. 2, pp. 42-48.

Baldwin, D. (1997) The Concept of Security', *Review of International Studies*, Vol. 23, No. 1, pp. 5-26.

Ball, N. (1997) *Demobilising and Reintegrating Soldiers: Lessons from Africa'*, In Krishna Kumar, (Eds.). Rebuilding Societies after Civil War: Critical Roles for International Assistance, (pp. 85-105). Boulder: Lynne Rienner.

Ball, N. (2002) *The Reconstruction and Transformation of War-torn Societies and State Institutions: How can External Actors Contribute*? In: Debiel, T & Klein, A. (Eds). Fragile Peace: State Failure, Violence and Development in Crisis Regions', pp. 33-55. London: Zed Books in Association with the Development and Peace Foundation.

Ball, N. and Fayemi, K. (2004) *Security Sector Governance in Africa: A handbook'*, London: Centre for Democracy and Development (www.ssrnetwork.net/document_library/detail/3155/security-sector-governance-in-Africa-a-handbook).

Ball, N. and Goor, L. (2006) *Disarmament, Demobilisation and Reintegration: Mapping Issues, Dilemmas and Guiding Principles'*, Working Paper, August. The Hague: Netherlands Institute for International Relations (Clingendael) Conflict Research Unit.

Ball, N. and Hendrickson, D. (2006) *Trends in Security Sector Reform (SSR): Policy, Practice and Research'*, International Development Research Centre (IDRC), Ottowa.

Ball, N. and Van de Goor, L. (2013) *The Challenges of Supporting Effective Security and Justice Development Programming'*, Washington DC: Centre for International Policy.

Ballentine, K. and Nitzschke, H. (2005) *The Political Economy of Civil War and Conflict Transformation'*, Berghof Research Centre for Constructive Conflict Management, https://www.berghof-foundation.org/fileadmin/redaktion/Publications/Handbook/Dialo gue_Chapters/dialogue3_ballentine_nitzschke.pdf. [Accessed: 06/09/2017].

Bankston, C.L, and Zhou, M. (2002) *Social Capital as a Process: The Meanings and Problems of a Theoretical Metaphor'*, Sociological Inquiry, Vol. 72, pp. 285-317.

Barash, D.P. and Webel, C.P (2014) *Peace and Conflict Studies'*, 3rd (Ed.), Thousand Oaks, CA. Sage

Barbier, E. B. *et al.* (2011) *The Value of Estuarine and Coastal Ecosystem Services*', Ecology Monographs, Vol. 81, No. 2, pp. 169–193.

Barkan, J.D (1993) Kenya: Lessons from a Flawed Election', *Journal of Democracy*, Vol. 4, No. 3, pp. 85–99.

Barnett, M. and Zürcher, C. (2007) *The Peace Builders Contract: How External Intervention Reinforces Weak Statehood*', Paper for the Research Partnership on Post-War Peacebuilding.

Barnett, M. *et al.* (2007) *Peacebuilding: What is in a Name*? Global Governance, No. 13, pp. 35-58.

Barnett, M. N. (2011) *Empire of Humanity: A History of Humanitarianism*', Ithaca, N.Y. and London: Cornell University Press.

Barth, F. (1969) Introduction', In: F. Barth (Ed.), *Ethnic Groups and Boundaries: The Social Organisation of Cultural Difference*', (pp. 9-38). Allen and Unwin, London.

Basedau, M. and Köllner, P. (2007) *Area Studies, Comparative Area Studies, and The Study of Politics: Context, Substance, and Methodological Challenges*', Zeitschrift für Vergleichende Politikwissenschaft, Vol. 1, pp. 105–124.

Basedau, M. and Lay, J. (2009) Resource Curse or Rentier Peace? The Ambiguous Effects of Oil Wealth and Oil Dependence on Violent Conflict', *Journal of Peace Research*, Vol. 46, No. 6, pp. 757–776.

Bates, R.H. (1983) *Modernisation, Ethnic Competition and the Rationality of Politics in Contemporary Africa*', In: D. Rothchild and V. A. Olorunsola

(Eds.), State Versus Ethnic Claims: African Policy Dilemmas, (pp. 152–71). Boulder, Co.: Westview Press.

Baumann, M. and Kuemmerle, T. (2016) The Impacts of Warfare and Armed Conflict on Land systems', *Journal of Land Use Science*, Vol. 11, No. 6, pp. 672–688.

Baxter, P. and Jack, S. (2008) *Qualitative Case Study Methodology: Study Design and Implementation for Novice Researchers'*, The Qualitative Report, Vol. 13, No. 4, pp. 544-559.

Bayart, J.F. (1993) *The state in Africa: The Politics of The Belly'*, 2nd (Ed.). London: Longman.

Becker, H.S. (1970) *Sociology work: Method and Substance'*, New Brunswick, NJ: Transaction Books

Beckker, H.W. (1970) *Sociological Work'*, Chicago: Aldine.

Bell, C. and Pospisil, J. (2017) Navigating Inclusion in Transitions from Conflict: The Formalised Political Unsettlement', *Journal of International Development*, Vol. 29, No. 5, pp. 576-593.

Bell, C. and Watson, C. (2006) *DDR: Supporting Security and Development'*, The EU's Added Value, London: International Alert, http://www.international-alert.org/pdf/EU_DDR_Aug_2006.Pdf

Bellina, S., Darbon, D., Eriksen, S., and Sending, O.J. (2009) *The Legitimacy of the State in Fragile Situations'*, Organisation for Economic Cooperation and Development DAC; development and aid committee, Norwegian Agency for Development Cooperation, Oslo, Norway.

Benard, C., Jones, G., Oliker, O., Thurston, Q., Stearns, K., and Cordell, K. (2008) *Women and Nation-Building'*, Santa Monica, CA: RAND Corporation, at http://www.rand.org/pubs/monographs/2008/RAND_MG579.pdf [Accessed 14/04/2018].

Bennett, J. (2010) *Aiding Peace: A Multi-donor Evaluation of Support to Conflict Prevention and Peacebuilding Activities in Southern Sudan 2005–2010'*, Brighton: ITAD.

Bennett, J., Pantuliano, S., Fenton, W., Vaux, A., and Brusset, E. (2010) *Aiding the Peace: A Multi-donor Evaluation of Support to Conflict Prevention and Peacebuilding Activities in Southern Sudan 2005—2010'*, Canadian International Development Agency (CIDA), Hove, East Sussex: ITAD. http://www.acdi-cida.gc.ca/acdi-cida/acdi-cida.nsf/eng.

Bercovitch, J. and DeRouen, K. (2005) *Managing Ethnic Civil Wars: Assessing the Determinants of Successful Mediation'*, Civil Wars, Vol.7, No. 1, pp. 98-116.

Bercovitch, J. and Gartner, S.S. (2006) *Is There Method in the Madness of Mediation? Some Lessons for Mediators from Quantitative Studies of Mediation'*, International Interactions, Vol. 32, No.4, pp. 329-354.

Berdal, M. (1996) *Disarmament and Demobilisation after Civil Wars: Arms, Soldiers, and the Termination of Conflict'*, Adelphi Paper No. 303. Oxford, UK: Oxford University Press.

Berdal, M. (2003) *How, New are New Wars? Global Economic Change and the Study of Civil Wars'*, in Global Governance, Vol.9, No.4, pp. 477-502.

Berdal, M. (2005) Beyond Greed and Grievance – and Not Too Soon', *Review of International Studies*, Vol. 31, No. 4, pp. 687-698.

Berdal, M. and Keen, D. (1997) *Violence and Economic Agendas in Civil Wars: Some Policy Implications'*, Millennium, Vol. 26, No. 3, pp. 795–818.

Berdal, M. and Malone, D. (2000) *Greed and Grievance: Economic Agendas in Civil Wars'*, Boulder, CO: Lynne Rienner.

Berdal, M. and Ucko, D.H. (2009) *Introduction: The Political Reintegration of Armed Groups after War'*, in Berdal and Ucko (Eds), Reintegrating Armed Groups after Conflict: Politics, Violence and Transition. London:

Berg, B.L. (2004) *Qualitative Research Methods for the Social Sciences'*, Boston: Pearson.

Berger, P.L (ed.) (2010) *Between Relativism and Fundamentalism: Religious Resources for a Middle Position'*, Grand Rapids, Michigan: William B. Eerdmans Publishing Company.

Berlin, I. (2001) *Nationalism: Past Neglect and Present Power'*, In: Isaiah Berlin, Henry Hardy and Roger Hausheer (Eds.), Against the Current: Essays in the History of Ideas, (pp. 333-355). Princeton, NJ: Princeton University Press.

Berman, B. (1998) *Ethnicity, Patronage and the African State: The Politics of Uncivil Nationalism'*, African Affairs, Vol. 97, No. 388, pp. 305-341.

Beshir, M. O. (1968) *The Southern Sudan: Background to Conflict'*, New York: Praeger.

Beswick, S.F. (1991) *The Addis Ababa Agreement: 1972-1983 Harbinger of the Second Civil War in the Sudan'*, Northeast African Studies, Vol. 13, No. 2 & 3, pp. 191-215.

Beswick, S.F. (2004) *Sudan's Blood Memory: The Legacy of War, Ethnicity, and Slavery in South Sudan'*, University of Rochester Press.

Bhabba, H. (1994) *The Location of Culture'*, New York: Routledge.

Bickman, L. and Rog, D. (2009) *Applied Research Design: A Practical Approach'*, In: L. Bickman and D. Rog (Eds.), Handbook of Applied Social Research Methods, 2nd (Ed.), pp. 3-43. Thousand Oaks, CA: Sage.

Biel, M.R and Ojok, D. (2018) *IGAD, Political Settlements and Peacebuilding in South Sudan: Lessons from the 2018 Peace Negotiation Processes'*, Konrad-Adenauer-Stiftung report (KAS), https://www.kas.de/c/document_library/get_file?uuid=aa8118eb-f1b8-5845-b628-606fd3c17361&groupId=280229[Accessed: 20/08/2019].

Binder, I. (2013) *The Discourse of Ethnicity in Sociology of International Relation'*, History, Babeş-Bolyai, University of Cluj-Napoca, pp. 221-238.

Bindi, I.T. and Tufekci, O. (2018) Liberal Peacebuilding in Sierra Leone: A Critical Exploration', *Journal of Asian and African Studies*, No, 2-05, pp. 1-16.

Bior, K.B. (2018) *Evaluation of the implementation of the SA of the Agreement on the Conflict in South Sudan (ARCSS): Implications for the Security Sector Reforms'*, Policy Brief, The Sudd Institute, Juba. South Sudan.

Blanchard, L. P. (2016) *Conflict in South Sudan and the Challenges Ahead'*, Congressional Research Service, https://fas.org/sgp/crs/row/R43344.pdf.[Accessed: 26/09/17].

Bloor, M., Fincham, B. and Sampson, H. (2007) *Qualities (NCRM) Commissioned Inquiry into the Risk to Well-Being of Researchers in Qualitative Research'*, Cardiff ESRC National Centre for Research Methods, Cardiff University Wales.

Blumer, H. (1969) *Symbolic Interactionism: Perspective and Method'*, Berkeley: University of California Press.

Bochner, A.P. (2007) *Notes towards an ethics of memory in auto-ethnographic Inquiry'*, In: Norman K. Denzin & Michael D. Giardina (Eds.), Ethical futures in Qualitative Research, (pp.196-208). Walnut Creek, Ca: Left Coast Press.

Boege, V., Brown, A. and Clements, K. (2008) *States Emerging from Hybrid Political Orders – Pacific Experiences Brisbane'*, The Australian Centre for Peace and Conflict Studies (ACPACS), Occasional Papers Series.

Boege, V., Brown, A., Clements, K., and Anna Nolan, A. (2009) *On Hybrid Political Orders and Emerging States: What is failing – States in the Global South or Research and Politics in the West?*' Berghof Handbook Dialogue Series, Vol. 8, pp. 15-35.

Boege, V., Brown, A., Clements, K., and Nolanet, A. (2009*) Building Peace and Political Community in Hybrid Political Orders*', International Peacekeeping, Vol. 16, No. 5, pp.599-615.

Boege, V., Brown, A., Clements, K., and Nolanet, A. (2009a) *Undressing the Emperor: A Reply to our Discussants*', In Martina Fischer & Beatrix Schmelzle (Eds), Building Peace in the Absence of States: Challenging the Discourse on State Failure, (pp. 15-31). Berlin: Berghof Research Centre.

Bogdan, R. C. and Biklen, S. K. (1982) *Qualitative research for education: An Introduction to Theory and Methods*', Boston: Allyn & Bacon

Bohannan, P. (1963) *Social Anthropology*', New York Holt, Rinehart and Winston.

Bohman, J. (2003) *How to Make a Social Science Practical: Critical Theory, Pragmatism, and Multiperspectival Theory*', Millennium, Vol. 21, No. 3, pp. 499-524.

Boland, R.J. (1985*) Phenomenology: A Preferred Approach to Research in Information Systems*', In: Research Methods in Information Systems, E. Mumford, R. A. Hirschheim, G. Fitzgerald, and A. T. Wood-Harper (Eds.), (pp. 193-201). North-Holland, Amsterdam.

Boland, R.J. (1991*) Information System Use as a Hermeneutic Process'*, In: Information Systems Research: Contemporary Approaches and Emergent Traditions, H-E. Nissen, H. K. Klein, and R. A. Hirschheim (Eds.), (pp. 439-464). North-Holland, Amsterdam.

Bonner, G. *et al.* (2002) Trauma for all: A pilot study of the subjective experience of physical restraint for mental health inpatients and staff in the UK', *Journal of Psychiatric and Mental Health Nursing*, Vol. 9, pp. 465–473.

Booth, K. (1991) Security and Emancipation', *Review of International Studies*, Vol. 17, No. 4, pp. 313-326.

Borger, J. (2008) *War Crimes: General Consensus that Al-Bashir behind Genocide'*, https://www.theguardian.com/world/audio/2008/jul/15/borger.sudan:[Accessed: 30/04/2017].

Bossuroy, T. (2008) *Ethnicity as a Resource in Social Capital'*, Typescript, Paris School of Economics, DIAL.

Boswell, A. (2019) *Insecure Power and Violence: The Rise and Fall of Paul Malong and the Mathiang Anyoor'*, Geneva: Small Arms Survey, Briefing Paper, Graduate Institute of International Studies, pp.1-20. http://www.smallarmssurveysudan.org/fileadmin/docs/briefing-papers/HSBA-BP-Mathiang-Anyoor.pdf [accessed: 20/11/2019].

Boutros-Ghali, B. (1992) *An Agenda for Peace: Preventive Diplomacy, Peacemaking and Peace-Keeping'*, United Nations: New York.

Bozus, L. (2013) *Applying the Governance Concept to Areas of Limited Statehood: Implications for International Foreign and Security Policy'*, In Governance without a State? Policies and Politics in Areas of Limited Statehood, (Ed.), T. Risse, (pp. 262–280). New York: Columbia University Press.

Braathen, E., Bøås, M., and Saether, G. (2000) *Ethnicity Kills? The Politics of War, Peace and Ethnicity in Sub-Saharan Africa'*, McMillan Press Ltd.

Brady, M. (2016) *Neoliberalism, Governmental Assemblages, and the Ethnographic Imaginary'*, University of Toronto Press, Toronto, Canada.

Bragg, C. (2006) *Challenges to Policy and Practice in the Disarmament, Demobilisation, Reintegration and Rehabilitation of Youth Combatants in Liberia'*, Sussex Migration Working Paper', No. 29, pp.1-23.

Branch, A. and Mampilly, Z. (2004) Winning the War, But Losing the Peace? The dilemma of SPLM/A Civil Administration and the Tasks Ahead', *Journal of Modern African Studies*, Vol. 43, No. 1, pp. 1–20.

Brandt, P.T., Mason, D., Gurses, M., Petrovsky, N., and Radin, D. (2008) *When and How the Fighting Stops: Explaining the Duration and Outcome of Civil Wars'*, Defence and Peace Economics, Vol. 19, No. 6, pp. 415-434.

Brannen, J. (1992) *Mixing Methods: Qualitative and Quantitative Research'*, London: Routledge.

Brannen, J. (2017) *Mixing Methods: Qualitative and Quantitative Research'*, New York, N.Y.: Routledge.

Bratton, M. and Masunungure, E. (2008) Zimbabwe's Long Agony', *Journal of Democracy*, Vol. 19, No. 4, pp. 41-55.

Breidlid, I.M. and Arensen, M.J. (2014) *Demystifying the White Army: Nuer Armed Civilians involvement in the South Sudanese Crisis'*, Conflict Trends, Vol. 3, pp.32–39.

Breitung, C., Paes, W., and van de Vondervoort, L. (2016) I*n Need of a Critical Re-think: SSR in South Sudan'*, BICC Working Paper, No. 6. https://www.bicc.de/publications/publicationpage/publication/in-need-of-a-critical-re-think-security-sector-reform-in-south-sudan-654/[Accessed: 20/03/2018].

Brethfeld, J. (2010) *Unrealistic Expectations: Current Challenges to Reintegration in Southern Sudan'*, Small Arms Survey, Geneva: Graduate Institute of International and Development Studies, HSBA Working Paper, No. 21, pp. 4-45.

Brett, R. and Specht, I. (2004) *Young Soldiers: Why They Choose to Fight'*, Boulder, CO: Lynne Rienner.

Brewer, C. (2010) *Disarmament in South Sudan'*, Case study No. 7, Centre for Complex Operations, Washington, DC, National Defence University.

Brinkerhoff, D. W. (2005) *Accountability and Good Governance: Concepts and Issues'*, International Development Governance, (Eds.), Ahmed Shafiqul Zafarullah and Habib Mohammad Huque. New York: CRC Press.

Britten, N. (1995) Qualitative Research: Qualitative Interviews in Medical Research', *British Medical Journal*, Vol. 3, No. 11, pp. 251-253.

Broch-Due, V. (2005) *Violence and belonging: Analytical Reflections'*, In: V. Broch-Due (ed.), Violence and belonging: The Quest for Identity in Post-Colonial Africa (pp.1-40). London: Routledge.

Brosche, J. (2009) *Sharing Power-Enabling Peace? Evaluating Sudan's Comprehensive Peace Agreement 2005'*, Uppsala: Uppsala University.

Brosche, J. (2014) *Masters of War: The Role of Elites in Sudan's Communal Conflicts'*, Uppsala: Uppsala University Press.

Brosche, J. and Höglund, K. (2016) Crisis of Governance in South Sudan: Electoral Politics in the World's Newest Nation', *Journal of Modern African Studies*, Vol. 54, No. 1, pp. 1–24.

Brosche, J. and Höglund, K. (2017) *Riek Machar: Warlord-Doctor in South Sudan'*, In Anders Themné, (Eds.), Warlord Democrats in Africa: Ex-military Leaders and Electoral Politics', (pp. 199-220). Nordic Africa Institute, Uppsala, Sweden.

Brown, J.A. (2014) *South Sudan's Slide into Conflict: Revisiting the Past and Reassessing Partnerships'*, Chatham House: The Royal Institute of International Affairs.

Brown, L.P. and Wycoff, M. A. (1987) *Policing Houston: Reducing Fear and Improving Service'*, Crime and Delinquency, Vol. 33, No. 1, pp. 71–89.

Brown, M.E. (1996) *The Causes and Regional Dimensions of Internal Conflict'*, In: Michael Brown, (Ed.), International Dimensional of Internal Conflict, pp. 571-602. Cambridge, MA: MIT Press.

Browning, C. S., (2018a) *Jesuis en terrase: Political Violence, Civilisational Politics, and the Everyday Courage to be'*, Political Psychology, Vol. 39, No. 2, pp. 243–226.

Brubaker, R. (2009) Ethnicity, Race and Nationalism', *Annual Review of Sociology*, Vol. 35, pp. 21-42.

Bryant, A. and Charmaz, K. (2007) *Grounded Theory Research: Methods and Practices'*, In: A. Bryant & K. Charmaz (Eds.), The Sage handbook of grounded theory (pp. 1-28). London, UK: Sage.

Bryden, A. and Hänggi, H. (2005) *Reforming and Reconstructing the Security Sector'*, In: Bryden, A., and Hänggi, H. (Eds.), Shaping a Security Governance Agenda in Post-Conflict Peacebuilding, (pp. 23-43). Geneva Centre for the Democratic Control of Armed Forces (DCAF).

Bryden, A. and Scherrer, V. (2012) *Disarmament, Demobilisation and Reintegration and SSR'*, Insights from U.N. Experience in Afghanistan, Burundi and the Democratic Republic of Congo', LIT Verlag Münster.

Bryden, M. (2014) *The Reinvention of Al-Shabaab'*, Centre for Strategic and International *Studies'*, https://www.csis.org/analysis/reinvention-al-shabaab[Accessed: 12/09/2016].

Bryman, A. (2004) *Social Research Methods,'* 2nd (Ed.), Oxford: Oxford University Press.

Bryman, A. (1988) *Quantity and Quality in Social Research'*, London: Allen & Unwin.

Bryman, A. (2001) *Social Research Method'*, Oxford: Oxford University Press.

Bryman, A. (2006b) Paradigm Peace and the Implications for Quality', *International Journal of Social Research Methodology*, Vol 9, pp. 111-126.

Burgess, S.F. (2008) *Fashioning Integrated Security Forces after Conflict'*, African Security, Vol.1, No. 2, pp. 69 – 91.

Bush, R.A. and Folger, J. P. (2005) *The Promise of Mediation. The Transformative Approach to Conflict'*, book San Francisco, CA: Jossey-Bass.

Butterfield, H. (1951) *History and Human Relations'*, London: Collins.

Buzan, B. (1981) *People, States and Fear: An Agenda for International Security Studies in the Post-Cold War Era'*, 1st (Ed) 1981, 2nd Edition. Hertfordshire: Harvester Wheatshcaf, 1991 and 2008 with a new preface from the author.

Buzan, B. (1991) *New Patterns of Global Security in the Twenty-First Century'*, International Affairs, Royal Institute of International Affairs 1944, Vol. 67, No 3, pp. 431-451.

Buzan, B. (1991) *People, States and Fear'*, Boulder, Colorado: Lynne Rienner Publishers.

Buzan, B. (1998) *Security, the State, the New World Order, and Beyond'*, On Security, (Ed.). Ronne D. Lipschutz. New York: Columbia University Press.

Buzan, B. (2006) *The War on Terrorism as the New Macro-Securitisation?* Oslo Workshop, pp. 1-25.

Byrne, A. (2009) *Experience and Content'*, The Philosophical Quarterly, Vol. 59, Issue 236, pp.429–451.

Cabestan, J. P. and Pavković, A. (2013*) Secessionism and Separatism in Europe and Asia: To have a State of One's Own'*, New York: Taylor and Francis.

Call, C. (2010) *Liberia's War Recurrence: Grievance over Greed'*, Civil Wars, Vol 12, No. 4, pp. 347-369.

Call, C. and Cook, S.E. (2003) *On Democratisation and Peacebuilding'*, Global Governance, Vol. 9, No. 2, pp. 233-46.

Call, C. and Wyeth, V. (2008) *Building States to Build Peace'*, Boulder: Lynne Rienner Publishers.

Call, C., and Cousens, E.M. (2008) *Ending Wars and Building Peace: International Responses to War-Torn Societies'*, Blackwell Publishing, International Studies Perspectives, Vol. 9, pp.1–21.

Campbell, D.T. (1988) *Methodology and Epistemology for Social Science'*, (Ed.), E. S. Overman, Chicago: University of Chicago Press.

Campbell, D.T. and Stanley C. (1963) *Experimental and Quasi-Experimental Designs for Research'*, N.Y.: Houghton Mifflin.

Caplan, R. (2005) *International Governance of War-Torn Territories: Rule and Reconstruction'*, Oxford: Oxford University Press.

Carney, T. (2007) *Some assembly required: Sudan's Comprehensive Peace Agreement'*, Washington, DC: U.S. Institute of Peace.

Castaneda, C. (2009) How Liberal Peacebuilding Might be Failing Sierra Leone', *Review of African Political Economy*, Vol. 36, No. 120, pp. 235-51.

Chabal, P. and Daloz, J.P. (1999) *Africa Works Disorder as a Political Instrument'*, Oxford, James Currey. Indiana University Press.

Chambers, R. (1997) *Whose Reality Counts? Putting the First Last'*, London: Intermediate Technology Publications.

Chambers, R. (1998) *Challenging the Professions: Frontiers for Rural Development'*, London: Intermediate Technology Publications.

Chandler, D. (1999) *Bosnia: Faking Democracy after Dayton'*, London: Pluto Press.

Chandler, D. (2006) *Empire in Denial: The Politics of State-building'*, London. Pluto Press.

Chandler, D. (2010) *Race, Culture and civil society: Peacebuilding Discourse and the Understanding of Difference'*, Security Dialogue, Vol. 41, No. 4, pp. 369-390.

Chandler, D. (2013) *Promoting democratic norms? Social Constructivism and the 'Subjective' Limits to Liberalism'*, Democratisation, Vol. 20, No. 2, pp. 215-239.

Chandler, D. (2015) Resilience and the 'Every day': Beyond the Paradox of 'Liberal Peace', *Review of International Studies*, Vol. 41, No. 1, pp. 27-48.

Chandra, K. (2001) *Cumulative Findings in the Study of Ethnic Politics'*, Vol. 12, No.1, pp. 7-11.

Chandra, K. (2012) *Constructivist Theories of Ethnic Politics'*, Oxford: Oxford University Press.

Chang, H. and Dodd, T. (2001*) International Perspectives on Race and Ethnicity: Annotated Bibliography'*, the Electronic Magazine of Multicultural Education.

Chassang, S. and Miquel, G.P. (2008) *Mutual Fears and Civil War'*, Bread Working Paper, 165. http://ipl.econ.duke.edu/bread/papers/working/165.pdf [Accessed: 27/07 2018].

Chazan, N., Mortimer, R., Ravenhill, J., Rothchild, D. (1992) *The Diversity of African Politics: Trends and Approaches'*, In: Politics and Society in Contemporary Africa, Palgrave, London.

Chen, C. (2015) *Negotiated Settlement and the Durability of Peace: Agreement Design, Implementation, and Mediated Civil Wars'*, Master thesis, Utah State University, pp. 1-44.

Chetail, V. and Jütersonke. (2015*) Peacebuilding: A Review of the Academic Literature'*, Geneva: GPP. Conciliation Resources', The International Contact Group on Mindanao, http://www.cr.org/featured-work/international-contact-group-mindanao[Accessed: 13/5/2017].

Childress, S. (2011) *South Sudan Seeks Statehood'*, Wall Street Journal: Africa News. https://www.wsj.com/articles/SB10001424052748704739504576067790998188326(Accessed: 16/12/2017].

Chirban, J.T. (1996) *Interviewing In-Depth: The Interactive-Relational Approach'*, Thousand Oaks, CA. Sage Publications.

Chua, A. (2003) *World on Fire: How Exporting Free Market Democracy Breeds Ethnic Hatred and Global Instability'*, New York: Doubleday.

Civic, A. and Miklaucic, (2011) *The State and the Use of Force: Monopoly and Legitimacy'*, in Monopoly of Force; the Nexus of DDR and SSR', (Ed), by Melanne A. Civic and Miklaucic, M. Centre for Complex Operations Institute for National Strategic Studies, National Defence University Press. Washington, DC.

Clandinin, D.J. and Connelly, F.M. (2000) *Narrative Inquiry: Experience and Story in Qualitative Research'*, San Francisco: Jossey-Bass.

Clapham, C. (1982) *Clientelism and the State'*, In: C. Clapham, ed., Private Patronage and Public Power: Political Clientelism in the Modern State, (pp. 1-35). New York: St Martin's Press.

Clapham, C. (1996) *Africa and the International System: The Politics of State Survival'*, Cambridge: Cambridge University Press.

Clapham, C. (2012) *From Liberation Movement to Government: Past Legacies and the Challenge of Transition in Africa'*, The Brent Hurst Foundation, Johannesburg, Oppenheimer & Son (Pty) Ltd.

Clark, J.N. (2009) The Limits of Retributive Justice: Findings of an Empirical Study in Bosnia and Herzegovina', Journal of International Criminal Justice, Vol. 7, No. 3, pp. 463-487.

Clark, J.N. (2014) *International Trials and Reconciliation: Assessing the Impact of the International Criminal Tribunal for the Former Yugoslavia'*, New York: Routledge.

Clarke, D. (2003) *Research Methods in Education'*, unpublished manuscript, Melbourne.

Clarke, L. (1995) Nursing research: Science, Vision and Telling Stories', *Journal of Advanced Nursing*, Vol. 21, pp.584-93.

Cleaver, F. (1998a) Gendered incentives and Institutions: Women, Men and the Management of water', *Journal of Agriculture and Human Values*, Vol.15, No. 4.

Cleaver, F. (1998b) *There's a Right Way to Do It – Informal Arrangements for Local Resource Management'*, Waterline, Vol. 16, No. 4. pp. 12-14.

Clement, C. (2009) *SSR in the DRC: Forward to the Past'*, In: TK editors, SSR in Challenging Environments, Geneva, DECAF Annual Yearbook.

Clement, C. (2015) *Stepping beyond the Ideological Clash: A Window of Opportunity for Effective Peacebuilding in South Sudan'*, Presented at Wilton Park's Peacebuilding in Africa, Geneva Centre for Security Policy, pp.1-13.

Cockett, R. (2010) *Sudan: Darfur and the Failure of an African State'*, New Haven, CT: Yale University Press.

Cohen, A. (1969) *Custom and Politics in Urban Africa: A Study of Hausa Migrants in a Yoruba Town'*, London: Routledge & Kegan Paul.

Cohen, J.L. (1999) *Changing Paradigms of Citizenship and the Exclusiveness of the Demos'*, International Sociology, Vol. 14, No. 3, pp. 245-68.

Cohen, R. (1978) Ethnicity: Problem and Focus in Anthropology', *Annual Review of Anthropology*, Vol.7: pp. 383-384.

Coleman J.S. (1958) *Relational Analysis: The Study of Social Organisations with Survey Methods'*, Human Organisation, Vol. 17, pp. 28–36.

Coleman, J.S. (1988) Social Capital in the Creation of Human Capital', *American Journal of Sociology*, Vol. 94, pp. 95-120.

Colletta, N. Kostner, J., Wiederhofer, M., and Kostner, M.(1996a) T*he Transition from War to Peace in Sub-Saharan Africa'*, Washington, DC: The World Bank.

Colletta, N., Kostner, J., Wiederhofer, M., and Kostner, M. (1996b) *Case Studies in War-to-Peace Transition: The Demobilisation and Reintegration of Ex-Combatants in Ethiopia, Namibia, and Uganda'*, Discussion Paper No. 331 (Africa Technical Department Series). Washington, DC: The World Bank.

Colletta, N.J. (1999) *The World Bank, Demobilisation, and Social Reconstruction'*, In: Jeffrey Boutwell and Michael T. Klare (Eds.), Light

Weapons and Civil Conflict: Controlling the Tools of Violence, (pp. 203–214). Lanham: Rowman and Littlefield.

Colletta, N.J. and Cullen, M.L. (2000) *The Nexus between Violent Conflict, Social Capital, and Social Cohesion: Case Studies from Cambodia and Rwanda'*, Washington DC: The World Bank: Social Capital Initiative.

Colletta, N.J. and Muggah, R. (2009) Rethinking Post-War Security Promotion', *Journal of Security Sector Management*, Vol. 7, No. 1, pp. 1–25.

Collier, P. (1998) *On Economic Causes of Civil War'*, Oxford Economic Papers, Vol.50, No.4, pp.563-573.

Collier, P. (2000a) Rebellion as a Quasi-criminal Activity', *Journal of Conflict Resolution*, Vol 44, No. 6, pp.839-853.

Collier, P. (2000b) *Doing Well out of War'*, in Berdal, M. and D.M. Malone (Eds.), Greed and Grievance: Economic Agendas in Civil Wars, (pp. 91-111). Boulder: Lynne Rienner Publishers.

Collier, P. (2007) *The Bottom Billion: Why the Poorest Countries are Failing and What Can Be Done About It'*, Oxford: Oxford University Press.

Collier, P. (2009) *Wars, Guns and Votes: Democracy in Dangerous Places'*, London: Random House.

Collier, P. and Hoeffler, A. (2004) *Greed and Grievance in Civil War'*, Oxford Economic Papers, Vol.56, No.4, pp.563-595.

Collier, P. and Hoeffler, A. (2007) *Civil War'*, In: T. Sandler and K. Hartley (Eds.), Handbook of Defence Economics', (pp. 712–39). Elsevier, Amsterdam.

Collier, P., Hoeffler, A. and Rohner, D. (2009) *Beyond Greed and Grievance: Feasibility and Civil War*', Oxford Economic Papers, Vol. 61, No.1, pp.1-27.

Collins, R.O. (2007) *Civil Wars in the Sudan*', History Compass, Vol 5, No. 6, pp. 1778- 1805

Collins, R.O. (1983) *Shadows in the Grass: Britain in the Southern Sudan, 1918-1956*', New Haven: Yale University Press.

Comaroff, J.L. (1996) *Ethnicity, Nationalism, and the Politics of Difference in an Age of Revolution*', In: The Politics of Difference: Ethnic Premises in a World of Power, (Ed.). McAllister Patrick and Edwin Wilmsen, Chicago, University of Chicago Press.

Connor, W. (1994) *Ethnonationalism: The Quest for Understanding*', Princeton: Princeton University Press.

Cooper, N. (2007) *On the Crisis of the Liberal Peace*', Conflict, Security and Development, Vol. 7, No. 4, pp. 605-616.

Cooper, N., Turner, M. and Pugh, M. (2011) The End of History and the Last Liberal Peacebuilder: A Reply to Roland Paris', *Review of International Studies*, Vol. 37, No. 4, pp. 1995-2007.

Copnall, J. (2014) *A Poisonous Thorn in Our Hearts: Sudan and South Sudan's Bitter and Incomplete Divorce*', Hurst Publishers, Great Russell Street, London WC1B 3PL.

Coppieters, B. (2003) *War and Secession: A Moral Analysis of the Georgian-Abkhazian Conflict*', In Bruno Coppieters and Richard Sakwa (Eds.),

Contextualising Secession: Normative Studies in Comparative Perspective. Oxford University Press.

Coser, L.A. (1967) Social Conflict and the Theory of Social Change', *The British Journal of Sociology*, Vol. 8, No. 3, pp. 197-207.

Cox, R.W. and Scechter, M.G. (2002) *The Political Economy of a Plural World: Critical Reflections on Power, Morals and Civilisation*', New York: Routledge.

Coyne, C. (2006) *Reconstructing Weak and Failed States: Foreign Intervention and the Nirvana Fallacy*', Foreign Policy Analysis, Vol. 2, No. 4, pp. 343-360.

Crabtree, B. and Miller, W. (1999) Doing Qualitative Research', 2nd (Ed.), London: Sage.

Cramer, C. (2006) *Civil War is Not a Stupid Thing: Accounting for Violence in Developing Countries*', London: Hurst & Co.

Cramer, C. (2010) *Unemployment and Participation in Violence*', Background paper for WDR 2011.Washington, DC: World Bank.

Creswell, J. (2003) *Research Design: Qualitative, Quantitative, and Mixed Method Approaches*', 2nd (Ed.), Thousand Oaks, Calif.: Sage Publications.

Creswell, J. W. (2007) *Qualitative Inquiry and Research Design: Choosing Among Five Approaches*', London. Sage Publications.

Creswell, J. W. (2009) *Research Design: Qualitative and Mixed Methods Approaches*', London: Sage.

Crotty, M. (1989) *The Foundations of Social Research'*, London: Sage.

Crotty, M. (2003) *The Foundations of Social Research: Meaning and Perspectives in the Research Process'*, 3rd (Ed.), London: Sage Publications.

Crowley, J. (1999) *The Politics of Belonging: Some Theoretical Considerations'*, In: Andrew Geddes and Adrian Favell (Eds.), The Politics of Belonging: Migrants and Minorities in Contemporary Europe Aldershot: Ashgate.

Crowther, D. and Lancaster, G. (2008) *Research Methods: A Concise Introduction to Research in Management and Business Consultancy'*, Butterworth-Heinemann.

Crowther, D. and Lancaster, G. (2008) *Research Methods'*, London: Routledge.

Cubitt, C. (2011) *African Peace and Conflict Journal'*, Vol. 4, No. 1, pp.1-101.

Cullis, J.O. (2017) Not everything that can be counted counts... British Journal of Haematology', Vol. 177, No. 4, pp. 505–506.

Cunningham, D. E. (2013) Who Should Be at the Table: Veto Players and Peace Processes in Civil War', *Penn Journal of Law and International Affairs*, Vol. 2, No. 1, pp. 38-47.

Cunningham, D.E. (2006) Veto Players and Civil War Duration', *American Journal of Political Science*, Vol. 50, No. 4, pp. 875–892.

Dagne, T. (2011) *The Republic of South Sudan: Opportunities and Challenges for Africa's Newest Country'*, CRS Report for Congress. Congressional Research Service.

Dahl, R. A. (1989) *Democracy and its Critics'*, Yale University Press: New Haven.

Daly, M. W. (2007) *Darfur's Sorrow: A History of Destruction and Genocide'*, Cambridge: Cambridge University Press.

Das, T. and Teng, B. (1998) *Between Trust and Control: Developing Confidence in Partner Cooperation in Alliances'*, The Academy of Management Review, Vol. 23, No. 3, pp. 491-512.

Davidsen, A. (2010) *To Survive, General Practice needs a Reintroduction of the Psychodynamic Dimension'*, Psychodynamic Practice, Vol. 16, No. 4, pp. 451–61.

Davidson, B. (1992) *Man's Burden: Africa and Roots of State the Curse of the Nation-State'*, Cambridge: Cambridge University Press.

Davidson, B. (1992) *The Black Man's Burden: Africa and the Curse of the Nation-State'*, Oxford: James Currey.

Davies, J. (2001) *Review', Agriculture, Ecosystems and Environment'*, Vol. 86, No. 1, pp. 107–109.

De Herdt, T. and J.P. Olivier de Sardan. (2015) *Introduction: The Game of the Rules'*, In: T. De Herdt and J.-P. Olivier de Sardan (Eds) Real Governance and Practical Norms in Sub-Saharan Africa: The Game of the Rules, pp. 2–16. London and New York: Routledge.

De Heredia, M. I. (2018) *The Conspicuous Absence of Class and Privilege in the Study of Resistance in Peacebuilding Contexts'*, International Peacekeeping, Vol. 25, No. 3, pp.325-348.

De Maio, J.L. (2009) *Confronting Ethnic Conflict: The Role of Third Parties in Managing Africa's Civil Wars'*, Lanham: Lexington Books.

De Soysa, I. (2000) *The Resource Curse: Are Civil Wars Driven by Rapacity or Paucity?'* In: Berdal, M. and Malone, D. Boulder, (Ed.), Greed and Grievance: Economic Agendas in Civil War, CO: Lynne Rienner.

De Soysa, I. (2002) Paradise is a Bazaar? Greed, Greed, and Governance in Civil War, 1989–99', *Journal of Peace Research*, Vol. 39, No. 4, pp. 395–416.

De Vries, L. and Schomerus, M. (2017) *South Sudan's Civil War Will Not End with a Peace Deal'*, Peace Review, Vol. 29, No. 3, pp. 333-340.

De Waal, A. (2000) *Who Fights? Who Cares? War and Humanitarian Action in Africa'*, (Eds.), Africa World Press.

De Waal, A. (2007) *Sudan: The Turbulent State'*, In; Alex de Waal (Eds.), War in Sudan and the Search for Peace. Harvard University Press, Cambridge, MA.

De Waal, A. (2014) *When Kleptocracy Becomes Insolvent: Root Causes of the Civil War in South Sudan'*, African Affairs, Vol. 113, No. 452, pp. 347–369.

De Waal, A. (2017) Peace and the Security Sector in Sudan, 2002–11', *African Security Review*, Vol. 26, No. 2, pp. 180-198.

De Waal, A. (2018) *The Political Marketplace Framework: Framing Paper Prepared for the First Political Markets Workshop'*, May 30-31, Martin School, University of Oxford.

De Waal, A. (2019) Sudan', In: *Comparing Peace Processes'*, (Eds.), by Alpaslan Özerdem and Roger Mac Ginty, Routledge.

De Waal, A. and Abdul Mohammed, A. (2014) *Breakdown in South Sudan'*, Foreign Affairs, http://www.foreignaffairs.com/print/137729[Accessed: 20/04/2017].

De Waal, A. and Pendle, N. (2018) *South Sudan: Decentralisation and the Logic of the Political Marketplace,'* In: Luka Biong Deng Kuol and Sarah Logan (Eds.) The Struggle for South Sudan: Challenges of Security and State Formation, London, IB Tauris.

DeNardo, J. (1985) *Power in Numbers: The Political Strategy of Protest and Rebellion'*, Princeton, NJ: Princeton University Press.

Deng, D. (2018) *Compound Fractures: Political Formations, Armed Groups and Regional Mediation in South Sudan'*, Institute for Security Studies, Vol. 21. pp. 1-24.

Deng, F. (1995) *War of Visions: Conflict of Identities in the Sudan'*, Washington, DC, Brookings Institution.

Deng, F. (2005) *Sudan's Turbulent Road to Nationhood'*, In: R.R. Laremont, ed. Borders, Nationalism, and the African State, Boulder: Lynne Rienner.

Deng, F. and Morrison, J.S. (2001) *U.S. Policy to end Sudan's War: Report of the CSIS Task Force on U.S.–Sudan Policy'*, Washington, DC: CSIS.

Deng, L.B. (2005a) *The Comprehensive Peace Agreement: will it also be dishonoured? Forced Migration Review'*, Vol. 24, pp.15-16.

Deng, L.B. (2005b) *The Sudan Comprehensive Peace Agreement: Will it be sustained?* Civil Wars, Vol. 7, pp. 244-257.

Deng, L.B. (2017) *Dinka Youth in Civil War: Between Cattle, Community, and Government'*, In: Madut, J.J, Schomerus M, Kuol, L.B, Breidlid, I.M, Arensen, M. J (Eds) Informal armies: community defence groups in South Sudan's Civil War. Saferworld, pp 1–6. https://www.saferworld.org.uk/downloads/informal-armies-final.pdf.

Denzin, N. K. and Lincoln, Y. S. (2000) *Introduction: the Discipline and Practice of Qualitative Research'*, In: N. K. Denzin and Y. S. Lincoln (eds) The Sage Handbook of Qualitative Research', London: Sage.

Denzin, N. K., and Lincoln, Y.S. (1994) *Handbook of Qualitative Research'*, Thousand Oaks, CA: Sage.

DeRouen, K. and Chowdhury, I. (2013) *Mediation and Civil War Peace Agreement Implementation'*, In APSA 2013 Annual Meeting Paper.

Di John, J. (2007) Oil abundance and Violent Political Conflict: A Critical Assessment', *The Journal of Development Studies*, Vol. 43, No. 6, pp. 961-986.

Diamond, L. (1996) Is the Third Wave Over?' *Journal of Democracy*, Vol.7, pp. 20–37.

Diamond, L. (2002) Thinking about Hybrid Regimes', *Journal of Democracy*, Vol. 13, pp. 21–35.

Diamond, L. (2008) *The Democratic Roll-back: The Resurgence of the Predatory State*', Foreign Affairs, Vol. 87, pp. 36–48.

DiMaggio, P.J. and Powell, W.W. (1991) Introduction. In W. W. Powell & P. J. DiMaggio (Eds.), *The new institutionalism in organisational analysis*, Chicago: University of Chicago Press.

Disarmament, Demobilisation and Reintegration- Fact Sheet. (2010) Report of the Secretary-General on the Sudan', United Nations (S681).

Dobbins, J. Dobbins, J., Jones, S. Keith Crane, K., Beth C.D. (2007) *Beginner's Guide to Nation-Building*', Santa Monica: RAND.

Dobbins, J., Jones, S. Keith Crane, K., Beth C.D. (2003) *America's Role in Nation-Building: From Germany to Iraq'*, Santa Monica, CA: RAND Corporation',
https://www.rand.org/pubs/monograph_reports/MR1753.html [Accessed: 06/03/2019].

Doki, C. and Ahmad, A.M. (2014) *Africa's Arms Dump: Following the Trail of Bullets in the Sudans*', Guardian Africa Network Sudan, https://www.theguardian.com/world/2014/oct/02/-sp-africa-arms-dump-south-sudan [Accessed: 16/01/2020].

Dorman, S.R. (2006) *Post-Liberation Politics in Africa: Examining the Political Legacy of Struggle'*, Third World Quarterly, Vol. 27, No.6, pp. 1085-1101.

Dowden, R. (1993) *Reflections on Democracy in Africa'*, African Affairs, Vol. 92, No. 369, pp. 607-13.

Downes, A.B. (2004) *The Problem with Negotiated Settlements to Ethnic Civil Wars'*, Security Studies, Vol. 13, No. 4, pp. 230-79.

Doyle, D. (2011) *Ripe Moments for Exiting Political Violence, an Heuristic Model from Northern Ireland and its Application in Kashmir'*, Dublin City University: Centre for International Studies School of Law and Government.

Doyle, M. (1983) *Kant, Liberal Legacies, and Foreign Affairs'*, Philosophy and Public Affairs, Vol. 12, No.3/4, pp. 323–53.

Doyle, M. (2005) *Three Pillars of the Liberal Peace'*, The American Political Science Review', Vol. 99, No.3, pp. 463-466.

Doyle, M. W. and Sambanis, N. (2000) International Peacebuilding: A Theoretical and Quantitative Analysis', *The American Political Science Review*, Vol. 94, No.4, pp. 779-801.

Doyle, M.D. and Sambanis, N (2006) Making War and Building Peace: The United Nations Peace Operations, Princeton University Press.

Drapeau, M.　(2004b) *Réflexion Épistémologique Sur La Recherche Qualitative E.T. La Psychanalyse: Refaire une place au rêve E.T. àl imaginaire [Epistemological reflection on qualitative research and psychoanalysis'*,

Redeeming the dream and the imaginary]. Le Coq-héron [The Rooster], Vol. 2, No. 177, pp. 124-129.

Drysdale, J. (1964) *The Somali Dispute'*, New York: Praeger Press.

Dryzek, J.S. (2005) *Deliberative Democracy in Divided Societies: Alternatives to Agonism and Analgesia'*, Political Theory, Sage Publications.

Du Toit, P. (1989) Bargaining About Bargaining: Inducing the Self-negating Prediction in Deeply Divided Societies–the Case of South Africa', *The Journal of Conflict Resolution*, Vol 33, No. 2. pp. 210–30.

Dudouet, V. (2006) *Transitions from Violence to Peace: Revisiting Analysis and Intervention in Conflict Transformation'*, Berghof Report No. 15. Berghof Research Centre for Constructive Conflict Management.

Dudouet, V. Civic, (2011) *Non-state Armed Groups and the Politics of Post-war Security Governance in Monopoly of Force; in the Nexus of DDR and SSR'*, (Ed.), In: Melanne A. Civic and Miklaucic, M. Centre for Complex Operations Institute for National Strategic Studies, National Defence University Press Washington, DC.

Duffield, M. (2001) *Global Governance and the New Wars'*, London: Zed Books.

Duffield, M. (2007) *Development, Security and Unending War, Governing the World of Peoples'*, Cambridge: Polity.

Dulic, T. (2011) *Peace Research and Source Criticism; Using Historical Methodology to Improve Information Gathering and Analysis'*, In: K. Höglund and M. Öberg (Eds.), Understanding Peace Research, Methods and Challenges (pp. 35-46). London/New York: Routledge.

Dunne, T. (2005) System, State and Society: How Does it All Hang Together? *Millennium-Journal of International Studies,* Vol. 34, No.1, p. 157-170.

Durkheim, E. (1973) Pacifism et Patriotism' translated', by N. Layne in, Sociological Inquiry, Vol. 43, No. 2, PP. 99–103.

Duursma, A. (2014) A current literature review of international mediation', *International Journal of Conflict Management*, Vol. 25, No. 1, pp. 81-98.

Eagleton, T. (1983) *Literary theory: An Introduction*', Oxford: Basil Blackwell

Ebo, A. (2007) *The Role of SSR in Sustainable Development: Donor Policy Trends and Challenges'*, Conflict, Security & Development, Vol. 7, No. 1, pp. 27-60.

Egnell, R. and Haldén, P. (2009) *Laudable, a historical and Overambitious: SSR meets state formation theory*', Conflict, Security and Development, Vol. 9, No. 1, pp. 27-54.

Eisenstadt, S.N. (1978) *Revolution and the Transformation of Societies: A Comparative Study of Civilisations*', New York, N.Y.: Free Press.

Ekeh, P. (1975) *Colonialism and the Two Publics in Africa: A Theoretical Statement*', Comparative Studies in Society and History, Vol. 17, No. 1, pp. 91-112.

El-Affendi, A. (2001) *The impasse in the IGAD peace process for Sudan: the limits of regional peacemaking?* African Affairs, Vol 100, pp.581–599.

Elaine, K. and Walters, B. (2014) Ethnicity and Civil War', Anniversary Special Issue, *Journal of Peace Research*, Vol. 51, No. 2, pp. 199–212.

El-Battahani, A. (2007) Tunnel vision or kaleidoscope: Competing concepts on Sudan identity and national integration', *African Journal on Conflict Resolution*, Vol. 27, No. 2, pp.37–61.

Elena, T. *et al.* (2011) Historical research in Archives: User Methodology and Supporting Tools', International Journal of Digital Library, Springer-Verlag.

Englebert, P and Tull, D.M (2008) *Post-conflict Reconstruction in Africa'*, International Security, Vol. 32, No. 4, spring 2008, pp. 106-139.

Eriksen, T. H. (2004) *What is Anthropology'*, London: Pluto Press.

Eriksen, T.H. (2002) *Ethnicity and Nationalism, Anthropological Perspectives'*, London: Pluto Press.

Eriksson, M. and Wallensteen, P. (2004) Armed Conflict, 1989–2003', *Journal of Peace Research,* Vol. 41, No. 5, pp. 625–636.

Esman, M. (1994) *Ethnic Politics'*, Ithaca, New York: Cornell University Press.

Esman, M. (2004) *An introduction to Ethnic Conflict'*, Polity Press, Ltd.

Etherington, K. (2006) *Chicken or Egg? An Exploration of The Relationships Between Physical and Psychological Symptoms with a Woman*

Diagnosed with Tourette's Syndrome', In: Counselling and Psychotherapy Research. Vol. 6, no. 2, pp138-146.

Etherington, K. (2007) *Ethical Research in Reflexive Relationships'*, Qualitative Inquiry, Vol. 13, No. 50, pp. 599 -616.

Evans, G. and Newnham, J. (1998) *Dictionary of International Relations'*, London: Penguin Books

Evans, G. and Sahnoun, M. (2002) *The Responsibility to Protect'*, Foreign Affairs. Vol. 81, pp. 99–110.

Evans, P.B., Rueschemeyer, D. and Skocpol, T. (1985) *Bringing the State Back'*, Cambridge University Press.

Eyoh, D. (1999) *Community, Citizenship, and the Politics of Ethnicity in Post-Colonial Africa'*, in E. Kalipeni and P. Zeleza (Eds), Sacred Spaces and Public Quarrels, (pp. 271–300). Trenton, NJ and Asmara: Africa World Press.

Fahcy, D. (2013) *Gold, Land, and Ethnicity in North-Eastern Congo'*, London: Rift Valley Institute.

Fay, B. (1987) *Critical Social Science'*, Cornell University Press, Ithaca, New York.

Fearon, J. (1998) *Bargaining, Enforcement, and International Cooperation'*, *International Organisation'*, Vol. 52, No, 2, pp. 269-305.

Fearon, J. (2004) Why Do Some Civil Wars Last So Much Longer than Others?' *Journal of Peace Research*, Vol. 41, pp. 275-302.

Fearon, J. (2005) Primary Commodity Exports and Civil War', *Journal of Conflict Resolution*, Vol. 49, No. 4, pp. 483–507.

Fearon, J. and David D. L. (2000) *Ordinary Language and External Validity: Specifying Concepts in the Study of Ethnicity*', Paper Presented at the October 2000 meeting of LICEP, University of Pennsylvania.

Fearon, J. and Laitin, D. (2003 Ethnicity, Insurgency, and Civil War', *American Political Science Review*, Vol. 97, pp. 75–90.

Fearon, J. and Latin, D. (2000) *Violence and the Social Construction of Ethnic Identity*', International Organisation, Vol 54, No. 4, pp. 845-877.

Fearon, J. D. (2004) Why Do Some Civil Wars Last So Much Longer than Others? *Journal of Peace Research*, Vol. 41, No. 3, pp. 275–301.

Fearon, J. D. and Laitin, D.D. (1996) Explaining Inter-ethnic Cooperation', *American Political Science Review*, Vol 90, pp. 715-735.

Fiedler, C. and Karina, M. (2017) *Post-conflict Societies: Chances for Peace and Types of International Support*', Briefing Paper, Bonn: German Development Institute/Deutsches Institutfür Entwicklungspolitik, Vol. 4. https://www.die-gdi.de/uploads/media/BP__4.2017.pdf.

Field, A. (2005) *Reliability Analyses*', In: Field, A. (Ed.), Discovering Statistics Using Spss, Sage, London.

Fischer, A. M. (2008) *Resolving the Theoretical Ambiguities of Social Exclusion with Reference to Polarisation and Conflict*', Working Paper No. 08-90. DESTIN, London School of Economics.

http://www.lse.ac.uk/internationalDevelopment/pdf/WP/WP90.pdf.

Fischer, M. and Schmelzle, B. (2009) *Building Peace in the Absence of States: Challenging the Discourse on State Failure*', Berlin: Berghof Research Centre.

Fithen, C (1999) *Diamonds and War in Sierra Leone: Cultural Strategies for Commercial Adaptation to Endemic Low-intensity Conflict*', In: London: Department of Anthropology, University College, London.

Foley, D. (2003) *Indigenous Epistemology and Indigenous Standpoint Theory*', Social Alternatives, Vol. 22, No, 1, pp. 44-52.

Fortin, J. (2016) *Deadly Attacks Leave Victims Wondering Why*', New York Times 17 April, https://www.nytimes.com/2016/04/18/world/africa/deadly-attacks-in-ethiopia-leave-victimswondering-why.html.

Fortna, V.P. (2003) *Inside and Out: Peacekeeping and the Duration of Peace after Civil and Inter-state Wars*', International Studies Review. Vol. 5, No. 4, pp.97-114.

Fortna, V.P. (2004) *Peace Time: Cease-Fire Agreements and the Durability of Peace*', Princeton, NJ: Princeton Univ. Press.

Foucault, M (1991) *Governmentality*', (trans. R Braidotti and revised C Gordon) In: Burchell G, Gordon C and Miller P (Eds) *The Foucault Effect: Studies in Governmentality*, (pp.87-104) Chicago: University of Chicago Press.

Foucault, M. (1980) *Power/Knowledge: Selected Interviews and Other Writings 1972-1977'*, (Ed.), C. Gordon. Brighton: Harvester.

Foucault, M. (1997a) *Ilfau défendre la société'*, *Cours au Collège de France 1976, Paris*: Gallimard/Seuil.

Foucault, M. (1997b) *Security, Territory, and Population'*, In: Michel Foucault, Ethics: Subjectivity and Truth', (Ed.), (pp. 67-71). By Paul Rainbow, New York: The New Press.

Frahm, O. (2012) *Defining the Nation: National Identity in South Sudanese Media Discourse'*, Africa Spectrum. Vol 1, pp.21-49.

Freire, P. (1974) *Education for a Critical Consciousness'*, New York, N.Y.: Continuum.

Freire, P. (2005) *Pedagogy of the Oppressed: 30th-anniversary edition'*, London, United Kingdom: Continuum.

Fritz, V. and Menocal, A.R. (2007) *Forthcoming Developmental States in the New Millennium: Concepts and Challenges for a New Aid Agenda'*, Development Policy Review. Vol. 25, Issue, 5, pp. 531-552.

Fritz, V. and Rocha Menocal, A.R. (2006) *(Re) building Developmental States: From Theory to Practice'*, Working Paper No. 274, London, ODI.

Fukuyama, F. (2004) *State-Building: A New Agenda'*, Cornell University Press.

Fukuyama, F. (2004) The imperative of Statebuilding', *Journal of Democracy*, Vol. 15, No. 2, pp. 17-31.

Fukuyama, F. and Levy, B. (2010) *Development strategies: Integrating Governance and Growth',* World Bank Policy Research Working Paper, Washington DC: World Bank. https://openknowledge.worldbank.org/bitstream/handle/10986/19 915/WPS5196.pdf?sequence=1.

Gabriele Pollini (2005) Socio-Territorial Belonging in a Changing Society, *International Review of Sociology*, Vol 15, No. 3, pp. 493-496.

Gadir, A. (2003) *Conflict Resolution and Wealth Sharing in Sudan: Towards an Allocation Formula',* http://www.arab-api.org/jodep/products/delivery/wps0305.pdf. [Accessed: 20/02/2017].

Gadir, A., Ibrahim, A., and El-Batahani, A. (2005) *The Sudan's Civil War: Why has it Prevailed for So Long?'* in Collier, P. and Sambanis, N. (Eds.), *Understanding Civil War: Evidence and Analysis*, Vol.1, (pp.193-220). Africa, Washington, DC: The World Bank.

Galbraith, P. W. and Van Hollen, Jr. (1988) *Chemical Weapons Use in Kurdistan: Iraq's Final Offensive',* Staff Report to the Committee on Foreign Relations, U.S. Senate, Washington, DC: U.S. Government Printing Office

Galbraith, P.W. (2003) *The Ghosts of 1991',* Washington Post, 12 April, Academic, Lexis-Nexis, University of Iowa Library, Iowa City, IA.

Gall, M.D and Borg, W. (2003) *Educational Research: An introduction',* 7th (Ed.), Boston, MA: A & B Publications.

Galtung, J. (1965) A Structural Theory of Aggression', *Journal of Peace Research*, Vol. 1, No. 2, pp. 95-119.

Galtung, J. (1976) *Three Approaches to Peace: Peacekeeping, Peacemaking, and Peacebuilding*', In: J. Galtung. Peace, War and Defence: Essays in Peace Research, Vol. 2, pp. 297-298.

Galtung, J. (1990) Cultural Violence', *Journal of Peace Research*, Vol. 27, No. 3, pp.291–305.

Galtung, J. (2001) *After Violence, Reconstruction, Reconciliation, and Resolution', Reconciliation, Justice and Coexistence*', (Ed.), Mohammed Abu-Nimer, Oxford, England: Lexington Books.

Galtung. J (1985) Twenty-Five Years of Peace Research: Ten Challenges and Responses', *Journal of Peace Research*, Vol. 22, pp. 141–158.

Garang, A. (2015) *The impact of external actors on the prospects of a mediated settlement in South Sudan*', Paper was Presented at the Academic Conference on International Mediation. The University of Pretoria, 2-4 June 2015, Pretoria, South Africa.

Garang, J. (1987) *The Call for Democracy in Sudan*', London: Kegan Paul International.

Garang, J. and Khalid, M. (1987) *John Garang Speaks*', London: Kegan Paul International.

Gates, S. and Strøm, K. (2008) *Power-sharing, Agency and Civil Conflict: Power-sharing Agreements, Negotiations and Peace Processes'*, Policy brief forms, pp.1-15.

Gazit, N. (2009) Social Agency, Spatial Practices and Power: The Micro-foundations of Fragmented Sovereignty in the Occupied Territories', *An International Journal of Politics, Culture and Society*, Vol. 22, No. 1, pp. 83-104.

Gebrehiwot, G. and Abeba, A. (2007) *Cross Border Cooperation in the IGAD Region: A study Commissioned by IGAD as Part of its Peace and Security Strategy Development Project'*, The Framework Vol. 1, pp. 2-62.

Gebreselassie, S. (2018) *Disarmament Process in the Greater Lakes Hampered by Availability of Guns and Lack of Trust'*, UNMIS News: https://unmiss.unmissions.org/disarmament-process-greater-lakes-hampered-availability-guns-and-lack-trust [Accessed 15/03/2018].

Geertz, C. (1967) *Old Societies and New States: The Quest for Modernity in Africa and Asia'*, New York: The Free Press.

Geertz, C. (1973) *The Interpretation of Cultures'*, New York: Basic Books.

Geertz, C. (1973) *Thick Description Toward an Interpretive Theory of Culture'*, In C. Geertz. Ed. The Interpretation of Cultures, New York: Basic Books.

Gellner, E. (1983) *Nations and Nationalism'*, Oxford: Basil Blackwell.

George, A.L. and Bennett, A. (2005) *Case Studies and Theory Development in the Social Sciences'*, The MIT Press.

Gephardt, R.J. (1988) *Ethno-statistics: Qualitative Foundations for Quantitative Research'*, Newbury Park, CA: Sage.

Gerrard, A.J. (2000) *What is a Mountain? Background Paper to Definition of Mountains and Mountain regions (English)',* Washington, DC: World Bank Group. pp. 1-9.

Gerring, J. (2004) What is a Case Study and What Is It Good for?', *American Political Science Review*, Vol. 98, No. 2, pp. 341-354.

Gerring, J. (2006) *Case Study Research: Principles and Practices'*, Cambridge University Press: Cambridge.

Gerring, J. (2007) *Is There a (Viable) Crucial-Case Method? Comparative Political Studies'*, Vol. 40, No. 3, pp. 231-253.

Geschiere, P. (2009) *The Perils of Belonging: Autochthony, Citizenship, and Exclusion in Africa and Europe Chicago'*, University of Chicago Press.

Gettleman J (2012a) *Accounts emerge in South Sudan of 3,000 Deaths in Ethnic Violence'*, New York Times 5 Jan. http://www.nytimes.com/2012/01/06/world/africa/in-south-sudan-massacre-of-3000-isreported.html

Gettleman, J. (2008) *Anarchy-Cursed Nation Looks to Bottom-Up Rule,'* New York Times, August 18, p. A6, http://www.nytimes.com/2008/08/18/world/africa/18somalia.html .

Gettleman, J. (2012b) *Born in Unity, South Sudan is Torn again'*, New York Times 12 Jan.

http://www.nytimes.com/2012/01/13/world/africa/south-sudan-massacres-followindependence.html

Gettleman, J. (2013) *Quandary in South Sudan: Should it lose its Hard-won Independence?* New York Times, 23 January. https://www.nytimes.com/2017/01/23/world/africa/quandary-in-south-sudan-should-it-loseits-hard-won-independence.html

Ghani, A. and Lockhart, C. (2008) *Fixing Failed States: A Framework for Rebuilding a Fractured World'*, Oxford: Oxford University Press.

Ghobarah, H.P. and Russett, B. (2003) Civil Wars Kill and Maim People, Long after the Fighting Stops', *American Political Science Review*, Vol 97, No. 2, pp.189-202.

Gilley, B. (2004) *Against the Concept of Ethnic Conflict'*, Third World Quarterly, Vol. 25, No. 6, pp. 1155-1166.

Gilpin, R. (1981) *War and Change in World Politics'*, Princeton: Princeton University Press.

Ginifer, J. (2003) *Reintegration of Ex-Combatants'*, In Meek, Sarah, Thokozani Thusi, Jeremy Ginifer, and Patrick Coke (Eds.). Sierra Leone: Building the Road to Recovery. Institute for Security Studies Monograph No. 80. Pretoria, South Africa: Institute for Security Studies.

Glaser, C. (1993) *Why NATO is Still Best: Future SA for Europe'*, International Security, Vol. 18, No. 1, pp. 5-50.

Glasser, B. G. and Strauss A.L. (1967) *The Discovery of Grounded Theory: Strategies for Qualitative Research'*, Chicago: Aldine Publishing Company.

Glassmyer, K. and Sambanis, N. (2008) *Rebel—Military Integration and Civil War Termination', Journal of Peace Research*, Vol.45, No. 3, pp. 365–384.

Glazer, N. and Moynihan, D. (1975) *Ethnicity: Theory and Experience'*, Cambridge, MA, Harvard University Press.

Gleditsch, K.S. (2004) *A revised list of Wars between and Within Independent States, 1816–2002'*, International Interactions, Vol.30, pp. 231–62.

Gleditsch, N.P., Wallensteen, P., Eriksson, M., Sollenberg, M., and Strand, H. (2002) Armed Conflict 1946–2001: A New Dataset', *Journal of Peace Research*, Vol. No, 39, pp. 615–37.

Glowacki, L. and Wrangham, R. (2015) *Warfare and Reproductive Success in a Tribal Population'*, Proceedings of the National Academy of Sciences, Vol 112, No. 2, pp. 348–353.

Goetze, C. and Guzina, D. (2008) *Peacebuilding, Statebuilding, Nation-building – Turtles All the Way Down?* Civil Wars, Vol. 10, No. 4, pp. 319-347.

Golafshani, N. (2003) *Understanding Reliability and Validity in Qualitative Research'*, the Qualitative Report, Vol. 8, No. 4, pp. 579-606.

Goldstein, D.M (2014) *Qualitative Research in Dangerous Places: Becoming an 'Ethnographer' of Violence and Personal Safety'*, The DSD Program is funded by the Open Society Foundations, The program is a partnership between OSF, the SSRC, pp. 21.

Gonzalez, M. (2009) *Local Histories: A Methodology for Understanding Community Perspectives on Transitional Justice*', In: Van Der Merwe *et al.* Assessing the Impact of Transitional Justice. Challenges for Empirical Research. Washington, D. C: University of Peace Press.

Goodhand, J. (2006) *Working in and on War, Civil War, Civil Peace*', Yanacopulos, H. and Hanlon, J., Open University in association with James Currey, Oxford and Ohio University Press, Athens.

Goodman, L. A. and Smyth, K. F. (2011) *A Call for a Social Network-oriented Approach to Services for Survivors of Intimate Partner Violence*', Psychology of Violence, Vol. 1, No. 2, pp. 79–92.

GoS (2007) *The National DDR Strategic Plan 2007, Khartoum, Sudan Government of South Sudan (GoSS)-Approved Budget 2012-2013*', Ministry of Finance and Economic Planning, Juba

Government of Sudan (2007*) The National DDR Strategic Plan*', Disarmament, Demobilisation and Reintegration Coordination Council, Khartoum.

Grafstein, R. (1981) *The Institutional Resolution of the Fact-Value Dilemma*', Philosophy of the Social Sciences, Vol. 11, No. 1, pp. 1–14.

Graham, S. (1992) *Most of the subjects were White and Middle Class: Trends in Published Research on African Americans in Selected APA Journals, 1970-1989*, American Psychologist, No. 47, pp. 629-639.

Gramsci, A. (1971) *Selections from the Prison Notebooks'*, New York, N.Y.: International Publishers.

Grawert, E. (2010) *After the Comprehensive Peace Agreement in Sudan'*, Woodbridge, Suffolk; Rochester, N.Y.: Boydell & Brewer.

Green, D.P. and Seher, R.L. (2003) *What Role Does Prejudice Play in Ethnic Conflict?* Annual Review of Political Science, Vol. 6, pp. 509-531.

Green, D.P., Stolovitch, D. Z. and Wong, J.S. (1998) Defended Neighbourhoods, Integration, and Racial Motivated crime', *American Journal of Sociology*, Vol. 104, pp. 372–403.

Green, E. (2006) *Redefining Ethnicity'*, *Development Studies Institute'*, London School of Economics; Paper prepared for presentation at the 47th Annual International Studies Association Convention, San Diego, CA.

Greenbank, P. (2003) The role of values in educational research: the case for reflexivity', *British Educational Research Journal*, Vol. 29, No.6, pp. 791-801.

Grieco, J, (1993) *Anarchy and the Limits of Cooperation: A Realist Critique of the Newest Liberal Institutionalism'*, In: David Baldwin ed., Neorealism and Neoliberalism: The Contemporary Debate.

Groger, L and Mayberry, P. (1999) *What We Didn't Learn Because of Who Would Not Talk to Us'*, Qualitative Health Research. Vol. 9, No. 6, pp. 829-835.

Grossman, H. (1999) *Kleptocracy and Revolutions', Oxford Economic Papers'*, No. 51, pp. 267-283.

Guba, E. (1981) *Criteria for Assessing the Trustworthiness of Naturalistic Inquiries'*, Educational Resources Information Centre Annual Review Paper, Vol. 29, pp.75-91.

Guba, E. G. and Lincoln, Y.S. (1994) *Competing Paradigms in Qualitative Research'*, In: N. K. Denzin & Y. S. Lincoln (Eds.), Handbook of Qualitative Research, pp. 105-117.

Gubrium, J.A. and Holstein, J.A. (2001) *Handbook of Interview Research: Context and Method'*, Thousand Oaks, CA. Sage Publications.

Guelke, A. (2012) *Politics in Deeply Divided Societies'*, Polity Press: Cambridge.

Guibernau, M. (2000) *Nationalism and Intellectuals in Nations without States: The Catalan Case'*, Political Studies, Vol.48, No. 5, pp. 989–1005.

Gurr, T. (1968) A Causal Model of Civil Strife: A Comparative Analysis Using New Indices', *American Political Science Review*, Vol 62, No. 4, pp. 1104–1124.

Gurr, T. (1970) *Why Men Rebel?* Princeton, NJ: Princeton University Press.

Gurr, T. (1993) *Why Minorities Rebel: A Global Analysis of Communal Mobilisation and Conflict since1945'*, International Political Science Review. Vol 14, pp. 161-201.

Gurr, T. (1994) *People Against States: Ethno-political Conflict and the Changing World System'*, International Studies Quarterly. Vol. 38, pp. 347-377.

Haass, R. (2014) *Tipperary International Peace Award'*, http://www.cfr.org/peace-conflict-and human-rights/richard-n-haasssremarks-upon-receiving-2013-tipperary-international-peace award/p33186.[Accessed: 07/04/2018].

Hagmann, T. and Péclard, D. (2010) *Negotiating Statehood: Dynamics of Power and Domination in Africa'*, Development and Change, Vol. 41, No. 4, pp. 539-562.

Hall, R. A. (2009) *From Rebels to Soldiers: An Analysis of the Philippine and East Timorese Policy Integrating Former Moro National Liberation Front (MNLF) and Falintil Combatants into the Armed Forces. SSRN Scholarly Paper'*, http://papers.ssrn.com/ abstract1450242 [Accessed 16/04/2017].

Hall, R. and Biersteker, T. (2002) The Emergence of Private Authority in Global Governance', *Cambridge Studies in International Relations*, Cambridge: Cambridge University Press.

Hambrecht, M. *et al.* (1993) *Evidence for a Gender Bias in Epidemiological Studies of Schizophrenia, Schizophrenia Research'*, No. 8, pp. 223-231.

Hamelink. C. J. (2002) Communication May Not Build Peace, But It Can Certainly Contribute to War', *Journal of Media Development*, Vol. 49, No. 2, pp. 36-37.

Hammersley, M. (1993) *What is Social Research*? Milton Keynes: Open University Press.

Hänggi, H., (2005) *Approaching Peacebuilding from a Security Governance Perspective*', In Bryden and H. Hänggi, (Eds.), Security Governance in Post-Conflict Peacebuilding (pp. 3-19). Münster and New Brunswick, NJ: Lit Verlag and Transaction Publishers.

Hannabuss, S. (1996) *Research Interviews*', New Library World. Vol. 97, No. 5, pp. 22-30.

Hansen, T. and Finn, S. (2006) Sovereignty revisited', *Annual Review of Anthropology*, Vol. 35, pp. 295–315.

Hanson, S. (2007) *Disarmament, Demobilisation, and Reintegration (DDR) in Africa*', Backgrounder, http://www.cff.org. Publication [Accessed 15/04/2016].

Hanzich, R. (2011) Struggles in South Sudan', *Harvard International Review*, Vol. 33, No. 1, pp. 38-41.

Harle, J. (2016) *Research and Knowledge Systems in Difficult Places, part 1, Research to Action*', The Global Guide to Research Impact. http://ebn.bmj.com/content/3/3/68.full [Accessed: 20/06/2016].

Harris, M. and Johnson, O. (2000) *Cultural Anthropology*, 5th (Ed.), Needham Heights, MA: Allyn and Bacon.

Harsch, E. (2005) *Reintegration of Ex-combatants when War ends: transforming Africa's Fighters into Builders*', Africa Renewal, https://www.un.org/africarenewal/magazine/october-2005/reintegration-ex-combatants[Accessed: 15/08/2019].

Hartzeil, C. and Hoddie, M. (2003) Institutionalising Peace: Power-Sharing and Post-Civil War Conflict Management', *American Journal of Political Science*, Vol 47, No. 2, pp. 318-332.

Hartzell, C, Hoddie, M. and Rothchild, D. (2001) *Stabilising the Peace after Civil War: An Investigation of Some Key Variables'*, International Organisation, Vol. 55, No. 1, pp. 183–208.

Hartzell, C. A. and Hoddie, M. (2007) *Crafting Peace: Power-Sharing Institutions and the Negotiated Settlement of Civil Wars'*, University Park PA: Pennsylvania State University Press.

Haug, W. (2001) Ethnic, Religious and Language Groups: Towards a Set of Rules for Data Collection and Statistical Analysis', *International Statistical Review*, Vol. 69, No.2, pp. 303-311.

Hayashi, P., Abib, G. and Hoppen, N. (2019) Validity in Qualitative Research: A Processual Approach', *The Qualitative Report*, Vol. 24, No. 1, pp. 98-112.

Hazen, J. M. (2010) *Understanding Reintegration within Post-conflict Peacebuilding: Making the Case for Reinsertion' First and Better Linkages Thereafter,'* In: Monopoly of Force; The Nexus of DDR and SSR', (Ed.), by Melanne A. Civic and Miklaucic, M. Centre for Complex Operations Institute for National Strategic Studies, National Defence University Press Washington, DC.

Healy, S. and Plaut, M. (2007) *Ethiopia and Eritrea: Allergic to Persuasion'*, Briefing Paper, African Affairs, Chatham House, The Royal Institute of International Affairs. London.

Hechter, M. (1986) *A Rational Choice Approach to Race and Ethnic Relations'*, In D. Mason, and R. J, Theories of Race and Ethnic Relations (pp. 268-277). Cambridge: Cambridge University Press.

Hechter, M. (1987) *Principles of Group Solidarity'*, Berkeley: University of California Press.

Heckathorn, D. D. (2011) *Snowball versus Respondent-Driven Sampling'*, Sociological Methodology. Vol. 41, No. 1, pp. 355–366.

Heger, L. and Salehyan, S.I. (2007) Ruthless Rulers: Coalition Size and the Severity of Civil Conflict', *International Studies Quarterly*, Vol. 51, No. 2, pp. 385-403.

Hegre, H. *et al.* (2001) Towards a Democratic Civil Peace? Democracy, Political Change, and Civil War, 1816-1992', *American Political Science Review*, Vol. 95, No. 1, pp. 16-33.

Henderson, E. A. (1998) The Democratic Peace through the Lens of Culture, 1820- 1989', *International Studies Quarterly*, Vol. 42, No, 3, pp. 461-484.

Hendricks, K. B. and Singhal, V.R. (2005) *An empirical Analysis of the Effects of Supply Chain Disruption on Long-run Stock Price Performance and Equity Risk of the Firm'*, Production and Operations Management, Vol. 14, No. 1, pp. 22-53.

Herath, O. (2016) A *Critical Analysis of Positive and Negative Peace'*, pp. 104-107. http://www.repository.kln.ac.lk/bitstream/handle/.../journal1%20% 281%29 [Accessed: 15/10/2017].

Herbst, J. (2000) *States and Power in Africa: Comparative Lessons in Authority and Control'*, Princeton: Princeton University Press.

Herring, E. and Rangwala, G. (2006) *Iraq in Fragments: The Occupation and Its Legacy'*, London: Hurst.

Herz, J. (1951) *Political Realism and Political Idealism: A Study in Theories and Realities'*, Chicago: University of Chicago Press.

Hesse-Biber, S. N. and Leavy, P. (2011) *The Practice of Qualification Research'*, 2nd (Eds.), Sage Publications, Inc. Oaks, California

Hindess, B. (1996) *Discourses of Power: From Hobbes to Foucault'*, Oxford: Blackwell Publishers Ltd.

Hippler, J. (2004*) Nation-states for Export? - Nation-building between Military Intervention, Crisis Prevention and Development Policy'*, (pp. 173-190). In: Jochen Hippler (Ed.), Nation-Building – A Key Concept for Peaceful Conflict Transformation. London.

Hippler, J. (2005) *Nation-Building - A Key Concept of Peaceful Conflict Transformation'*, London Pluto Press, pp. 3-14.

Hirshleifer, J (2001) *The Dark Side of the Force: Economic Foundations of Conflict Theory'*, Cambridge: Cambridge University Press.

Hobbes, T. [1651] 1996. *Leviathan*', (Ed.), Richard Tuck. Cambridge: Cambridge University.

Hobbs, D. (2006) *Fieldwork'*, In V. Jupp (Ed.), The Sage Dictionary of Social Research Methods', (pp. 120-122). London: Sage Publications Ltd.

Hoddie, M. and Hartzell. C. (2003) Civil War Settlements and the Implementation of Military Power-Sharing Arrangements', *Journal of Peace Research*, Vol. 40, No. 3, pp. 303-320.

Hoffman, J. and Graham, P. (2009) *Introduction to Political Theory'*, London: Pearson Longman.

Hoffmann, K. (2014) Ethnogovernmentality: The Making of Ethnic Territories and Subjects in Eastern Congo', PhD Thesis. University of Roskilde, Roskilde.

Hoffmann, K. and Vlassenroot, K. (2014) *Armed Groups and the Exercise of Public Authority, The Cases of the Mayi Mayi and Raya Mutomboki in Kalehe, South Kivu'*, Peacebuilding. Vol. 2, No. 2, pp. 202–20.

Höglund, K. and Oberg, M. (2011) *Understanding Peace Research: Methods and Challenges'*, New York: Taylor & Francis.

Høigilt, J., Falch, A. and Rolandsen, O. H. (2010) *The Sudan Referendum and Neighbouring Countries: Egypt and Uganda'*, Oslo: Peace Research Institute Oslo.

Holsti, K. (1996) *The State, War, and the State of War'*, Cambridge: Cambridge University Press.

Hooks, B. (1989) *Talking Back: Thinking Feminist, Thinking Black'*, Boston, MA: South End Press.

Horkheimer, M. (1982) *Critical Theory'*, New York: Seabury Press.

Horowitz, D. L. (1985) *Ethnic Groups in Conflict'*, Berkeley: University of California Press.

Horowitz, D. L. (1998) Structure and Strategy in Ethnic Conflict', *Paper Prepared for the Annual World Bank Conference on Development Economics*, Washington, DC.

Horwitz, T. (1991) *First Sounds of Defiance Emanating from Iraqis'*, Globe and Mail (Canada), Academic, Lexis-Nexis, University of Iowa Library, Iowa City, IA.

Howell, J. (1978) *Horn of Africa: Lessons from the Sudan Conflict'*, International Affairs. Vol. 54, No. 3, pp. 421-36.

HSBA (2011) *Women's Security and the Law in South Sudan Grow and Oxfam'*, Geneva: HSBA.

HSBA (2012) *Sudan Human Security Baseline Assessment, DDR in South Sudan'*, Geneva: HSBA.

Htun, M. (2004) *Is Gender like Ethnicity? The Political Representation of Identity Groups'*, Perspectives on Politics, Vol.2, No, 3, pp. 439-458.

Hughes, C., Öjendal, J. and Schierenbeck, I. (2015) *The Struggle versus the Song—the local turn in Peacebuilding: An introduction'*, Third World Quarterly. Vol. 36, No. 5, pp. 817–824.

Humphreys, M and Weinstein, J. (2005) *Handling and Manhandling Civilians in Civil War'*, Unpublished Manuscript.

Humphreys, M. (2005) Natural Resources, Conflict, and Conflict Resolution: Uncovering the Mechanisms', *Journal of Conflict Resolution*, Vol. 49, No.4, pp. 508 – 537.

Humphreys, M. and Weinstein, J. (2004) *What the Fighters Say'*, Centre for Globalisation and Sustainable Development Working Paper, Columbia University.

Humphreys, M. and Weinstein, M. (2008) Who Fights? The Determinants of Participation in Civil War', Midwest Political Science Association, *American Journal of Political Science*, Vol. 52, No. 2, pp. 436-455.

Huntington, S. (1996) *The Clash of Civilisations and the Remaking of World Order'*, New York: Simon & Schuster.

Hurworth, R. (2003) *Overview of Qualitative Methods'*, Unpublished Manuscript, Melbourne.

Hutchinson S. (1996) *Nuer Dilemmas: Coping with Money, War, and the State'*, University of California Press, Berkeley.

Hutchinson, J. and Smith, A. (1996) *Ethnicity'*, Oxford University Press, Oxford and New York.

Hutchinson, S. (2000) *Nuer Ethnicity Militarised'*, Anthropol Today. Vol. 16, No. 3, pp. 6–13.

Hutchinson, S. (2001) A Curse from God? Religious and Political Dimensions of the post-1991 Rise of Ethnic Violence in South Sudan', *Journal of Modern African Studies*, Vol. 39, No. 2, pp. 307–331.

Hutchinson, S. and Pendle. N.R (2015) *Violence, Legitimacy, and Prophecy: Nuer struggles with uncertainty in South Sudan*', Am Ethnol. Vol 42, No. 3, pp. 415–430.

Hutton, L. (2014) *South Sudan: From Fragility at Independence to a Crisis of Sovereignty*', Netherlands Institute of International Relations Clingendael', pp. 4-48. https://www.clingendael.org/sites/default/files/pdfs/South%20Sudan.pdf [Accessed: 15/10/2017].

Hyden, G. (1996) *Rethinking Theories of the State: An Africanist Perspective*', Africa Insight, Vol. 26, No. 1, pp. 26 - 35.

Ibhawoh, B (2010) *Beyond Instrumentalism and Constructivism: Reconceptualising Ethnic Identities in Africa*', Humanities Today, Vol. 1. No.1, pp. 221-9.

IDDRS, (2006) *Integrated DDR Standards*', United Nations, New York, http://pksoi.army.mil/doctrine_concepts/documents/UN Guidelines/IDDRS. Pdf [Accessed 20/03/2017].

Idris, A. H. (2001) *Sudan's Civil War: Slavery, Race, and Formational Identities*', Lewiston, N.Y.: Edwin Mellen Press.

Idris, A. H. (2005) *Conflict and Politics of identity in Sudan*', New York, Palgrave Macmillan.

Idris, A.H. (2010) *I Hate to Choose: Personal Reflections on the Referendum'*, http://www.sudantribune.com/I-hate-to-Choose-Personal,37003, [Accessed: 06/07/2018].

IGAD (2011) IGAD Support for the new Republic of South Sudan. Available at: http://www.un.org/en/ecosoc/julyhls/pdf12/south_sudan_igad_br ochure.pdf, [Accessed: 11/09/2017].

Ignatieff, M. (1996) *There's No Place Like Home: The Politics of Belonging'*, In: S. Dunant and R. Porter (Eds), The Age of Anxiety. London: Virago.

Ignatieff, M. (2003) *Empire Lite: Nation-Building in Bosnia, Kosovo and Afghanistan'*, London: Vintage.

Ihonvbere, J. (1996a) *The Crisis of Democratic Consolidation in Zambia'*, Civilisations. Vol. 43, No. 2, pp. 83-109.

Ihonvbere, J. (1996b) *Economic Crisis, civil society and Democratisation: The Case of Zambia'*, Trenton, NJ: Africa World Press.

Ikenberry, D. and Ramnath, D. (2000) *Underreaction'*, Working Paper. Rice University.

Ingrid, V.B. and Rustad, S.A. (2018) *Conflict Trends in Africa, 1989–2017, Conflict Trends'*, Vol. 6. Oslo: PRIO.

International Crisis Group (2012) *Conflict Minerals in DRC'*, http://www.crisisgroup.org/en/publication-type/key-issues/country/conflict-minerals-in-drc.aspx [Accessed: 27/12/2017/].

International Crisis Group. (2003a) *Sudan: Towards an Incomplete Peace'*, Nairobi and Brussels: International Crisis Group.

International Crisis Group. (2003b) *Sudan's Other Wars'*, Nairobi and Brussels: International Crisis Group, Nairobi and Brussels: International Crisis Group.

International Crisis Group. (2005) *The Khartoum–SPLM Agreement: Sudan's Uncertain Peace'*, Nairobi and Brussels: International Crisis Group.

International Crisis Group. (2011) *Divisions in Sudan's Ruling Party and the Threat to the Country's Future Stability'*, Nairobi and Brussels: International Crisis Group.

International Crisis Group. (2019) *Salvaging South Sudan's Fragile Peace Deal'*, Brussels.

Isajiw, W. (2000) Approaches to Ethnic Conflict Resolution: Paradigms and Principles', *International Journal of Intercultural Relations*, Vol. 24, No.1, pp.105-24.

Isike, C. and Okeke-Uzodike, U. (2010) *Moral Imagination, Ubuntu and African Women: Towards Feminising Politics and Peace-building in KwaZulu-Natal'*, Gandhi Marg. Vol. 31, No. 4, pp. 679-709.

Iyob, R and Khadiagala, G.M. (2006) *Sudan: The Elusive Quest for Peace'*, Colorado: Lynne Rienner Publishers.

Jabareen, Y. (2013) Conceptualising Post-Conflict Reconstruction and Ongoing Conflict Reconstruction of Failed States', *International Journal of Politics, Culture, and Society*, Vol. 26, No. 2, pp. 107-125.

Jabri, V. (2007) *War and the Transformation of Global Politics*', Basingstoke & New York: Palgrave Macmillan.

Jackson, P. (2015) *Introduction: Security and Development*', In: P. Jackson (Ed.), Handbook of International Security and Development (pp. 1-18). Cheltenham: Edward Elgar Publishing.

Jackson, R.H. (1990) *Quasi-States: Sovereignty, International Relations and the Third World*', Cambridge: Cambridge University Press.

Jacoby, T. and Ozerdem, A. (2008) The Role of the State in the Turkish Earthquake of 1999', *Journal of International Development*, Vol. 20, No. 3, pp. 297–310.

James, C. and Oplatka, I. (2015) *An Exploration of the notion of the 'Good Enough School'*, Management in Education, Vol. 29, No. 2, pp. 77–82.

James, L. (2011) *From Slaves to Oil*', In: J. Ryle, J. Willis, S. Baldo and J.M. Jok, (Eds). The Sudan Handbook. London: James Currey and the Rift Valley Institute.

Jarstad, A. K. (2009) *The Prevalence of Power-sharing: Exploring the Patterns of Post-election Peace*', Africa Spectrum, Vol. 44, No. 3, pp. 41-62.

Jenkins, R. (1997) *Rethinking Ethnicity*', London: Sage.

Jenne, E. (2006) *National Self-Determination: A Deadly Mobilising Device'*, In: Hannum and E. Babbitt (Ed.), Negotiating Self-Determination (pp. 7-36). Lanham: Lexington.

Jennings, K. M. (2009) The Political Economy of DDR in Liberia: A gendered Critique', *Conflict, Security and Development*, Vol. 9, No. 4, pp.475-494.

Jervis, R. (1976) *Perception and Misperception in International Relations'*, Princeton University Press.

Jervis, R. (1978) *Cooperation under the Security Dilemma'*, World Politics. Vol. 30, No. 2

Johnson, D. (1986) Judicial Regulation and Administrative Control: Customary Law and the Nuer, 1898–1954', *The Journal of African History'*, Vol. 27, No. 01, pp. 59–78.

Johnson, D. (2003) *The Root Causes of Sudan's Civil Wars'*, Indiana University Press.

Johnson, D. (2010) *When Boundaries Become Borders: The Impact of Boundary-making in Southern Sudan's Frontier Zones'*, London: Rift Valley Institute.

Johnson, D. (2014) The Political Crisis in South Sudan', *African Study Review*, Vol.57, No. 3, pp. 167–174.

Johnson, H. (2011) *Waging Peace in Sudan: The Inside Story of the Negotiations that ended Africa's Longest Civil War'*, Brighton, UK: Sussex Academic Press.

Johnson, H. (2016) *South Sudan: The Untold Story from Independence to the Civil War'*, London: IB Tauris.

Johnson, K. and Hutchison, M. L. (2012) Hybridity, Political Order and Legitimacy: Examples from Nigeria', *Journal of Peacebuilding and Development*, Vol. 7, No. 2, pp. 37–52.

Johnson, M.J. (2002) *In-depth Interviewing'*, In J. F. Gubrium & J.A. Holstein (Eds.), Handbook of Interview Research: Context and methods (pp. 103-120). London: Sage.

Jok, A., Leitch, R. and Vandewint, C. (2004) *A study of Customary Law in Contemporary Southern Sudan'*, World Vision International and the South Sudan Secretariat of Legal and Constitutional Affairs. Juba; South Sudan.

Jok, M.J. (2005) *War, changing ethics and the position of youth in South Sudan'*, In: Jon Abbink and Ineke van Kessel (Eds), Vanguard or Vandals: Youth, Politics and Conflict in Africa (Brill, Leiden.

Jok, M.J. (2011) *Diversity, Unity, and Nation-Building in South Sudan'*, Special Report, Washington: United States Institute of Peace.

Jok, M.J. (2012) *Insecurity and Ethnic Violence in South Sudan: Existential Threats to the State'*, The Sudd Institute, Issue Paper No. 1.

Jok, M.J. (2012) *South Sudan: Building a Diverse Nation'*, In: Heinrich Böll Foundation and Toni Weis (Eds.), Sudan after Separation: New Approaches to a New Region, Heinrich Böll Foundation, Berlin.

Jok, M.J. (2013) *Mapping Sources of Conflict and Insecurity in South Sudan'*, Special Report No. 1. The Sudd Institute. Juba; South Sudan.

Jok, M.J. (2014*) South Sudan and the Prospect of Peace amidst Violent Political Wrangling'*, Juba; The Sudd Institute. South Sudan

Jok, M.J. (2014) *South Sudan and the Prospects for Peace amidst Violent Political Wrangling'*, Policy Brief, No. 4, The Sudd Institute. Juba; South Sudan.

Jok, M.J. (2015) *Negotiating the end to the current Civil War in South Sudan: What Lessons can Sudan's Comprehensive Peace Agreement Offer?* Inclusive Political Settlements Papers, No. 19, Berghof Foundation, Berlin.

Jok, M.J. (2015) *The Paradox of Peace in Sudan and South Sudan; Why the Political Settlements Failed to Endure'*, Berghof Foundation Operations GmbH – CINEP/PPP, pp. 1-17.

Jok, M.J. (2017) *Introduction: The State, Security and Community Defence Groups in South Sudan'*, In: Jok, M.J., Schomerus M, Kuol LBD, Breidlid IM, Arensen M.J. (Eds.), Informal Armies: Community Defence Groups in South Sudan's Civil War. pp 1–6. Saferworld. London.

Jok, M.J. and Hutchinson, S.E. (1999) *Sudan's Prolonged Second Civil War and the Militarisation of Nuer and Dinka Ethnic Identities'*, African Studies Review. Vol. 42, No. 2, pp. 125–145.

Jones I.R. (2001) *Habermas or Foucault or Habermas and Foucault? The implications of a shifting debate for medical sociology'*, In: G. Scambler (Ed.), Habermas Critical Theory and Health London, (pp. 163–181). Routledge.

Jones, B. F and Olken, B.A. (2005) Do Leaders Matter? National Leadership and Growth Since World War II', *The Quarterly Journal of Economics*, Vol. 120, Issue 3, pp. 835–864.

Jones, M. (2011) *Somaliland and South Sudan—the Challenging Road Ahead*', http://www.southsudannation.com/somalilandsschallengesahead%2078.htm [Accessed: 05/04/2018].

Jooma, M. (2007) *Dual realities: Peace and War in the Sudan – An update on the implementation of the CPA*', Institute for Security Studies, Situation Report, www.issafrica.org/uploads/.

Jooma, M. (2005) *Feeding the Peace: Challenges Facing Human Security in Post-Garang South Sudan*', Pretoria: Institute for Security Studies. http://www.reliefweb.int/library/documents/2005/iss-sdn-23aug.pdf.

Joseph, R. (1991) Africa: The Rebirth of Political Freedom', *Journal of Democracy*, Vol. 2, No. 4, pp. 11–24.

Joshi, M. and Mason, T. D. (2011) *Civil War Settlements, Size of Governing Coalition, and Durability of Peace in Post–Civil War States*', International Interactions, Vol. 37, No. 4, pp. 388-413.

Josselson, R. (1996) *Ethics and Process in the Narrative Study of Lives*', London: Sage.

Justice Africa, (2001) *Prospect for peace in Sudan: Briefing November 2001*', http://www.sudanarchive.net. [Accessed 13/01/2018].

Justice Africa. (2002a) *Prospect for peace in Sudan: Briefing June–July 2002*', http://www.sudanarchive.net [Accessed: 02/01/ 2018].

Justino, P. (2013) *Research and Policy Implications from a Micro-level Perspective on the Dynamics of Conflict, Violence and Development*', In: P. Justino, T. Brück, and P. Verwimp (Eds.), A Micro-Level Perspective on the Dynamics of Conflict, Violence and Development', Oxford: Oxford University Press.

Justino, P. (2016) Supply and Demand Restrictions to Education in Conflict-affected Countries: New Research and Future Agendas', *International Journal of Educational Development*, Vol. 47, pp. 76–85.

Jütting, J. (2003) I*nstitutions and Development: A Critical Review*', OECD Development Centre Working Papers, No. 210, OECD Publishing, Paris. https://doi.org/10.1787/341346131416.

Kabeer, N. (2000) *Social Exclusion, Poverty and Discrimination: Towards an Analytical Framework*', IDS Bulletin, Vol. 31, No. 4, pp. 83-97

Kahmann, E. (2003*) Conceptualising Security Governance*', Cooperation and Conflict, Vol. 38, No. 1, pp. 5–26.

Käihkö, I. (2014) *Once a Combatant, Always a Combatant?' Mats Utas blog*, (http://matsutas.wordpress.com/2014/01/07/once-a-combatant-always-a-combatant-by-ilmari-kaihko.

Kaldor, M. (1999) *New and Old Wars: Organised Violence in a Global Era*', Stanford, CA: Stanford University Press.

Kaldor, M. (2001; 2006) *New and Old Wars, organised violence in a global era'*, Stanford: Stanford University Press.

Kaldor, M. (2009) *New Wars: Counter-Insurgency or Human Security'*, The Broker: http://www.thebrokeronline.eu/en/Dossiers/ [Accessed 4 June 2017].

Kalyvas, S. (2001*) New and Old Civil Wars: A Valid Distinction*?' World Politics. Vol. 54, pp. 99-118.

Kalyvas, S. (2006) *The Logic of Violence in Civil War'*, Cambridge: Cambridge University Press.

Kalyvas, S. and Kocher, M. (2007) *How 'Free' Is Free Riding in Civil Wars? Violence, Insurgency and the Collective Action Problem'*, World Politics. Vol. 59, pp. 177–216.

Kameir, E.W. (2011) *The Political Economy of South Sudan: A Scoping Analytical Study'*, The African Development Bank. https://www.afdb.org/fileadmin/uploads/afdb/Documents/Project -and-Operations/2011%20Political_Economy_South_Sudan_- _24_October_20111.pdf.

Kandeh, J.D. (1992) *Politicisation of Ethnic Identities in Sierra Leone'*, African Studies Review. Vol. 35, pp. 81-99.

Kaplan, R. (1993) *Balkan conflicts: A Journey through History'*, New York: St. Martin's Press.

Karazsia, Z. (2015) Evaluating the Success of Disarmament, Demobilisation, and Reintegration Programs: The Case of Congo-

Brazzaville', *Journal of Interdisciplinary Conflict Science*, Vol. 1, No. 2, pp.1-34.

Kareva, I. (2011) *Prisoner's Dilemma in Cancer Metabolism'*, PLoS One. Vol. 6, No. 12.

Karl, M. and Engels, F. [1968] (1848) *The Communist Manifesto'*, Middlesex: Penguin.

Karp, A. (2006) *Trickle and Torrent: State Stockpiles'*, Small Arms Survey 2006: Unfinished Business; Chapter 2 (Appendix I), p. 61. Oxford: Oxford University Press.

Kasfir, N. (1977*) Southern Sudanese Politics since the Addis Ababa Agreement'*, African Affairs. Vol. 76, No. 303, pp. 143-66.

Kauffmann, C. (1996) *Possible and Impossible Solutions to Ethnic Civil Wars'*, International Security, Vol. 20, pp. 136-175.

Kaufman, S. (2006) *Symbolic Politics or Rational Choice? Testing Theories of Extreme Ethnic Violence'*, International Security, Vol.30, No. 4, pp.45-86.

Kaufmann, C. (2005) *Rational Choice and Progress in the Study of Ethnic Conflict: A Review Essay'*, Security Studies. Vol.14, No. 1, pp. 178-207.

Keating, V.C. and Wheeler, N.J. (2013) *Concepts and Practices of Cooperative Security: Building Trust in the International System'*, In: V. Mastny & Z. Liqun (Eds.), The Legacy of the Cold War: Perspectives on Security, Cooperation, and Conflict (pp. 57-78). Lanham, MD: Lexington Books.

Keen, D. (1998) *The Economic Functions of Violence in Civil Wars'*, Adelphi Paper 320. Oxford: Oxford University Press.

Keen, D. (2001) *War and Peace: What's the Difference?* In: Adebajo, A. and C.L. Sriram (Eds.). Managing Armed Conflict in the 21st Century (pp. 1-22). London: Frank Cass.

Keen, D. (2009) *A Tale of Two Wars: Great Expectations, Hard Times'*, Conflict, Security and Development, Vol.9, No, 4, pp. 515-534.

Keen, D. (2012) *Greed and Grievance in Civil War'*, International Affairs, Vol. 88, No. 4, pp.757-777.

Keili, F.L. (2008) *Small arms and light weapons transfer in West Africa: a stock-taking'*, Disarmament Forum 4.

Kellner, D. (1989) *Critical Theory, Marxism and Modernity'*, Cambridge: Polity Press. Keohane, R.O. and Nye, J.S. (Eds) 1971 Transnational Relations and World Politics. Massachusetts: Harvard University Press.

Kellner, D. (1990) *Critical Theory and the Crisis of Social Theory'*, Sociological Perspectives, Vol. 33, No. 1, pp. 11–33.

Keohane, R.O. (2005) *After Hegemony: Cooperation and Discord in the World Political Economy'*, Princeton: Princeton University Press.

Keriga, L. and Bujra, A. (2009) *Social Policy, Development and Governance in Kenya: A Profile on Healthcare Provision in Kenya'*, Nairobi. Dpmf.

Kerr, P. (2013) *Human Security'*, In: Collins, A. 3rd (Ed.), Contemporary Security Studies (pp. 104-116) Oxford University Press.

Kettl, D.F. (1999) The Future of Public Administration', *Journal of Public Affairs Education*, Vol. 5, No. 2, pp. 127-133.

Kettl, D.F. (2015) *The Job of Government: Interweaving Public Functions and Private Hands'*, Public Administration Review, Vol. 75, No. 2, pp. 219-229.

Khalid, M. (1990) *The Government They Deserve: The Role of the Elite in Sudan's Political Evolution'*, London: Kegan Paul.

Khalid, M. (2003) *War and Peace in Sudan: A Tale of Two Countries'*, London: Keegan Paul Ltd.

Kidder, L. and Fine, M. (1987) *Qualitative and Quantitative Methods: When Stories Converge, Multiple Methods in Program Evaluation, New Directions for Program Evaluation'*, No. 35. San Francisco, CA: Jossey-Bass.

Kieh, G.K. (1996) The Taproots of the Liberian Civil War', *Twenty-First Century Afro-Review*, Vol. 2, No. 3, pp. 123-152.

Kieh, G.K. (2011) *Warlords, Politicians and the Post-First Civil War Election in Liberia'*, African and Asian Studies, Vol. 10, pp. 83-99.

Kilroy, W. (2008) *Disarmament, Demobilisation and Reintegration (DDR) as a participatory process: involving communities and beneficiaries in post-conflict disarmament programmes'*, In: European Consortium for Political Research (ECPR) Second Graduate Conference, 25-27 August 2008, Universitat Autònoma Barcelona.

Kilroy, W. (2010) *Disarmament, Demobilisation, and Reintegration: The co-evolution of concepts, practices, and understanding'*, Working Papers. N.Y.: Ralph Bunche Institute for International Studies.

Kilroy, W. (2014) *Does a more participatory approach to reintegrating Ex-Combatants lead to better outcomes? Evidence from Sierra Leone and Liberia'*, Conflict, Security and Development. Vol. 14, No. 3, pp. 275-308.

Kim, K. (2007) Clinical Competence among Senior Nursing Students after their Preceptorship experiences', Journal *of Professional Nursing*, Vol. 23, No. 6, pp. 369-375.

Kim, S. (2003) *Research Paradigms in Organisational Learning and Performance: Competing Modes of Inquiry'*, Information Technology, Learning, and Performance Journal, Vol. 21, No. 1, pp. 9-18.

Kimenyi, M. (2012) *Future engagement between South Sudan and the Republic of Sudan'*, In: South Sudan, one year after independence: Opportunities and Obstacles for Africa's Newest Country, The Brookings Africa Growth Initiative.

Kimenyi, M. and Mbaku, J. (2011) *South Sudan: Avoiding State Failure'*, the Brooking Institution.

King, G., Robert O. Keohane, R.O. and Sidney, V. (1994) *Designing social inquiry: In Scientific inference in Qualitative Research'*, Princeton: Princeton University Press.

King, J.A., Morris, L.L. and Fitz-Gibbon, C. T. (1987) *How to Assess Program Implementation'*, Beverly Hills, CA: Sage.

Kingma, K (2000) *Demobilisation in Sub- Saharan Africa: The Development and Security Impacts*', London: Macmillan.

Kingma, K. (2001) *Demobilisation and Reintegration of Ex-Combatants in Post-War and Transition Countries: Trends and Challenges of External Support*', Eschborn, Germany: GTZ.

Kisiangani, E. (2011) South Sudan and The Pitfalls of Power', *African Security Review*, Vol. 20, pp. 91-95.

Klabbers, J. (2008) *Treaty Conflict and the European Union*', Cambridge: Cambridge University Press.

Klain, E. (2009) *Croatia: The Participant in Large-Group Conflict*', In: Carter Judy, C, Irani George, I. and Vamik, V., (Ed.), Regional and Ethnic Conflicts: Perspectives from the Front Lines. New Jersey: Pearson.

Klaus, K. and Mitchell, M. I. (2015) Land grievances and the mobilisation of electoral violence: Evidence from Côte d'Ivoire and Kenya', *Journal of Peace Research*, Vol. 52, No, 5, pp. 622–635.

Klein, A. (2002) *The Horn of Turbulence: Political Regimes in Transition*', In: Debiel, T and Klein, A., (Eds). Fragile Peace: State Failure, Violence and Development in Crisis Regions, (pp. 156 – 170). London: Zed Books in Association with the Development and Peace Foundation.

Klopp, J.M. (2002) *Can Moral Ethnicity Trump Political Tribalism? The Struggle for Land and Nation in Kenya*', African Studies, Vol. 61, No. 2, pp. 269-94.

Knight, W.A. (2008) *Disarmament, Demobilisation, and Reintegration and Post-Conflict Peacebuilding in Africa: An Overview'*, African Security, Vol. 1, No. 1, pp. 24-52.

Knopf, K.A. (2016) *Ending South Sudan's Civil War. Council Special Report'*, Vol. No. 77. Council on Foreign Relations, New York.

Knotter, C. (2019) *The de facto Sovereignty of Unrecognised States: Towards a Classical Realist Perspective?* Ethno-politics, Vol.18, No. 2, pp. 119-138.

Knox, C. (2012) *The Secession of South Sudan: A Case Study in African Sovereignty and International Recognition'*, Political Science Student Work Paper 1. https://digitalcommons.csbsju.edu/polsci_students/1[Accessed: 14/08/2018].

Koenig, T., Spano, R. and Thompson, J. (2019) *Human Behaviour Theory for Social Work Practice'*, Singapore: Sage Publications.

Kohnert, D. (2010) *Democratisation via Elections in an African 'Narco-State'?* The Case of Guinea-Bissau', GIGA Working Papers Series.

Körppen, D. (2011) *Space Beyond the Liberal Peacebuilding Consensus – A Systemic Perspective'*, In: Daniela Körppen, Norbert Ropers and Hans J. Giessmann (Eds.). The Non-Linearity of Peace Processes: Theory and Practice of Systemic Conflict Transformation (pp. 77-96) Opladen/Farmington Hill: Barbara Budrich Publications.

Krahmann, E. (2003) *Conceptualising Security Governance'*, Cooperation and Conflict. Vol. 38, No. 1, pp. 5-26.

Kraidy, M.M. (2002) *Hybridity in Cultural Globalisation'*, Communication Theory, Vol.12, No. 3, pp. 316-339.

Krain, M. and Myers, M. (1997) *Democracy and Civil War: A Note on the Democratic Peace Proposition'*, International Interactions, Vol. 23, No, 1, pp. 109-18.

Krasner, S.D., and Risse, T. (2014) *External Actors, State-Building, and Service Provision in Areas of Limited Statehood: Introduction'*, Governance, Vol. 27, No. 4, pp. 545-567.

Krause, J. (2018) *Resilient Communities: Non-violence and Civilian Agency in Communal War'*, Cambridge: Cambridge University Press.

Krebs, R.R. (2014) *Military Disintegration: Canary in the Coal Mine?* In: Licklider R (Ed.), New Armies from Old: Merging Competing Military Forces after Civil Wars (pp. 245–58). Washington, DC: Georgetown University Press.

Kriesberg, L. (2001) *Changing forms of Coexistence'*, In: Abu-Nimer, Mohammed (Ed) Reconciliation, Justice, and Coexistence (Chapter 3, pp. 47-64). Oxford, UK: Lexington Books.

Kron J. (2010) *Peace Hovers in Sudan, but most Soldiers Stay Armed'*, New York Times, Online: http://www.nytimes.com/2010/12/31/world/africa/31sudan.html[Accessed: 10/02/2017].

Kruger, D. (1988) *An introduction to Phenomenological Psychology'*, 2nd (Ed.). Cape Town, South Africa: Juta.

Kuhn, T. S. (1962) *The Structure of Scientific Revolutions'*, Chicago: The University of Chicago Press.

Kulusika, S.E. (1998) *Southern Sudan: Political and Economic Power Dilemmas and Options'*, London: Minerva Press.

Kumar, K. (1998) *Post-Conflict Elections, Democratisation and International Assistance*; London: Lynne Rienner.

Kumar, K. (1999) *Promoting Social Reconciliation in Post-Conflict Societies: Selected Lessons from USAID's Experience'*, USAID Program and Operations Assessment Report No. 24. Centre for Development Information and Evaluation, U.S. Agency for International Development.

Kumar, R. (1996) *Research: A way of thinking. Research Methodology'*, A step-by-step guide for beginners, Melbourne, VIC, Longman, pp. 1-13.

Kumnar, K. (1998) *Post-conflict Elections and International Assistance'*, In: Krishna Kumnar (Ed.), Post-Conflict Elections, Democratisation, and International Assistance (pp. 5-14). Boulder, CO: Lynne Rienner Publishers.

Kuol, D.K. (2018) *Confronting the Challenges of South Sudan's Security Sector: A Practitioner's Perspective'*, African Centre for Strategic Studies, Special Report, No. 4, https://africacenter.org/spotlight/confronting-the-challenges-of-south-sudans-security-sector-a-practitioners-perspective/[Accessed: 28/07/2019].

Kupchan, C. (1998) *After Pax Americana: Benign Power, Regional Integration, and the Sources of a Stable Multi-polarity'*, International Security, Vol. 23, No. 2, pp. 40-79.

Kuperman, A.J. (2013) *A Model Humanitarian Intervention? Reassessing NATO's Libya Campaign'*, International Security. Vol. 38, No. 1, pp. 105-136.

Kustov, A. (2017) *How Ethnic Structure affects Civil Conflict: A model of Endogenous Grievance'*, Conflict Management and Peace Science. Vol. 34, No. 6, pp. 660–679.

Kvale, S. (1996) *Interviews: An Introduction to Qualitative Research Interviewing'*, London: Sage.

Kydd, A.H. (1997) *Sheep in Sheep's Clothing'*, Security Studies, Vol. 7, No. 1, pp. 114–154.

Kydd, A.H. (2005) *Trust and Mistrust in International Relations'*, Princeton, NJ: Princeton University Press.

Kymlicka, W. (1995) *Multicultural Citizenship: A Liberal Theory of Minority Rights'*, Oxford: Oxford University Press.

Kymlicka, W. (1995) *The Rights of Minority Cultures'*, Oxford: Oxford University Press.

Lacher, W. (2012) *South Sudan: International State-building and its Limits'*, SWP Research Paper. Berlin: German Institute for International and Security Affairs.

Lacina, B. (2006) Explaining the severity of civil wars', *Journal of Conflict Resolution*, Vol. 50, No. 2, pp. 276-289.

Lagrange, M. A. (2010) *Insurgencies in South Sudan: A Mandatory Path to Build a Nation?* Small Wars Journal (pp.1-7). https://smallwarsjournal.com/blog/journal/docs-temp/620-lagrange.pdf. [Accessed: 26/04/2017].

Lagu, J. and Alier, A. (1985) *Protest from the First-Generation Leadership of the South'*, Hom of Africa, Vol. 8. No.1, pp. 47-51.

Lake and Rothschild, D. (1998) *The International Spread of Ethnic Conflict: Fear, Diffusion, and Escalation'*, Princeton, NJ: Princeton University Press.

Lake, D. and Rothchild, D. (1996) *Containing Fear: The Origins and Management of Ethnic Conflict'*, International Security. Vol. 21, No. 2, pp. 41-75.

Lamb, G. and Stainer, T. (2018) The Conundrum of DDR Coordination: The Case of South Sudan. Stability', *International Journal of Security and Development*, Vol. 7, No. 1, pp. 1–16.

Lamoureaux, S. and Sureau, T. (2019) Knowledge and Legitimacy: The Fragility of Digital Mobilisation in Sudan', *Journal of Eastern African Studies*, Vol. 13, No, 1, pp. 35-53.

Lange, M. (2004) *British Colonial Legacies and Political Development'*, World Development, Vol. 32, No. 6, pp. 905–22.

Lapin, L.L. (1987) *Statistics for Modern Business Decisions'*, Harcourt Publishers Ltd. Wallingford, United Kingdom.

Laqueur, W. (1968) *Revolution, International Encyclopedia of the Social Sciences'*, Vol. 13, pp. 501-507.

Larson, G., Biar, A. and Pritchett, L. (2013) *South Sudan's Capability Trap: Building a State with Disruptive Innovation'*, Harvard University Center for International Development Working Paper No. 268. Cambridge, MA: MIT Press.

Laudati, A. (2011) Victims of discourse: Mobilising narratives of fear and insecurity in post-conflict South Sudan —The case of Jonglei State', *African Geographical Review*, No. 30, Vol. 1, pp. 15–32.

Lax, D.A. and Sebenius, J.K. (1991) Negotiating Through an Agent', Journal of Conflict Resolution. Vol. 35, No. 3, pp. 474-493.

Le Billon, P. (2008) Diamond wars? Conflict diamonds and geographies of resource wars', *Annals of the Association of American Geographers*, Vol. 98, No. 2, pp. 345–372.

Le Billon, P. and Cervantes, A. (2009) Oil Prices, Scarcity and Geographies of War', *Annals of the Association of American Geographers*, Vol. 99, No. 5, pp. 836-844.

LeBrun, E. and Jonah, L. (2014) *Weapons Tracing in Sudan and South Sudan – Introduction'*, Small Arms Survey 2014: Women and Guns; (pp. 213-214). Cambridge University Press.

Lederach, J.P. (2001a) *Building Peace. Sustainable Reconciliation in Divided Societies*', Washington DC, U.S.: United States Institute of Peace Press.

Lederach, J.P. (2001b) *Civil Society and Reconciliation, Turbulent Peace: The Challenges of Managing International Conflict*', (Ed.), Chester A. Crocker, Fen Osler Hampson, and Pamela Aall. Washington: United States Institute of Peace Press.

Lederach, J.P. (2003) *The Little Book of Conflict Transformation*', Intercourse, PA: Good Books.

Leibfried, S. and Zürn, M. (2005) *Transformations of the State*? UK: Cambridge University Press.

Lema, A. (2000) *Causes of Civil War in Rwanda: The Weight of History and Socio-Cultural Structures*', In: 'Ethnicity Kills? The Politics of War, Peace and Ethnicity in Sub-Saharan Africa, McMillan Press Ltd.

Lemay-Herbert, N. (2009) State-building without Nation-building? Legitimacy, State Failure and the Limits of the Institutional Approach', *Journal of Intervention and Statebuilding*, Vol. 3, No.1, p. 21-45.

Leonardi, C. (2007) *Liberation or Capture: Youth in-between 'Hakuma', and 'Home' during Civil War and its Aftermath in Southern Sudan*', African Affairs. Vol. 106, No, 424, pp. 391-412.

Leonardi, C. (2011) Paying Buckets of Blood for the Land: Moral Debates over Economy, War and State in Southern Sudan', *The Journal of Modern African Studies*, Vol. 49, No, 2, pp. 215-240.

Leonardi, C., Moro, L.N., Santschi, M., and Deborah, H.I. (2010) *Local Justice in Southern Sudan*', United States Institute for Peace, Washington DC.

LeRiche, M. (2014) *Sudan 1972-1983*', In: New Armies from Old, Merging Competing Military Forces after Civil War, Roy Licklider, (Eds.), Washington, DC: Georgetown University Press.

LeRiche, M. and Arnold, M. (2012) *South Sudan: From Revolution to Independence*', New York: Columbia University Press.

Lesch, A.M. (1998) *The Sudan: Contested National Identities*', Bloomington: Indiana University Press.

Leuprecht, C. (2010) International Security Strategy and Global Population Aging', *Journal of Strategic Security*, Vol. 3, No. 4, pp. 27-48.

Levin, D.M. (1988) *The opening of vision: Nihilism and the Postmodern Situation*', London: Routledge.

Lewis, I. (1983) *Nationalism and Self-Determination in the Horn of Africa*', London: Ithaca Press.

Leysens, A.J. (2006) Social Forces in Southern Africa: Transformation from Below? *Journal of Modern African Studies*, Vol. 44, No. 1, pp. 31-58.

Licklider, R. (1995) The Consequences of Negotiated Settlements in Civil Wars, 1945-1993', *American Political Science Review*, Vol. 89, pp. 681-690.

Lincoln, Y.S. and Guba, E.A. (1985) *Naturalistic Inquiry*', Beverly Hills, CA: Sage.

Lindley C.A. (2005) *Story and Narrative Structures in Computer Games*', In: Developing Interactive Narrative Content: Sagas/Sagasnet Reader, Bushoff, B. (Ed.), Munich: High Text.

Linklater, A. and Suganami, H. (2006) *The English School of International Relations: A Contemporary Reassessment*', Cambridge: Cambridge University Press.

Lonsdale, J. (1994) *Moral Ethnicity and Political Tribalism*', In: P. Kaarsholm and J. Hultin (Eds.), Inventions and Boundaries: Historical and Anthropological Approaches to the Study of Ethnicity and Nationalism, Roskilde University.

Lotze, W., Yvonne, K., and de Carvalho, G. (2008) *Peacebuilding Coordination in African Countries: Transitioning from Conflict: Case Studies of the Democratic Republic of the Congo, Liberia and South Sudan*', Occasional Paper Series: Vol. 3, No. 1, Durban: Accord.

Luborsky, M. (1994) *The Identification and Analysis of Themes and Patterns*', In: Gubrium, J. and Sankar, A. (Eds.), Qualitative Methods in Aging Research. Sage; Thousand Oaks, CA.

Luckham, R. and Kirk, T. (2013*) Understanding Security in the Vernacular in hybrid political contexts: a Critical Survey*', Conflict, Security and Development. Vol. 13, No. 3, pp.339-359.

Lujala, P. (2010) The Spoils of Nature: Armed Civil Conflict and Rebel Access to Natural Resources', *Journal of Peace Research*, Vol. 47, No. 1, pp. 15–28.

Lunde, L. (2002) *Economic Driving Forces of Conflict (Econ Report 27/01)*', Oslo: Econ Institute.

Lunde, L., Taylor, T., and Huser, A. (2003) *Commerce or Crime? Regulating Economies of Conflict*', Fafo Report 424. Oslo: Fafo Institute.

Lyman, P. and Knopf, K. A. (2016) *To save South Sudan, Put it on Life Support*', Financial Times (July 20). http://blogs.ft.com/beyond-brics/2016/07/20/to-save-south-sudan-put-it-on-life-support/ [Accessed: 06/09/2018].

Lynch, G. (2011) *I Say to You: Ethnic Politics and the Kalenjin in Kenya*', Chicago: Chicago University Press.

Lynch, M. (2013) *Civilian-on-civilian Violence: An Ethnography of Choices during Civil War*', ProQuest, UMI Dissertations Publishing.

Lyons, T. (2002) *Post-conflict Elections: War Termination, Democratisation, and Demilitarising Politics*', Working Paper No. 20. Arlington, VA: Institute of Conflict Analysis and Resolution, George Mason University.

Lyons, T. (2002) *The Role of Post-Settlement Elections*', Ending Civil Wars: The Implementation of Peace Agreements', (Ed.) by Elizabeth M. Cousens, Donald Rothchild, and Stephen John Stedman. Boulder, CO: Lynne Rienner.

Maanen, J. V. (1996) Commentary: On the Matter of Voice', *Journal of Management Inquiry*, Vol. 5, No. 4, pp. 375–381.

Mac Ginty, R. (2006) *No War, No Peace: The Rejuvenation of Stalled Peace Processes and Peace Accords'*, New York: Palgrave Macmillan.

Mac Ginty, R. (2010) *Hybrid Peace: The Interaction between Top-Down and Bottom-Up Peace'*, Security Dialogue, Vol. 41, No.4, pp. 391–412.

Mac Ginty, R. (2011) *International Peacebuilding and Local Resistance: Hybrid Forms of Peace'*, Palgrave Macmillan.

Mac Ginty, R. (2012) Against Stabilisation', Stability, *International Journal of Security and Development*, Vol. 1, No. 1, pp. 20-30.

Mac Ginty, R. (2014) *Everyday Peace: Bottom-up and Local Agency in Conflict-affected Societies'*, Security Dialogue, Vol 45, No. 6, pp. 548–564.

Mac Ginty, R. and Richmond, O. (2007) *Myth or Reality: Opposing Views on the Liberal Peace and Post-war Reconstruction'*, Global Society, Vol. 21, No.4, pp. 491-497.

Mac Ginty, R. and Sanghera, G. (2012) Hybridity in Peacebuilding and Development: An Introduction', *Journal of Peacebuilding and Development*, Vol.7, No. 2, pp. 3–8.

Mack, A. (2005) *Human Security Report 2005: War and Peace in the 21st Century'*, New York and Oxford: Oxford University Press.

Mack, A. (2007) *Global Patterns of Political Violence'*, Working Paper, New York: International Peace Academy.

Madut-Arop, A. (2006) *Sudan's Painful Road to Peace; A Full Story of the Founding and Development of the SPLM/SPLA'*, North Charleston, SC: Book Surge.

Mailer, M. and Poole, L. (2010) *Rescuing the Peace in Southern Sudan'*, Joint NGO Briefing Paper.

Major, C. H. and Savin-Baden, M. (2011) *Integration of Qualitative Evidence: Towards Construction of Academic Knowledge in Social Science and Professional Fields'*, Qualitative Research, Vol. 11, No. 6, pp. 645–663.

Makombe, G. (2017) *An Expose of the Relationship between Paradigm, Method and Design in Research'*, The Qualitative Report, Vol. 22, No. 12, pp. 3363-3382.

Malejacq, R. (2016) *Warlords, Intervention, and State Consolidation: A Typology of Political Orders in Weak and Failed States'*, Security Studies, Vol. 25, No. 1, pp. 85-110.

Malesevic, S. (2004) *The Sociology of Ethnicity'*, London, GB: Sage Publications Ltd, 2004.

Malesevic, S. (2006) *Identity as Ideology: Understanding Ethnicity and Nationalism'*, New York: Palgrave Macmillan.

Malwal, B. (1985) *The Sudan: A Second Challenge to Nationhood'*, New York: Thornton Books.

Malwal, B. (2014) *Sudan and South Sudan: From One to Two'*, Palgrave MacMillan.

Mamdani M. (2017) *Can the African Union save South Sudan from Genocide?* New York Times 8 Jan. https://www.nytimes.com/2017/01/08/opinion/canafrican-union-save-south-sudan-fromgenocide.html [Accessed: 14/09/2018].

Mamdani, M. (1996) *Subject and Citizen'*, Princeton: Princeton University Press.

Mampilly, Z. (2011) *Rebel Rulers: Insurgent Governance and Civilian Life during War'*, Ithaca: Cornell University Press.

Manning, C. (2003) *Local-level Challenges to Post-conflict Peacebuilding, International Peacekeeping'*, No.10, Vol 3, pp. 25–43.

Mansfield, E.D. and Snyder, J. (2002) *Democratic Transitions, Institutional Strength, and War'*, International Organisation, Vol. 56, No. 2, pp. 297-337.

Mansfield, E.D. and Snyder, J. (2005) *Electing to fight: Why emerging Democracies go to War'*, Cambridge: MIT Press.

Marijan, B. (2015) *Neither War nor Peace: Everyday Politics, Peacebuilding and the Liminal Condition of Bosnia-Herzegovina and Northern Ireland'*, Theses and Dissertations (Comprehensive). Paper 1770.

Markakis, J. (1999) *Nationalism and Ethnicity in the Horn of Africa'*, In: Paris Yeros (Ed.), Ethnicity and Nationalism in Africa: Constructivist Reflections and Contemporary Politics, (pp. 65-80). Basingstoke: Macmillan.

Markula, P. and Silk, M. (2011) *Paradigmatic Approaches to Physical Culture'*, In: P. Markula and M. Silk (Eds.), Qualitative Research for Physical Culture (pp. 24-56). New York: Palgrave.

Marshall, M. and Cole, B. (2008) *Global Report on Conflict, Governance and State Fragility'*, Foreign Policy Bulletin, Vol. 18, No. 1, pp. 3-21.

Marshall, M. G. and Gurr, T. R (2005) *Peace and Conflict 2005: A Global Survey of Armed Conflicts, Self-Determination Movements, and Democracy'*, College Park: Centre for International Development and Conflict Management, University of Maryland.

Marwick, A., Blackwell, L. and Lo, K. (2016) *Best Practices for Conducting Risky Research and Protecting Yourself from Online Harassment'*, (Data & Society Guide). New York: Data & Society Research Institute.

Mason, J. (2002) *Qualitative Researching'*, London: Sage, 2nd (Ed.), — (2006) Six Strategies for Mixing Methods and Linking Data in Social Science Research, Real Life Methods NCRM Node Working Paper.

Mastropaolo, A. (2012) *Is democracy a Lost Cause? Paradoxes of an Imperfect Invention'*, Translated by Clare Tame, Publications from the ECPR Press.

Mathew, S, Boyd, R. (2011) *Punishment Sustains Large-scale Cooperation in Pre-state Warfare'*, Proc Natl Acad Sci, Vol. 108, No, 28, pp. 11375–11380.

Mathews, J. (1997) *Power Shift'*, Foreign Affairs, Vol. 76, No. 1, pp.50–66.

Mattes, M. and Savun, B. (2009) Fostering Peace after Civil War: Commitment Problems and Agreement Design', *International Studies Quarterly*, Vol. 53, No. 3, pp. 737-759.

Matthew, R. (2005) William James on Emotion and intentionality', *International Journal of Philosophical Studies,* Vol. 13, No. 2, pp. 179-202.

Maynard, D. (1989) *On the Ethnography and Analysis of Discourse in Institutional Settings'*, In: J. Holstein and G. Miller. (Ed.), In: Perspectives on Social Problems, Vol. 1, pp. 127–46.

Mayring, P. (2000) *Qualitative Inhaltsanalyse, Grundlagen und Techniken'*, 7th (Eds.), Weinheim: Deutscher Studien Verlag.

Mayring, P. König, J., Birk, N. and Hurst, A. (2000) *Opfer der Einheit, Eine Studie zur Lehrerarbeitslosigkeit in den neuen Bundesländern'*, Opladen; Leske & Budrich.

Mazurana, D.E., McKay, S.A., Carlson, K.C., and Kasper, J.C. (2002) *Girls in fighting forces and groups: Their recruitment, participation, Demobilisation, and Reintegration'*, Peace and Conflict: Journal of Peace Psychology, Vol 8, No. 2, pp. 97-123.

Mbaku, J.M and Smith, J.E. (2012) *South Sudan-One Year after Independence: Opportunities and Obstacles for Africa's Newest Country'*, Brookings Africa Growth Initiative.

Mc Fate, S. (2010) *The Link Between DDR and SSR in Conflict-Affected Countries'*, Special Report, No. 238, USIP. Washington.

McEvoy, C. and LeBrun, E. (2010) *Uncertain future: armed violence in Southern Sudan'*, Geneva: HSBA.

McMullin, J.R. (2013) Integration or Separation? The stigmatisation of Ex-Combatants after war', *Review of International Studies*, Vol. 39, pp. 385-414.

Mcneish, H. and Nicholls, P. (2014) *Hunger amid tragedy for South Sudan Refugees'*, As Fears Grow of New Violence in the World's Newest Nation, Refugees in Ethiopia Relive the Terror of the Conflict. https://www.aljazeera.com/indepth/features/2014/11/[Accessed: 02/07/2017].

Mearsheimer, J. (1994) *The False Promise of International Institutions'*, International Security, Vol. 19, No 3, pp. 5-49.

Mearsheimer, J. (2001) *The Tragedy of Great Power Politics'*, New York: W.W. Norton & Company.

Mecca, J.T., Gibson, C., Giorgini, V., Medeiros, K. E., Mumford, M. D., and Connelly, S. (2015) *Researcher Perspectives on Conflicts of Interest: A Qualitative Analysis of Views from Academia'*, Science and Engineering Ethics, Vol. 21, No. 4, pp. 843–855.

Meek, S. and Malan, M. (2004) Identifying Lessons from DDR Experiences in Africa', Institute for Security Studies, Monograph No. 106. Pretoria, South Africa: Institute for Security Studies.

Mehler, A. (2004) *Oligopolies of Violence in Africa South of the Sahara'*, In: Nord-Süd-Aktuell, Vol. 18, No. 3, p. 539-548.

Mehler, A. (2009) *Hybrid Regimes and Oligopolies of Violence in Africa: Expectations on Security Provision from Below'*, In: Martina Fischer and Beatrix Schmelzle (Eds.), Building Peace in the Absence of States: Challenging the Discourse on State Failure, Berghof Handbook Dialogue Series, No. 8.

Mehreteab, A. (2007) *Border Conflict' –1998-2000 and its Psychological Impact on the Youth'*, Conference paper in Healy, Op.cit. pp. 23-77.

Melber, H. (2009a) Southern African Liberation Movements as Governments and the Limits to Liberation', *Review of African Political Economy*, Vol. 121, pp. 453-461.

Melber, H. (2009b) *Namibian Politics: The Pathology of Power and Paranoia'*, the Namibian, Windhoek, A Weekly Electronic Forum for Social Justice in Africa.

Merriam S. B. (2009) *Qualitative Research: A Guide to Design and Implementation'*, 3rd (Ed.), San Francisco, CA: Jossey-Bass.

Messner, J.J., Haken, N., Taft, P., Blyth, H., Lawrence, K., Graham, S.P. (2017) *Fragile States Index*. (T.F. Peace, Ed.). [PDF file]. http://fundforpeace.org/fsi/2017/05/14/fragile-states-index-2017-annual-report/951171705-fragile-states-index-annual-report-2017.

Meyer C. B. (2001) *A Case in Case Study Methodology'*, Field Methods, Vol. 13, No. 4, pp. 329–352.

Meyer, J.W., & Scott, W.R. (1983b) *Centralisation and the Legitimacy Problems of Local Government'*, In J.W. Meyer & W.R. Scott (Eds.), Organisational environments: Ritual and rationality, (pp. 199-215). Beverly Hills, CA: Sage.

Miall, H. (2004) *Conflict Transformation: A Multi-Dimensional Task'*, Berghof Handbook for Conflict Transformation, Berghof Research Centre for Constructive Conflict Management, Berlin.

Migdal, J. (1988) *Strong Societies and Weak States: State-Society Relations and State Capabilities in the Third World*, Princeton: Princeton University Press.

Miles, M. B. and Huberman, A. (1984) *Qualitative Data Analysis*, London: Sage.

Miles, M.B. and Huberman, A.M. (1994) *Qualitative Data Analysis*, 2nd (Ed.), Newbury Park, CA: Sage.

Milgram, S. and Jodelet, D. (1976) *Psychological Maps of Paris*, In: Proshansky, Ittelson, Rivlin (Eds.) Environmental psychology: People and their physical settings, pp. 104-124). New York, Holt Rinehart and Winston.

Miller, C. (2005) A *Glossary of Terms and Concepts in Peace and Conflict Studies*, 2nd (Ed.), University of Peace, Africa Programme, from http://www.africa.upeace.org/documents/GlossaryV2.pdf.

Mitchell, C. (2012) *Introduction: Linking National-Level Peacemaking with Grassroots Peacebuilding*, In: Mitchell, C.R & Hancock, L.E. (Eds.), Local Peacebuilding and National Peace: Interaction between Grassroots and Elite Processes (pp. 1-18). London: Continuum International Publishing Group.

Mittelman, J.H. and Chin, C.N. (2005) *Conceptualising Resistance to Globalisation'*, In L. Amoore (ed.), the Global Resistance Reader, London: Routledge.

Mkutu, K.A. (2008) Uganda: Pastoral Conflict and Gender Relations', *Review of African Political Economy*, Vol. 35, No. 116, pp. 237-254.

Molloy, D.J. (2013) *An Unlikely Convergence: The Evolution of Disarmament Demobilisation and Reintegration (DDR) Theory and Counter-insurgency (COIN) Doctrine',* PhD Dissertation Tokyo University of Foreign Studies.

Montalvo, *et al.* (2002) *The Effect of Ethnic and Religious Conflict on Growth',* Available at: <http://www.econ.upf.edu/~montalvo/sec1034/jde.pdf[Accessed: 26/12/2018].

Moore, B. Jr. (1966) *Social Origins of Democracy and Dictatorship',* Boston: Beacon Press.

Morgan, J. and Olsen, W. (2008) Defining Objectivity in Realist Terms', *Journal of Critical Realism,* Vol. 7, No. 1, pp.107-132.

Morrisey, E.L. (2010) *Lessons from the Past: Power Transitions and the Future of U.S. –China Relations',* Washington DC: Georgetown University.

Morrison, J. (2004) *Sudan at the Crossroads',* Whitehall Papers, Vol. 62, No. 1, pp.23-30.

Morrow, R.A. and Brown, D.D. (1994) *Critical Theory and Methodology',* London: Sage.

Morrow, S. (2005) Quality and trustworthiness in qualitative research in counselling psychology', *Journal of Counselling Psychology,* Vol. 52, No. 2, pp. 250-260.

Moustakas, C. (1994) *Phenomenological Research Methods',* Thousand Oaks, CA: Sage.

Mouton, J. (2010) *Research Designs in the Social Sciences'*, Class Notes. African Doctoral Academy Summer School, Stellenbosch: University of Stellenbosch.

Mueller, J. (2000) *The Banality of Ethnic War'*, International Security, Vol. 25, No.1, pp. 42-70.

Muggah, R and O'Donnell, C. (2015) Next-generation Disarmament, Demobilisation and Reintegration', Stability: *International Journal of Security and Development*, Vol. 4, No. 1. pp. 1–12.

Muggah, R and Rieger, M. (2012) *Negotiating Disarmament and Demobilisation in Peace Processes: what is the State of the Evidence?* Noref Report, pp.1-11. https://www.files.ethz.ch/isn/155994/84c0656455ff43ac35123eaf64 9015f9.pdf [Accessed: 12/05/2017].

Muggah, R, Nat Colletta, N. and de Tessières, S. (2009) *Alternatives to Conventional Security Promotion: Rethinking the Case of Southern Sudan,'* In HSBA. http://smallarmssurveysudan.org/pdfs/HSBA-Sudan-conference-papers.pdf.

Muggah, R. (2005) *Securing Haiti's Transition: Reviewing Human Insecurity and the Prospects for Disarmament, Demobilisation, and Reintegration'*, Occasional Paper 14, Geneva: Small Arms Survey.

Muggah, R. (2005a) *No Magic Bullet: A Critical Perspective on Disarmament, Demobilisation and Reintegration (DDR) and Weapons Reduction in Post-conflict Contexts'*, the Round Table, Vol.94, No, 379, pp. 239–252.

Muggah, R. (2005b) *Listening for a Change! Participatory Evaluations of DDR and Arms Reduction in Mali, Cambodia and Albania'*, UNIDIR/2005/23. Geneva: United Nations Institute for Disarmament Research.

Muggah, R. (2005c) *Securing Haiti's Transition: Reviewing Human Insecurity and the Prospects for Disarmament, Demobilisation, and Reintegration'*, Occasional Paper 14, Geneva: Small Arms Survey.

Muggah, R., Molloy, D. and Halty, M. (2009) *Disintegrating DDR in Sudan and Haiti? Practitioners views to overcome integration inertia'*, In: Muggah, R. (Ed.), Security and Post-conflict Reconstruction: Dealing with Fighters in the Aftermath of War, (pp. 206–225). New York, N.Y.: Routledge.

Muller, E. N. (1972) A Test of a Partial Theory of Potential for Political Violence', *American Political Science Review*, Vol 66, No, 3, pp. 928–959.

Muller, E.N. (1985) Income Inequality, Regime Repressiveness, and Political Violence', *American Sociological Review*, Vol. 50, pp. 47-61.

Muller, E.N. and Weede E. (1990) Cross-National Variations in Political Violence: A Rational Action Approach', *Journal of Conflict Resolution*, Vol. 34, No, 4, pp. 624–51.

Multi-Country Demobilisation and Reintegration Program (2010) *MDRP Final Report: Overview of Program Achievements'*, Washington, DC: World Bank.

Munive, J. (2013a) *Context Matters: The conventional DDR template is Challenged in South Sudan'*, International Peacekeeping, Vol. 20, No. 5, pp. 585–599.

Munive, J. (2013b) *Disarmament, demobilisation and reintegration in South Sudan: The limits of conventional peace and security templates'*, Copenhagen: Danish Institute for International Studies', http://pure.diis.dk/ws/files/58204/RP2013_07_Jairo_Disarmament_SouthSudan_web.jpg.pdf [Accessed; 20/03/2018].

Munive, J. (2014) Invisible Labour: The Political Economy of Reintegration in South Sudan', *Journal of Intervention and Statebuilding*, Vol. 8, No. 4, pp. 334-356.

Munive, J. and Stine, J. (2012) *Revisiting DDR in Liberia: Exploring the power, agency and interests of local and international actors in the 'making' and 'unmaking' of combatants'*, Conflict, Security and Development, Vol, 12, No, 4, pp. 359-385.

Münkler, H. (2005) *The New Wars'*, Cambridge: Polity Press.

Murdoch, J.C. and Sandler, T. (2002) Economic growth, civil wars, and Spatial Spillover', *Journal of Conflict Resolution*, Vol 46, pp. 91-110.

Murshed, S. (2002) Conflict, Civil War and Underdevelopment: An Introduction', *Journal of Peace Research*, Vol. 39, Vol 4, pp. 387–393.

Murshed, S. and Tadjoeddin, M. (2009) Revisiting the Greed and Grievance Explanations for Violent Internal Conflict', *Journal of International Development*, Vol.21, No 1, pp.87-111.

Musso, G. (2011) *From one Sudan to two Sudan: from war to Peace*? ISPI - Working Paper, Africa Program.

Mutengesa, S. (2013) *Facile Acronyms and Tangled Processes: A Re-Examination of the 1990s 'DDR' in Uganda'*, International Peacekeeping, Vol. 20, No. 3, pp. 338-356.

Myrdal, G. (1972) How Scientific Are the Social Sciences?' *Journal of Social Issues*, Vol. 28, pp. 151-70.

Narayan, D., Raj Patel, R., Schafft, K., Rademacher, A. and Koch-Schulte, S. (1999) *Can Anyone Hear Us*? Washington D. C.: World Bank.

Natsios, A. S. (2012) *Sudan, South Sudan and Darfur: What Everyone Needs to Know'*, New York: Oxford University Press.

Nelson, C. (2004) *Learning from Clients, Assessment Tool for Microfinance Practitioners'*, the Small Enterprise Education and Promotion Network (SEEP), Washington D. C.

Newman, E. (2001) Human Security and Constructivism', *International Studies Perspectives*, Vol 2, No, 3, pp. 239–251.

Newman, E. (2009) *Conflict Research and the Decline of Civil War'*, Civil Wars. Vol. 11, No. 3, pp. 255-278.

Newman, E. (2013) *The International Architecture of Peacebuilding'*, In: R. Mac Ginty (Ed.), Routledge handbook of peacebuilding (pp. 266–276). London: Routledge.

Newman, E., Paris, R. and Richmond, O.P. (2009) *New perspectives on liberal peacebuilding'*, New York: United Nations University Press.

Nezam, T. and Alexandre, M. (2009) *Disarmament, Demobilisation and Reintegration*', Social Development Department Working Paper; no. 119. Conflict, Crime, and Violence, Washington, DC: World Bank.

Nichols, R. (2011) *DDR in South Sudan*', HSBA, Small Arms Survey, Geneva, Switzerland, http://www.smallarmssurveysudan.org/fileadmin/docs/archive/DDR/DDR-South-Sudan-Sept-2011.pdf.[Accessed: 04/07/2017].

Nitzschke, H. (2003) *Transforming War Economies: Challenges for Peacemaking and Peacebuilding*', IPA Conference Report, New York: International Peace Academy.

Nnoli, O. (1995) *Ethnicity and Development in Nigeria*', Aldershot: Avebury.

Noblit, G.W., and Hare, R.D. (1988) *Meta-ethnography: synthesising Qualitative Studies*', Newbury Park: Sage.

Nordlinger, E. A. (1972) *Conflict Regulation in Divided Societies: Occasional Papers in International Affairs No. 29*', Cambridge, Mass.: Harvard University. Centre for International Affairs, American Behavioural Scientist, Vol. 15, No. 6, pp. 952–952.

Nordstrom, C. (2004) *Shadows of War: Violence, Power, and International Profiteering in the Twenty-First Century*', Berkley/Los Angeles: University of California Press.

North, D. Wallis, J. and Weingast, B. (2009) *Violence and Social Orders: A conceptual framework for Interpreting Recorded Human History*', Cambridge, Cambridge University Press.

Nyaba, P.A. (2014) *South Sudan: The Crisis of Infancy'*, Cape Town: The Centre for Advanced Studies of African Society.

Nyaba, P.A. (2000) *Politics of Liberation in South Sudan: An Insider's View'*, Kampala, Uganda: Foundation Publishers.

Nyaba, P.A. (2019) *South Sudan: Elites, Ethnicity, Endless Wars and the Stunted State'*, Dares-Salaam: Mkuki na Nyota.

Nyadera, I.N. (2018) *South Sudan Conflict from 2013 to 2018 Rethinking the causes, Situation and Solutions'*, Accord, https://www.accord.org.za/ajcr-issues/south-sudan-conflict-from-2013-to-2018.[Accessed: 28/04/2019].

O'Brien, A. (2009) *Shots in the Dark: The 2008 South Sudan Civilian Disarmament Campaign'*, HSBA Working Paper No. 16. Geneva: Small Arms Survey. http://smallarmssurveysudan.org/pdfs/HSBA-SWP-16-South-Sudan-Civilian-Disarmament-Campaign.pdf.

OECD (2007) *Handbook on Security Sector Reform (SSR): Supporting Security and Justice'*, Paris.

OECD (2012) *Peacebuilding and State-Building Priorities and Challenges: A Synthesis of Findings from Seven Multi-Stakeholder Consultations'*, International Dialogue on Peacebuilding and State-building, Dili, Timor-Leste.

Olson, M. (1965) *The Logic of Collective Action'*, Cambridge, MA: Harvard University Press.

Omondi, P. (2011) *Climate Change and Inter-community Conflict over Natural Resources in Jonglei State, South Sudan*', Boma Development Initiative Report, London: Minority Rights Group International.

Omosulu, R. (2013) The Main Features and Constraints of Social Science's Research Methods', *International Journal of Development and Sustainability*, Vol. 2 No. 3, pp. 1907-1918.

Opongo, E. (2017) *An Assessment of Illicit Small Arms and Light Weapons Proliferation and Fragility Situations: Burundi*', Nairobi: Regional Centre on Small Arms and Light Weapons.

Organski, A.F. (1958) *World Politics*', New York: Knopf.

Osaghae, E. (1995) *Structural Adjustment and Ethnicity in Nigeria*', Research Report No. 98. Uppsala: Nordic Africa Institute.

Osaghae, E. (1999) *The Post-Colonial African State and its Problems*', In: P. McGowan and P. Nel (Eds.), Power, Wealth and Global Order, Cape Town: University of Cape Town Press.

Osaghae, E. (2005) The state of Africa's Second Liberation', Interventions: *International Journal of Post-colonial Studies*, Vol. 7, No. 1, pp. 1-20.

Osuala, E. C. (2001) *Introduction to Research Methodology*, 3rd (Ed.), Africana-First Publishers Limited, Onitsha.

Ottaway, M. (2002) *Rebuilding State Institutions in Collapsed States*', Development and Change, Vol. 33, No. 5, pp. 1001–23.

Otterbein, K.F. (2004) *How War Began'*, College Station: Texas A&M Press.

Owegi, J., Ruth, T. and Kwambai, J. (2014) *Militarisation of Ethnic Conflict, Paradigms of Military Ethnicity, Intervention and Prevention'*, A presentation at the University of Nairobi for the Institute for Diplomacy and International Studies, pp.1-15.

Owen, J.M. (1994) *How Liberalism Produces Democratic Peace'*, International Security, Vol. 19, No. 2, pp. 87-125.

Oyugi, W. (2003) *The Politics of Transition in Kenya, 1999-2003: Democratic Consolidation or Deconsolidation'*, In: W.O. Oyugi *et al.* Eds. The Politics of Transition in Kenya: From KANU to NARC, Nairobi: Heinrich Böll Foundation.

Özerdem, A. (2012) *A Re-conceptualisation of Ex-combatant Reintegration: Social Reintegration Approach'*, Conflict, Security and Development, Vol. 12, No. 1, pp. 51-73.

Ozkirimli, U. (2000) *Theories on Nationalism: A Critical Introduction'*, St. Martin's Press, New York.

Paffenholz, T. and Spurk, C. (2006) *Civil Society, Civic Engagement, and Peacebuilding'*, Social Development Papers: Conflict Prevention and Reconstruction, Paper No. 36.

Paffenholz, T., Abu-Nimer, M. and McCandless, E. (2005) Peacebuilding and development: Integrated approaches to evaluation', *Journal of Peacebuilding and Development*, Vol. 2, No. 2, pp. 1-5.

Pareto, V. (1935) *The Mind and Society'*, London: Jonathan Cape Limited.

Paris, R. (2004) *At War's End: Building Peace after Civil Conflict*, Cambridge: Cambridge University Press.

Paris, R., and Sisk, T. D. (2009) *The Dilemmas of State Building: Confronting the Contradictions of Post-war Peace Operations'*, New York: Routledge.

Parkinson, S.E. (2013) Organising rebellion: Rethinking high-risk mobilisation and social networks in war', *American Political Science Review*, Vol.10, No.3, p. 418.

Patton, M.Q. (1987) *How to Use Qualitative Methods in Evaluation'*, California: Sage Publications, Inc.

Patton, M.Q. (1990) *Qualitative Evaluation and Research Methods'*, Sage Publications, Newbury Park London New Delhi.

Patton, M.Q. (2002) *Qualitative Research and Evaluation Methods'*, 3rd (Ed.), Thousand Oaks, CA: Sage.

Paudel, D. (2016) *Ethnic Identity Politics in Nepal: Liberation from, or Restoration of Elite Interest?* Asian Ethnicity, pp. 1-18.

Pavkovic, A. and Radan, P. (2007) *Creating New States: Theory and Practice of Secession'*, Aldershot: Ashgate Publishing Limited.

Pavković, A. and Radan, P. (2011) *The Ashgate Research Companion to Secession'*, Farnham, UK; Burlington, VT: Ashgate Publishing.

Pelto, P., and Pelto, G. (2007) *Studying Knowledge, Culture and Behaviour in applied Medical Anthropology'*, Med Anthropol Q, Vol. 11, No. 2, pp. 147-63.

Pelto, P.J., and Pelto, G.H. (1997) *Ethnography: The Fieldwork Enterprise'*, In: J. Honigmann (Ed.), Handbook of Social and Cultural Anthropology, (pp. 241-288). New Delhi: Rawat Publications, India.

Pendle, N. (2015) They are Now Community Police: Negotiating the Boundaries and Nature of the Government in South Sudan through the identity of militarised cattle keepers', *International Journal of Minority Group Rights*, Vol. 22, No 3, pp. 410–434.

Persson, T., Roland, G. and Tabellini, G. (1997) Separation of Powers and Political Accountability', *Quarterly Journal of Economics*, Vol. 112, pp.1163-1202.

Petersen, R.D. (2001) *Resistance and Rebellion: Lessons from Eastern Europe'*, New York: Cambridge University Press.

Plummer, K. (1995) *Telling Sexual Stories: Power, Change, and Social Worlds'*, London: Routledge

Polese, A. and Santini, R.H. (2018) *Limited Statehood and its Security Implications on the Fragmentation Political Order in the Middle East and North Africa'*, Small Wars and Insurgencies, Vol. 29, No. 3, pp.379-390.

Polit, D.F. and Beck, C. T. (2004) *Nursing Research: Appraising Evidence for Nursing Practice'*, 7th (Ed.), Philadelphia, PA: Wolters Klower/Lippincott Williams & Wilkins.

Ponce, O. and Pagán-Maldonado, N. (2015) A mixed methods Research in Education: Capturing the complexity of the profession', *International Journal of Educational Excellence*, Vol. I, No. 1, pp. 111-135.

Porto, J.G. and Parsons, I. (2003) *Sustaining the Peace in Angola: an Overview of Current Demobilisation, Disarmament and Reintegration'*, Bonn, Bonn International Centre for Conversion, ISS Paper 27.

Posner, D. (2005) *Institutions and Ethnic Politics in Africa'*, Cambridge, Cambridge University Press.

Powell, G.B (1982) *Contemporary Democracies: Participation, Stability, and Violence'*, Cambridge: Harvard University Press.

Powell, R. (2004) The Inefficient Use of Power: Costly Conflict with Complete Information', *American Political Science Review*, Vol. 98, No. 2, pp. 231-242.

Powell, R. (1999) *In the Shadow of Power'*, Princeton: Princeton University Press.

Powell, R. (2006) *War as a Commitment Problem'*, International Organisation, Vol. 60, pp. 169–203.

Powney, J. and Watts, M. (1987) *Interviewing in Educational Research'*, London: Routledge & Kegan, Paul.

Prendergast, J. (1991) *The Political Economy of Famine in Sudan and the Horn of Africa'*, Issue: A Journal of Opinion, Vol. 19, No. 2, pp. 49-55.

Pritchett, L., Woolcock, M., and Andrews, M. (2012) *Looking Like a State: Techniques of Persistent Failure in State Capability for Implementation'*, UNU-WIDER Working Paper, No. 63.

Prunier, G. (1995) *The Rwanda Crisis: History of a Genocide'*, New York: Columbia University Press.

Pugel, J. (2009) *Measuring Reintegration in Liberia: Assessing the Gap between Outputs and Outcomes'*, In: Muggah, R. (Ed.), Security and Post-Conflict Reconstruction: Dealing with Fighters in the Aftermath of War. New York: Routledge.

Pugh, A.J. (2011) *Distinction, boundaries or bridges? Children, Inequality and the uses of Culture'*, Poetics, Vol. 39, No. 1, pp. 1-18.

Pugh, M.C. and Sidhu, P.S. (2003) *The United Nations and Regional Security: Europe and Beyond'*, Boulder, Colorado: Lynne Rienner Publishers.

Putnam, R. (1993) *Making Democracy Work: Civic Traditions in Modern Italy'*, Princeton, N.J.: Princeton University Press.

Qu, S. Q. and Dumay, J. (2011) The qualitative Research Interview', *Qualitative Research in Accounting and Management*, Vol. 8, No. 3, pp. 238-264.

Quinn, J., Mason, D. Gurses, M. (2007) *Sustaining the Peace: Determinants of Civil War Recurrence'*, International Interactions, Vol. 33, No. 2, pp.167-193.

Rabianski, J.S. (2006) *Primary and Secondary Data: concepts, Errors and Issues'*, Appraisal Journal, Vol. 71, No. 1, pp. 43-55.

Radon, J. and Logan. S. (2014) South Sudan: Governance Arrangements, War, and Peace', *Journal of International Affairs*, Vol. 68, No. 1 pp. 147–167.

Ramanathan, R. (2008) *The Role of Organisational Change Management in Offshore Outsourcing of Information Technology Services'*, Universal Publisher.

Ramose, M. (1999) *African Philosophy through Ubuntu'*, Harare: Mond Books.

Ramsbotham, O.W, T and Miall, H. (2009) *Contemporary Conflict Resolution'*, 2nd (Ed.), Cambridge: Polity Press.

Rands, R.B. and LeRiche, M. (2012) *Security Responses in Jonglei State in the Aftermath of Inter-ethnic Violence'*, London: Saferworld, Available at: http://www.burtonrands.com/documents

Ranger, T. (1991) *Missionaries Migrants and the Mayinka: The Invention of Ethnicity in Zimbabwe'*, In: Leroy Vail (Ed.), Creation of Tribalism in Southern Africa, Berkeley: University of California Press.

Rasmussen, J. (2018) *Parasitic Politics: Violence, Deception, and Change in Kenya's Electoral Politics'*, In: M. S. Kovacs, & J. Bjarnesen (Eds.), Violence in African Elections. Between Democracy and Big Man Politics, (pp.176-196). Zed Books, Africa Now.

Reed, S.K. (2016) The structure of ill-structured (and well-structured) problems re-visited', *Educational Psychology Review*, Vol. 28, No. 4, pp. 691–716.

Reeves E. (2013) The Coup Attempt in South Sudan: What we know. Sudan Tribune, http://www.sudantribune.com/spip.php?article49226 [Accessed 06/04/2017].

Reilly, B. (2002) *Elections in Post-Conflict Scenarios: Constraints and Dangers'*, International Peacekeeping, Vol.9. No. 2, pp. 118–139.

Reilly, B. (2006) *Political Engineering and Party Politics in Conflict-Prone Societies'*, Democratisation Vol.13, No. 5 pp. 811–27.

Reno, W. (1999) *Warlord Politics and African States'*, Boulder, CO: Lynne Rienner Publishers

Reno, W., (2000) *Shadow States and the Political Economy of Civil Wars'*, In Berdal, M. & Malone, D.M. (Eds.), Greed and Grievance: Economic Agendas in Civil Wars, London: Lynne Rienner Publishers.

Reychler, L. (2001) *From Conflict to Sustainable Peacebuilding: Concepts and Analytical Tools'*, In: Reychler, L & Paffenholz, J. (Eds.), Peacebuilding: A Field Guide, (pp. 3-20). London: Lynne Rienner Publishers.

Richards, L. and Richards, T. (1994) *From Filing Cabinet to Computer'*, In A. Bryman & R. G. Burgess (Eds.), Analysing qualitative data (pp. 146-172). London: Routledge.

Richards, P. (2002) Militia conscription in Sierra Leone', *Comparative Social Research*, No. 20, pp. 255-276.

Richards, P. (2005) *To fight or to farm? Agrarian dimensions of the Mano River conflict (Liberia and Sierra Leone'*, African Affairs, Vol. 104, No. 417, pp. 571-590.

Richmond O.P. (2012) *Beyond Local Ownership and Participation in the Architecture of International Peacebuilding'*, Ethno-politics, Vol. 1, No. 4, pp. 354-357.

Richmond, O.P. (2002) *Maintaining Order, Making Peace'*, London: Palgrave.

Richmond, O.P. (2013) *Failed Statebuilding versus Peace Formation'*, Cooperation and Conflict, Vol. 48, No. 3, pp. 378-400.

Richmond, O.P. (2005) *The Transformation of Peace'*, London: Palgrave.

Richmond, O.P. (2008) *Peace in IR'*, London: Routledge.

Richmond, O.P. (2009) *The Romanticisation of the Local: Welfare, Culture and Peacebuilding'*, The International Spectator, Vol. 44, No. 1, pp. 149-169.

Richmond, O.P. (2013) *Failed Statebuilding versus Peace Formation'*, Cooperation and Conflict, Vol. 48, No. 3, pp. 378–400.

Richmond, O.P. (2011a) *Critical Agency, Resistance, and a Post-colonial civil society'*, Cooperation and Conflict, Vol. 46, No. 4, pp. 419-440.

Richmond, O.P. (2011b) *A Post-Liberal Peace'*, London: Routledge.

Richmond, O.P. and Franks, J. (2009) *Liberal Peace Transitions: Between Statebuilding and Peacebuilding'*, Edinburgh: Edinburgh University Press.

Riehl, V. (2001) *Who is Ruling in South Sudan? The Role of NGOs in Rebuilding Socio-Political Order*', Studies on Emergencies and Disaster Relief, Uppsala: The Nordic Africa Institute.

Risse, T. (2010) *Governance without a State? Policies and Politics in Areas of Limited Statehood*', Columbia University Press, New York, N.Y.

Rodaway, P. (1995) *Exploring the Subject in Hyper-Reality*', In: Steve, Pile & Nigel, Thrift. Eds. Mapping the Subject: Geographies of Cultural Transformation', London; New York: Routledge.

Rodney, W. (1972) *How Europe Underdeveloped Africa*', Washington, DC: Howard University Press.

Rogier, E. (2005) *No More Hills Ahead? The Sudan's tortuous Ascent to Heights of Peace*', The Hague: Netherlands Institute of International Relations.

Rolandsen, O.H. (2005) *Guerrilla government: Political changes in the Southern Sudan during the 1990s*', Oslo: Nordiska Afrikainstitutet.

Rolandsen, O.H. (2011) A Quick Fix? A Retrospective Analysis of the Sudan Comprehensive Peace Agreement', *Review of African Political Economy*, Vol. 38, No 130, pp. 551-564.

Rolandsen, O.H. (2015) Another Civil War in South Sudan: the failure of Guerrilla Government? *Journal of Eastern African Studies*, Vol.9, No. 1, pp. 163-174.

Rolandsen, O.H. and Breidlid, I.M. (2012) *A Critical Analysis of Cultural Explanations for the Violence in Jonglei State, South Sudan*', Conflict Trends, Vol.1, pp. 49–56.

Rolandsen, O.H. and Breidlid, I.M. (2013) *What is Youth Violence in Jonglei*', The Peace Research Institute Oslo (PRIO) Paper', https://www.prio.org/utility/DownloadFile.ashx?id=367&type=publicationfile [Accessed: 10/03/2020].

Rosen, D.M. (2005) *Armies of the Young: Child Soldiers in War and Terrorism*', New Jersey: The Rutgers Series in Childhood Studies).

Ross, M.H. (2004) What do we know about Natural Resources and Civil War? *Journal of Peace Research*, Vol. 41, pp.337–56.

Ross, M.H. (2007) *Cultural Contestation in Ethnic Conflict*', Cambridge Studies in Comparative Politics, Cambridge: Cambridge University Press.

Rotberg, R. (2004) *The Failure and Collapse of Nation-States: Breakdown, Prevention and Repair*', In: R. Rotberg (Ed.), When States Fail: Causes and Consequences, Princeton University Press, Routledge.

Rotberg, R. (2007) The Challenge of Weak, Failing, and Collapsed States', Leashing the Dogs of War, pp. 83-94.

Rothchild, D. and Roeder, G. (2005) *Power-sharing as an Impediment to Peace and Democracy*,' In: P. G Roeder and D. Rothchild (eds.), Sustainable Peace: Power and Democracy after Civil Wars (pp. 29-50). Ithaca, N.Y.: Cornell University Press.

Rottenburg, R. and Komey, G. (2011) *The Genesis of Recurring wars in Sudan: Rethinking the violent conflicts in the Nuba Mountains / South Kordofan'*, Work Paper, Affiliation: Lost Research Group, University of Halle.

Rozema, Z. *et al.* (2008) *Governance for Sustainable Development: A Framework'*, Sustainable Development, John Wiley & Sons, Ltd., vol. Vol. 16, No. 6, pp. 410-421.

Rubin, H.J. Rubin, I.S. (2004) *Qualitative interviewing: The Art of Hearing Data'*, 2nd (Ed.), Thousand Oaks, CA. Sage Publications.

Rubinstein, R. (1990) The Environmental Representation of Personal Themes by Older People', *Journal of Aging Studies*, Vol. 4, No. 2, pp. 131–8.

Ruggeri, A., Dorussen, H., and Gizelis, T. (2017) *Winning the peace locally: U.N. peacekeeping and local conflict'*, International Organisation, Vol. 71, No, 1, pp. 163–185.

Russett, B.M., O'neal, J.R. and Cox, M. (2000) *Clash of Civilizations, or Realism and Liberalism Déjà Vu?* Some Evidence.

Ruzicka, J. and Wheeler, N.J. (2010) *The Puzzle of Trusting Relationships in the Nuclear Non-Proliferation Treaty'*, International Affairs, Vol. 86, No. 1, pp. 69-85.

Ryan, G. and Bernard, R. (2000) *Data Management and Analysis Methods'*, In: N. Denzin & Y. Lincoln (Eds.), Handbook of Qualitative Research (pp. 769–802). Thousand Oaks, CA: Sage.

Saferworld (2008) *Developing Integrated Approaches to Post-Conflict Security and Recovery: A Case Study of Integrated DDR in Sudan'*, London and Nairobi: Saferworld.

Saferworld, (2012) *Civilian disarmament in South Sudan: A Legacy of Struggle'*, http://www.saferworld. org.uk/downloads/pubdocs/South Sudan civilian disarmament.pdf.

Salant, P. and Dillman, D. A. (1994) *How to Conduct your own Survey'*, John Wiley & Sons, Inc.

Samatar, A. and Samatar, A.I. (1987) The Material Roots of the Suspended African State: Arguments from Somalia', *The Journal of Modern African Studies*, Vol. 25, No. 4, pp. 669-690.

Sambanis, N. (2000) *Partition as a Solution to Ethnic War: An Empirical Critique of the Theoretical Literature'*, World Politics, Vol. 52, pp. 437-483.

Sambanis, N. (2001) Do Ethnic and Non-ethnic Civil Wars have the same causes? A theoretical and Empirical Inquiry', *Journal of Conflict Resolution*, Vol. 45, No. 3, pp.259-282.

Sambanis, N. (2004) What is Civil War? Conceptual and Empirical Complexities of an Operational Definition', *Journal of Conflict Resolution*, Vol. 48, pp. 814-585.

Sandelowski, M. (1995) *Focus on Qualitative Methods: Sample Size in Qualitative Research'*, Research in Nursing and Health, Vol.18, pp.179-183.

Sanford, V. (2006) *The Moral Imagination of Survival: Displacement and Child Soldiers in Guatemala and Colombia'*, In: S. McEvoy-Levy (Ed.) Troublemakers or Peacemakers? Youth and Post Accord Peacebuilding, (pp. 49–80). Notre Dame, University of Notre Dame.

Sawant, A.B. (1998) *Ethnic Conflict in Sudan in Historical Perspective'*, International Studies, Vol. 35, No. 3. New Delhi: Sage Publications, pp. 343-363.

Schedler, A. (2001) *Measuring Democratic Consolidation'*, St Comp Int Dev, Vol.36, pp.66–92.

Schelling, T.C. (1960) *The Strategy of Conflict'*, Cambridge, MA: Harvard University Press. Schelling, T.C. (1966) Arms and Influence', New Haven, CT: Yale University Press.

Schermerhorn, R. A. (1970) *Comparative Ethnic Relations: A Framework for Theory'*, New York, Random House.

Scheurich, J.J and Delamont, K. B. (2005) *Foucault's Methodologies: Archaeology and Genealogy'*, In: N.K. Denzin & Y. S. Lincoln (Eds.), The Sage Handbook of Qualitative Research (3rd ed., pp. 841-868). Thousand Oaks: Sage Publications.

Scheurich, J.J. (1995) A Postmodernist Critique of Research Interviewing', *Qualitative Studies in Education*, Vol. 8, No.3, pp. 239–252.

Scheye, and Peake, G. (2005) To Arrest Insecurity: Time for a Revised SSR Agenda', *Conflict, Security and Development*, Vol. 5, No. 3, pp. 295-327.

Scheye, E. and McLean, A. (2006) *Enhancing the Delivery of Justice and Security in Fragile States'*, Organisation for Economic Cooperation and Development - Development Assistance Committee (OECD/DAC) Network on Conflict, Peace and Development Co-operation, Paris (CPDC).

Schilling, J. (2012) *Raiding Pastoral Livelihoods: Motives and Effects of Violent Conflict in North-Western Kenya'*, Pastoralism Res Policy Pract, Vol. 2, No. 25, pp.1-16.

Schirch, L. (2008) Strategic Peacebuilding- State of the Field', Peace Prints: *South Asian Journal of Peacebuilding'*, Vol. 1, No. 1, pp. 1-17.

Schlee, Y. and Watson, E. (2009) *Changing Identifications and Alliances in Northeast Africa'*, New York: Berghahn.

Schmeidl, S. (2009) *Prêt-a-Porter States: How the McDonaldization of State-Building Misses the Mark in Afghanistan'*, http://www.berghofhandbook. [Accessed: 23/11/2017].

Schomerus, M. (2008a) *Perilous border: Sudanese communities affected by conflict on the Sudan/Uganda border'*, London: Conciliation Resources.

Schomerus, M. (2008b) *Violent Legacies: Insecurity in Sudan's Central and Eastern Equatoria'*, Working Paper 13. Human Security Baseline Assessment. Geneva: The Small Arms Survey.

Schomerus, M. and Allen, T. (2010) *Southern Sudan at Odds with itself: Dynamics of Conflict and Predicaments of Peace'*, Development Studies Institute, LSE. London.

Schroeder, M., and Lamb, G. (2018) The Illicit Arms Trade in Africa: A Global Enterprise', *Small arms proliferation and control in Southern Africa.* https://www.researchgate.net/publication/326462123_The_Illicit_Arms_Trade_in_Africa_A_Global_Enterprise [Accessed: 08/05/2019].

Schultz, A. l. (1967) *The Phenomenology of the Social World*', Evanston, IL: North-Western University Press.

Scott, G. (2002) Recruitment and Allegiance: The Micro-foundations of Rebellion', *Journal of Conflict Resolution*, Vol 26, pp. 111-30.

Scott, J. (1990) *A Matter of Record: Documentary Sources in Social Research*', Cambridge: Polity Press.

Scroggins, D. (2002) *Emma's War*', New York: Pantheon Security Responses in Jonglei State, (Final).pdf.

Sedra, M. (2006) *SSR in Afghanistan: The Slide towards Expediency*', International Peacekeeping, Vol. 13, No. 1, pp. 94–110.

Sedra, M. (2013) *The Hollowing-out of the Liberal Peace Project in Afghanistan: The Case of SSR*', Central Asian Survey, Vol. 32, No. 3, pp. 371–387.

Sedra, M. (2018) Adapting SSR to Ground-Level Realities: The Transition to a Second-Generation Model', *Journal of Intervention and Statebuilding*, Vol. 12, No. 1, pp. 48-63.

Segovia, A. (2009) *Transitional Justice and DDR: The Case of El Salvador*', New York: ICTJ.

Sekaran, U. (1992) *Research Methods for Business: A Skills-Building Approach*', New York: Wiley and Sons.

Selby, J. (2007) *The Political Economy of the Israeli-Palestinian and Indo-Pak Peace Processes: Full Research Report'*, ESRC End of Award Report, RES-228-25-0010. Swindon: ESRC.

Senehi, J. (2009) *The Role of Constructive, Transcultural Storytelling in Ethno-political Conflict Transformation in Northern Ireland'*, In Carter Judy, I. George, V. Vamik. (Ed)., Regional and Ethnic Conflicts: Perspectives from the Front Lines. New Jersey: Pearson.

Senehi, J., Flaherty, M., Sanjana, C., Kirupakaran, L.K., Matenge, M. and Skarlato, O.

Senghaas, D. (2002) *The Clash within Civilisations: Coming to terms with Cultural Conflicts'*, 1st English (Ed.), Routledge, New York.

Sesay, A., Ukeje, C. and Gbla, O. (2009) *Post-War Regimes and State Reconstruction in Liberia and Sierra Leone'*, Dakar, Council for the Development of Social Science Research in Africa.

Shapcott, R. (2004) IR as Practical Philosophy: Defining a 'Classical Approach', *The British Journal of Politics and International Relations*, Vol. 6, No. 3, pp. 271–291.

Sharkey, H. (2008) *Arab Identity and Ideology in Sudan: The Politics of Language, Ethnicity, and Race'*, African Affairs, Vol. 107, pp. 21-43.

Shaw, T.M. and Mbabazi, P. (2007) *Two Uganda's and a Liberal Peace? Lessons from Uganda about Conflict and Development at the Start of a New Century'*, Global Society, Vol. 24, No. 4, pp.567-78.

Shinn D.H. (2004) *Addis Ababa Agreement: Was it destined to Fail and are there Lessons for the Current Sudan Peace Process*? Annales d'Ethiopie, Vol. 20, pp. 239-259.

Siebert, H. (2014) *National dialogue and legitimate change', Legitimacy and Peace Processes: from Coercion to Consent'*, Accord//ISSUE 25//www.c-r.org Conciliation Resources Burghley Yard, London.

Simangan, D. (2017) *The Limits of Liberal Peacebuilding and Pitfalls of Local Involvement Cambodia, Kosovo, and Timor-Leste in retrospect'*, PhD Thesis. The Australian National University, Canberra, Australia.

Simmons, M. and Dixon, P., eds. (2006) *Peace by piece: Addressing Sudan's Conflicts'*, London: Conciliation Resources.

Singh, G. (2000) *Ethnic Conflict in India'*, New York: St Martin's Press.

Sisk, T.D. (1996) *Power-Sharing and International Mediation in Ethnic Conflict'*, Perspective Series, United States Institute of Peace, Washington DC.

Sisk, T.D. (2002) *Spiritual Intelligence: The Tenth Intelligence that Integrates all other Intelligence'*, Gifted Education International, Vol. 16, No. 3, pp. 208–213.

Skocpol, T. (1979) *States and Social Revolutions'*, Cambridge, MA: Cambridge University Press.

Small Arms Survey (2006–2007) *Anatomy of civilian disarmament in Jonglei state: Recent experiences and implications'*, Sudan Issue Brief Number 3 (2nd Ed.) Human Security Baseline Assessment.

http://www.smallarmssurveysudan.org/fileadmin/docs/issue-briefs/HSBA-IB-03-Jonglei.pdf. [Accessed 20/08/2017].

Small Arms Survey (2011) *Failures and Opportunities, Rethinking DDR in South Sudan'*, HSBA Issue Brief No 17, Small Arms Survey, Geneva.

Small Arms Survey (2012a) *Reaching for the Gun: Arms Flows and Holdings in South Sudan'*, HSBA Issue Brief No 19. Small Arms Survey, Geneva.

Small Arms Survey, (2012b) *My neighbour, my enemy', Inter-tribal violence in Jonglei'*, HSBA Issue Brief No 21. Small Arms Survey, Geneva.

Smith, A.D. (1988) *Ethnic Origins of Nations'*, London, UK: Blackwell.

Smith, A.D. (1983) *Theories of Nationalism'*, London.

Smith, A.D. (1998) *Nationalism and Modernism'*, London: Routledge

Smith, A.D. (2004) *Towards a Strategic Framework for Peacebuilding: Getting their Act Together'*, the Royal Norwegian Ministry of Foreign Affairs.

Smith, M.G. (1986) *Pluralism, Race and Ethnicity in Selected African Countries'*, In J. Rex and D. Mason (Eds.), Theories of Race and Ethnic Relations Cambridge: Cambridge University Press.

Smith, T.L. (1999) *Decolonizing Methodologies: Research and Indigenous Peoples'*, London, New York, Dunedin: Zed Books and University of Otago Press

Snow, D.M. (1996) *Uncivil Wars: International Security and the New Internal Conflicts'*, London: Lynne Rienner Publishers, Inc.

Snowden, J. (2012) *Work in Progress: Security Force Development in South Sudan through February 2012*', HSBA Working Paper, No. 27. Small Arms Survey, Geneva.

Solomon, C., Ginifer, J. (2008) *Disarmament, Demobilisation and Reintegration in Sierra Leone –Case Study*', Centre for International Cooperation and Security, University of Bradford.

Sørbø, G.M. (2010) Local Violence and International Intervention in Sudan', *Review of African Political Economy*, Vol. 37, No. 124, pp. 173–186.

South, A. (2018) Hybrid Governance and the Politics of Legitimacy in the Myanmar Peace Process', *Journal of Contemporary Asia*, Vol. 48, No. 1, pp. 50-66.

Spear, J. (1996) *Arms Limitations, Confidence-Building Measures, and Internal Conflict*', In: M.E. Brown (Ed.), The International Dimensions of Internal Conflict, CSIA Studies in International Security Cambridge, Mass.: The MIT Press.

Spear, J. (2002) *Disarmament and Demobilisation*', In: S.J Stedman *et al.* (Ed.), Ending Civil Wars: The implementation of peace agreements (pp. 141-82). Boulder, CO: Lynne Rienner.

Spikes, D. (1993) *Angola and the Politics of Intervention: From Local Bush War to Chronic Crisis in Southern Africa*', McFarland & Co. Publishers, Jefferson, N.C. and London.

SPLM/A News Agency, (2002) *Government Forces Evacuate Torit*, http://www.Sudan Net/news/press/postedr/176.Shtml [Accessed 21/12/2016].

SSDDRC and UNDP (2006) *Jonglei Community Security and Arms Control (CSAC)*', Program Initial Emergency Phase.

Stahl, I. (1972) *Bargaining Theory: Computer Programs*', The Economic Research Institute, Stockholm. Sweden.

Stake, R. (1978) *The Case study Method in Social Inquiry*', Educational Researcher, Vol. 7, No. 2, pp. 5-8.

Stake, R. (1995) *The Art of Case Study Research*', Thousand Oaks, CA: Sage.

Stake, R. (1998) *Case studies'*, In: Denzin N. K, Lincoln Y. S. Strategies of Qualitative Inquiry, (pp. 86–109). Thousand Oaks, CA: Sage.

Stedman, S. (1991) *Peacemaking in Civil War: International Mediation in Zimbabwe*', 1974-1980. Boulder: Lynne Rienner.

Stedman, S. (1997) *Spoiler Problems in Peace Processes*', International Security, Vol 22, No. 2, pp. 5-53.

Stedman, S. (2001) *Implementing Peace Agreements in Civil Wars: Lessons and Recommendations for Policymakers*', International Peace Academy (IPA) Policy Paper Series on Peace Implementation, New York: Centre for International Security and Cooperation.

Stedman, S. (2001) *International Implementation of Peace Agreements in Civil Wars*', In Turbulent Peace, Washington DC U.S.: U.S. Institute of Peace.

Steenkamp, C. (2011) In the Shadows of War and Peace: Making Sense of Violence after Peace Accords', *Conflict, Security and Development*, Vol. 11, No. 3, pp. 357–383.

Stewart, F. Brown, G. and Mancini, L. (2005) *Why Horizontal Inequalities Matter: Some Implications for Measurement*', Crise Working Paper No. 19, Oxford: Centre for Research on Inequality, Human Security and Ethnicity.

Stewart, F. (2000) *Crisis Prevention: Tackling Horizontal Inequalities*', Oxford Development Studies, Vol 28, No 3, pp.245-262.

Stewart, F. (2003) Conflict and the Millennium Development Goals', *Journal of Human Development*, Vol 4, No 3, pp. 325-352.

Stewart, F. (2004) *Social Exclusion and Conflict: Analysis and Policy Implications*', Report prepared for the UK Department for International Development, London

Stewart, F. (2004) *The relationship between Horizontal Inequalities, Vertical Inequality and Social Exclusion*', Crise Newsletter, Winter.

Stewart, F. (2008) *Horizontal Inequalities and Conflict: Explaining Group Violence in Multiethnic Societies*', Basingstoke: Palgrave Macmillan.

Stewart, F. (2011) *Horizontal Inequalities as a Cause of Conflict*', World Development Report Background Paper, a Review of Crise Findings.

Stockholm Initiative on (SIDDR) (2006) *Final Report*', Ministry for Foreign Affairs, Sweden.

Stone, L. (2011) *Rethinking DDR in Post-Independence Sudan*', the SAS report, Global Policy Forum, https://www.globalpolicy.org/security-council/index-of-countries-on-the-security-council-agenda/sudan/50424-rethinking-ddr-in-post-independence-sudan.html [Accessed: 24/05/2017].

Strauss, A. and Corbin, J.M. (1990) *Basics of qualitative research: Grounded Theory Procedures and Techniques*', Sage Publications, Inc.

Stringer, E.T. (1999) Action research', 2nd (Ed.), Thousand Oaks, CA: Sage.

Stringham, N. and Forney, J. (2017) It Takes a Village to Raise a Militia: Local Politics, the Nuer White Army, and South Sudan's Civil Wars', *The Journal of Modern African Studies*, Vol 55, No. 2, pp. 177-199.

Stubbs, J.M. (1934) *Notes on Beliefs and Customs of the Malwal Dinka of Bahr el Ghazal Province*', Sudan Notes Rec, Vol. 17, pp. 243-54.

Stubbs, J.M. Morison, C.G. (1938) *The Western Dinkas, their Land and their Agriculture*', Sudan Notes Rec, Vol. 21, pp. 251-65.

Suchman, M. (1995). Managing Legitimacy: Strategic and Institutional Approaches', The *Academy of Management Review*, Vol. 20, No. 3, pp. 571-610.

Sudan Human Security Baseline Assessment (HSBA) (2012) *Small Arms Survey'*, No. 47 Avenue Blanc, Geneva, Switzerland http://www.smallarmssurveysudan.org.

Sudman, S. (1985) *Efficient Screening Methods for the Sampling of Geographically Clustered Special Populations'*, Marketing Res. Vol. 22, pp. 20-29.

Suleiman, M. A. (2011) *Britain Looking into Debt Relief for Sudan: Envoy'*, Sudan Tribune: Plural news and Views on Sudan, http://www.sudantribune.com/Britain-looking-into-debt-relief,37988. [Accessed 19/02/2016].

Suri, H. (2011) *Purposeful Sampling in Qualitative Research Syntheses'*, Qualitative Research Journal, Vol.1. No.2, pp. 63-75.

Swarbrick, P. (2007) *Avoiding Disarmament Failure: The Critical Link in DDR; An Operational Manual for Donors, Managers, and Practitioners'*, Geneva: Small Arms Survey, http://www.smallarmssurvey.org.[Accessed: 27/08/2018].

Swift, J.J. (1996) *Desertification: Narratives, Winners and Losers'*, In: Leach M. and Mearns, R. (Eds.), the lie of the Land, Oxford: James Currey publishers.

Sylvester, A. (1977) *Sudan Under Nimeiri'*, London: Bodley Head.

Tadjbakhsh, S. (2011) *Rethinking the Liberal Peace: External Models and local alternatives'*, Routledge Cass Series on Peacekeeping, Routledge, Milton Park, UK.

Tarimo, A. (2010) Politicisation of Ethnic Identities: The Case of Contemporary Africa', *Journal of Asian and African Studies*, Vol. 45, No. 3, pp. 297–308.

Tasić, S. and Feruh, M (2012) Errors and Issues in Secondary Data Used in Market Research Data, socioeconomic', *The Scientific Journal for Theory and Practice of Socioeconomic Development*, Vol. 1, No. 2, pp. 326-335.

Tatiana, C. and Pangburn, A. (2018) *What Works in Security Interventions: Rethinking DDR in Today's Violent Conflicts'*, Peace and Security, https://blogs.lse.ac.uk/crp/2018/10/03/what-works-in-security-interventions-rethinking-ddr-in-todays-violent-conflicts/[Accessed: 08/04/2020].

Taylor, I. (2007) *What fit the liberal peace in Africa*? Global Society, Vol. 21, No. 4, pp. 553-566.

Tellis, W. (1997) *Introduction to Case Study'*, The Qualitative Report, Vol. 3, No. 2. pp. 1-14.

Temitope, O. (2014) Ethnic Conflict and African Women's Capacity for Preventive Diplomacy', *International Research Journal*, Global Journals Inc. pp. Vol. 1, 4 Issue, 2. pp. 61-66.

Terpstra, N. and Frerks, G. (2017) *Rebel Governance and Legitimacy: Understanding the Impact of Rebel Legitimation on Civilian Compliance with the LTTE Rule'*, Civil Wars, Vol. 19, No. 3, pp. 279-307.

Thakur, S. and Venugopal, R. (2018) *Parallel Governance and Political order in Contested Territory: Evidence from the Indo-Naga Ceasefire'*, Asian Security, Vol. 15, No. 3, 285-303.

The Comprehensive Peace Agreement between the Government of the Republic of Sudan and the Sudan People's Liberation Movement/Sudan People's Liberation Army', January 2005. Available at: http://www.sd.undp.org/doc/CPA.pdf.[Accessed: 02/10 2016].

The CPA Monitor-Monthly Report on the Implementation of the CPA', UNMIS, https://unmis.unmissions.org/sites/default/files/CPA%20Monitor%20December%202009.pdf[Accessed on 20/12/2017].

The CPA Monitor-Monthly report on the Implementation of the CPA', UNMIS, December 2010. https://unmis.unmissions.org/sites/default/files/CPA%20Monitor%20December%202009.pdf[Accessed on 20/12/2017].

The Department for International Development (DFID) (2004) Non-State Justice and security system. London.

The Government of the Republic of South Sudan (2011b) South Sudan', Available at: http://geography.about.com/gi/o.htm?zi=1/XJ&zTi=1&sdn=geography&cdn=education&tm=184&gps=326_6_1366_618&f=00&su=p284.13.342.ip_&tt=2&bt=0&bts=0&zu=http%3A//www.goss.org/[Accessed: /10/16/2016].

The United Nations (2000) *Report of the Panel of Experts on Violations of the Security Council Sanctions against UNITA'*, U.N. Document S/2000/203.

The United Nations (2000) *The Role of United Nations Peacekeeping in Disarmament, Demobilisation, and Reintegration*', Report of the Secretary-General.

The World Bank (2017) World Bank Annual Report', Washington, DC: World Bank Group. http://documents.worldbank.org/curated/en/143021506909711004/pdf/119779-BR-REPLACE-ON-FRINDAY-OUO-9-SecM2017-0254-1-World-Bank-Annual-Report-2017-Rev-09292017.pdf. [Accessed: 17/09/2019].

The World Bank. (1993) *Demobilisation and Reintegration of Military Personnel in Africa: The Evidence from Seven Country Case Studies*', Discussion Paper: Africa Regional Series. Washington, DC: The World Bank.

Themnér, A. and Ohlson, T. (2014) *Legitimate Peace in Post-civil War States: Towards Attaining the Unattainable, Conflict, Security AND Development*', Vol.14, No. 1, pp. 61-87.

Thomas, E. (2015) *South Sudan: A Slow Liberation*', London: Zed Books.

Thompson, J.B. (2012) *Rethinking the Clinical vs. Social Reform Debate: A Dialectical Approach to Defining Social Work in the 21st Century*', PhD Dissertation, University of Kansas, Lawrence, KS, USA.

Thorne, S. (2000) *Data Analysis in Qualitative Research Evidence-Based Nurse*', Vol. 3, Issue, 3, pp. 68-70.

Tilly, C. (1969) *Collective Violence in European Perspective*', In: Violence in America, H. O. Graham and T. R. Gurr (Eds.), (pp. 4-45). New York: Bantam.

Tilly, C. (1975) *The Formation of National States in Western Europe*', Princeton University Press, Princeton, NJ.

Tilly, C. (1990) *Coercion, Capital, and European States, A.D. 990–1992*', Cambridge, MA: Wiley-Blackwell.

Tilly, C. (1990) *Coercion, Capital, and European States, AD 990-1990*', Studies in Social Discontinuity, Basil Blackwell, Inc. 3 Cambridge Centre, Cambridge, Massachusetts, USA.

Timonen, V., Foley, G. and Conlon, C. (2018) *Challenges When Using Grounded Theory: A Pragmatic Introduction to Doing GT Research*', International Journal of Qualitative Methods.

Titeca, K. and De Herdt, T. (2011) *Real Governance Beyond the Failed State: Negotiating Education in the Democratic Republic of the Congo*', African Affairs, Vol. 10, No. 439, pp. 213–31.

Toft, M. (2003) *The Geography of Ethnic Violence: Identity, Interests, and the Indivisibility of Territory*', Princeton University Press.

Toft, M. (2007) *Getting Religion? The Puzzling Case of Islam and Civil War*', International Security, Vol.31, No 4, pp.97-131.

Toft, M. (2010) *Securing the Peace: The Durable Settlement of Civil Wars*', Princeton NJ: Princeton University Press.

Toki, M. (2004) *Peace-building and the Process of Disarmament, Demobilisation, and Reintegration: the Experiences of Mozambique and Sierra Leone*', Institute for International Cooperation. Japan: Japan International Cooperation Agency, IIC/JR 03-64.

Torjesen, S. (2006) *The Political Economy of Disarmament, Demobilisation and Reintegration (DDR): Selective Literature Review and Preliminary Agenda for Research*', Paper No. 709. Oslo: Norwegian Institute of International Affairs.

Torjesen, S. (2013) Towards a Theory of Ex-Combatant Reintegration', *International Journal of Security and Development*, Vol. 2, No. 3, pp. 1-13.

Torjesen, S. and MacFarlane, S. Neil. (2007) *R before D: The Case of Post-Conflict Reintegration in Tajikistan*', Conflict, Security and Development, Vol 7, No 2, pp. 311–332.

Touray, O. (2005) *The Common African Defence and Security Policy*', African Affairs, Vol. 104, No. 417, pp. 635-656.

Tschirgi, N. (2004) *Political Economy of Armed Conflicts and Peacebuilding*', Conflict, Security and Development, Vol. 4, No. 3, pp. 377-382.

Tsebelis, G. (2000) Veto Players and Institutional Analysis', Governance: *An International Journal of Policy and Administration*, Vol. 13, No. 4, pp. 441-474.

Tsebelis, G. (2002) *Veto Players: How Political Institutions Work*', Princeton, NJ: Princeton University Press.

Turse, N. (2016) New Nation, Long War: In South Sudan, It's Hard to Tell the Soldiers from the Criminals', https://theintercept.com/2016/06/16/in-south-sudan-its-hard-to-tell-the-soldiers-from-the-criminals/[Accessed: on 13/03/2017].

Turyamureeba, R. (2014) *The CPA-DDR Program in South Sudan: What went wrong?* ALC Research Report, No. 7, pp. 1-29.

United Nations Department of Peacekeeping Operations (UNDPO) (2010) *DDR in Action: the Democratic Republic of the Congo*', DDR in peace operations – a retrospective, United States: United Nations.

UNMIS (2006) *United Nations Mission in Sudan, CPA Monitor: Monthly Report on the implementation of the CPA*', December 2006, http://www.unmis.org.

UNSG, (2012a) *Report of the Secretary-General on South Sudan*', UN Doc. S/2012/486, 26 June.

UNSG, (2012b) *Report of the Secretary-General on South Sudan*', UN Doc. S/2012/820, 8 November.

UNSG, (2013) *Report of the Secretary-General on South Sudan*', UN Doc. S/2013/140, 12 March.

Vale, R. J. (2011) *Is the Sudan Conflict best Understood in terms of Race, Religion, or Regionalism? Katholieke Universiteit Leuven*', https://www.e-ir.info/pdf/8854 [Accessed: 25/1/2017].

Vallings, C, Moreno-Torres, M. (2005) *Drivers of Fragility: What Makes States Fragile?* PRDE Working Paper 7. London: Department for International Development, pp. 1–31.

Van Evera, S. (1994) *Hypotheses on Nationalism and War'*, International Security, Vol. 18, No. 4, pp.5-39.

Van Evera, S. (2001) *Primordialism Lives!; APSA-CP: Newsletter of the Organised Section in Comparative Politics of the American Political Science Association'*, Vol. 12, No. 1, pp. 20-22.

Vangen, S and Huxham, C. (2003) Nurturing Collaborative Relations: Building trust in inter-organisational collaboration', *The Journal of Applied Behavioural Science*, Vol. 39, No. 1, pp. 5–31.

Varese, F. (2010) *General Introduction', what is Organised Crime?* In: Varese F (Ed.) Organised Crime, Vol. 1. London and New York: Routledge.

Vinck, P., Pham, P.N and Kreutzer, T. (2011) *Talking Peace: A population-based Survey on Attitudes about Security, Dispute Resolution, and Post-conflict Reconstruction in Liberia'*, Berkeley, CA: Human Rights Centre, University of California, Berkeley.

Vlassenroot, K. (2016) *The Challenges of Multi-Layered Security Governance in Ituri'*, JSRP Policy Brief 3: http://www.lse.ac.uk/internationalDevelopment/research/JSRP/downloads/JSRP-Brief-3.pdf.

Wa Thiong'o, N. (1986) *Decolonising the Mind Delhi'*, Worldview Publication.

Waever, Ole. (1998) *Securitisation and Desecuritisation*', On Security, (Ed.), Ronnie D. Lipschutz. New York: Columbia University Press.

Wagner, R.H. (1993) *The Causes of Peace. In: Roy Licklider, Stopping the Killing: How Civil Wars End*', (Eds.), (pp. 235-268). New York: New York University Press.

Wai, O.M. (1981) *The African-Arab Conflict in the Sudan*', New York: Africana Publishing Company.

Waihenya, W. (2006) *The Mediator: Gen. Lazaro Sumbeiywo and the Southern Sudan peace Processes*', Nairobi: Kenway Publications.

Wakoson, E.N. (1984) *The Origin and Development of the Anya-Nya movement, 1955–1972*', In: Beshir, M.O. (Ed.), Southern Sudan: Regionalism and Nationalism, Khartoum.

Wakoson, E.N. (1993) *The Politics of Southern Self-Government 1972-83*', in M. W. Daly & Ahman Alawad Sikainga, (Eds), Civil War in the Sudan', London: British Academic Press, pp. 27-50.

Wallenstein, I. (1980) *The Modern World-System II: Mercantilism and the Consolidation of the European World-Economy, 1600-1750*', San Diego, CA: Academic Press.

Wallis, J. (2017) *Is Good Enough Peacebuilding Good Enough? The potential and pitfalls of the Local Turn in Peacebuilding in Timor-Leste*', The Pacific Review, Vol. 30, No. 2, pp. 251-269.

Walsham, G. (1993) *Interpreting Information Systems in Organisations*', John Wiley & Sons, Inc. New York, United States.

Walsham, G. (1995) Interpretive Case Studies in is Research: Nature and Method', *European Journal of Information Systems*, Vol. 4, No. 2, pp. 74–81.

Walter, B. (1995) *Designing Transitions from Civil War: Demobilisation, Democratisation, and Commitments to Peace'*, International Security, Vol 24, No. 1, pp. 127.

Walter, B. (1997) *The Critical Barrier to Civil War Settlement'*, International Organisation, Vol 51, No. 3, pp. 335-364.

Walter, B. (2002) *Committing to Peace: The Successful Settlement of Civil Wars'*, Princeton, NJ: Princeton University Press.

Warner, L.A. (2016) The Disintegration of the Military Integration Process in South Sudan (2006–2013) Stability', *International Journal of Security & Development*, Vol. 5, No. 1, pp. 1–20.

Wassara, S. (2002) Conflict and State Security in the Horn of Africa: Militarisation of Civilian Groups', *African Journal of Political Science*, Vol 7 No. 2. pp. 39-60.

Wassara, S. (2007) *Traditional Mechanisms of Conflict Resolution in Southern Sudan'*, Berghof Foundation for Peace Support, Berlin-Germany.

Wassara, S. (2015) South Sudan: State Sovereignty Challenged at Infancy', *Journal of Eastern African Studies*, Vol. 9, No. 4, pp. 634-649.

Wassara, S. and Kurimoto, E. (2017) Negotiating statehood: Handling crisis of South Sudan. In: Gebre, Yntiso, Itaru Ohta and Motoji

Matsuda, (Eds.), *African Virtues in the Pursuit of Conviviality: Exploring Local Solutions in Light of Global Prescriptions'*, Bamenda, Langaa.

Webb, K. (1995) *An Introduction to Problems in the Philosophy of Social Sciences'*, New York, A Cassell Imprint, New York.

Weber, M. (1946) *Politics as a Vocation'*, In: From Max Weber: Essays in Sociology, translated by H. H. Gerth and C. Wright Mills, Oxford University Press.

Weber, M. (1978) *Ethnic Groups'*, In: G. Roth, & C. Wittich, (Ed.), Economy and Society, Vol. 1, (pp. 389-95). Berkeley: University of California Press.

Weber, M. (1979) *Economy and Society: An Outline of Interpretive Sociology'*, (Eds.), Wittich, C. and Roth, G. Berkeley: University of California Press.

Webster, M. (1985) *Webster`s Ninth new Collegiate Dictionary*. Meriam - Webster Inc.

Weinstein, J.M. (2005) Resources and the Information Problem in Rebel Recruitment', *Journal of Conflict Resolution*, Vol. 49, pp. 598–624.

Wendt, A. (1992) *Anarchy is What States Makes of It'*, International Organisation, Vol. 46, No. 2, pp. 391–425.

Wendt, A. (1994) Collective Identity Formation and the International State', *American Political Science Review*, Vol. 88, No. 2, pp. 384-396.

Wennmann, A. (2009) *Getting Armed Groups to the Table: Peace Processes, the Political Economy of Conflict and the Mediated State'*, Third World Quarterly, Vol. 30, No. 6, pp. 1123–38.

Wesley, M. (2008) *The State of the Art on the Art of State Building'*, Global Governance, No.14: pp. 369-385.

Wheeler, N.J. (2012) Trust-Building in International Relations', Peace Prints, *South Asian Journal of Peacebuilding*, Vol. 4, No. 2, pp. 1-13.

Wickham, M. and Woods, M. (2005) *Reflecting on the strategic use of CAQDAS to manage and report on the qualitative research process'*, The Qualitative Report, Vol. 10, No. 4, pp.687-702.

Wight, P. (2017) South Sudan and the Four Dimensions of Power-Sharing: Political, Territorial, Military, and Economic', *African Conflict and Peacebuilding Review*, Vol. 7, No. 2, 1-35.

Wild, H., Jok, J.M. and Patel, R. (2018) The militarisation of Cattle Raiding in South Sudan: How a Traditional Practice became a tool for political violence', *International Journal Humanitarian Action*, Vol 3, No. 2, pp.1-11.

Wilkof, M.V., Brown, D.W., and Selsky, J.W. (1995) When the Stories are Different: The Influence of Corporate Culture Mismatches on Inter-organisational Relations', *The Journal of Applied Behavioural Science*, Vol. 31, No. 3, pp. 373–388.

Willems, R. Kleingeld, J., and van Leeuwen, M. (2010) *Connecting Community Security and DDR: Experiences from Burundi'*, The Hague:

Working Group on Community Security and Community-based DDR in Fragile States, Peace, Security and Development network.

Willems, R., Kleingeld, J., and Rouw, H. (2009) *Security Promotion in Fragile States: Can Local Meet National*, The Hague: Working Group on Community Security and Community-based DDR in Fragile States, Peace, Security and Development Network.

Williams, G. (1984) *The Genesis of Chronic Illness: Narrative Reconstruction*', Sociology of Health and Illness, Vol. 6, No. 2, pp. 175–200.

Williams, P. (2004) *Peace Operations and the International Financial Institutions: Insights from Rwanda and Sierra Leone,*' International Peacekeeping, Vol. 11, No. 1, pp.103-23.

Williamson, O.J. (2000) The new institutional economics: Taking stock, looking ahead', *Journal of Economic Literature*, Vol. 38, pp.595-613.

Williamson, O.J. (2006) *The disarmament, demobilisation and reintegration of child soldiers: Social and Psychological Transformation in Sierra Leone*', Intervention, Vol. 4, No. 3, pp. 185–205.

Willis, J., Battahani, A., and Woodward, P. (2009) *Elections in Sudan: Learning from Experience*', Rift Valley Institute, Commissioned by the UK Department for International Development (DFID) https://riftvalley.net/sites/default/files/publicationdocuments/RVI%20Elections%20in%20Sudan_0.pdf.[Accessed: 25/08/2018].

Wilson, J.Q. (1989) *Bureaucracy: What Government Agencies do and why they do it*', New York, N.Y.: Basic Books.

Wolff, S. (2004) *The Institutional Structure of Regional Consociations in Brussels, Northern Ireland, and South Tyrol'*, Nationalism and Ethnic Politics, Vol.10, No.3, pp. 387-414.

Wolff, S. (2006) *Ethnic Conflict: A Global Perspective'*, Oxford University Press.

Wolff, S. (2007) Conflict resolution between power-sharing and power dividing, or beyond?' Political Studies Review, Vol. 5, No. 3, pp. 363-79.

Wolfsfeld, G. (2004) *Media and the Path to Peace'*, New York: Cambridge University Press.

Wondu, S. and Lesch, A. (1999) *Battle for peace in Sudan: an analysis of the Abuja conferences 1992–1993'*, Lanham, MD: University Press of America.

Wood, E.J. (2008) The Social Processes of Civil War: The Wartime Transformation of Social Networks', *Annual Review of Political Science*, Vol.11, No.1, pp. 539-561.

Woodward, P. (1990) *Sudan 1898-/989: The Unstable State'*, Boulder: Lynne Rienner Publishers.

Woodward, P. (1995) *Balkan Tragedy: Chaos and Dissolution after the Cold War'*, Washington, DC: Brookings Institution.

Woolcock, M. (1998) *Social Capital and Economic Development: Towards a Theoretical Synthesis and Policy Framework'*, Theory and Society, Vol. 27, No. 2, pp. 151-208.

World Bank, (2006) *World Development Indicators'*, World Bank, Washington DC.

Yamokoski, A. and Dubrow, J. (2008) *How Do Elites Define Influence? Personality and Respect as Sources of Social Power'*, Sociological Focus, Vol. 41. pp. 319-336.

Yang, P. (2000) *Ethnic Studies: Issues and Approaches'*, New York: State University of New York Press.

Yeros, P. (1999) *Ethnicity and Nationalism in Africa: Constructivist Reflections and Contemporary Politics'*, Basingstoke: Macmillan Press.

Yiftachel, O. (1992) *The State, Ethnic Relations and Democratic Stability: Lebanon, Cyprus and Israel'*, Geo Journal, Vol. 28, pp. 319–332.

Yin, R. (1984) *Case Study Research: Design and Methods'*, Newbury Park, CA: Sage.

Yin, R. (1994) *Case Study Research: Design and Methods*, London: Sage.

Yin, R. (2003) *Case study Research: Design and Methods'*, 3rd (Ed.), Thousand Oaks, CA: Sage.

Ylonen, A. (2012) *Limit of Peace through Statebuilding' in Southern Sudan: Challenges to State Legitimacy, Governance and Economic Development during the CPA Implementation, 2005-2011'*, Journal of Conflictology, Vol. 3, No. 2, pp. 28–40.

Ylonen, A. (2005) *Grievances and the Roots of Insurgencies: Southern Sudan and Darfur'*, Peace, Conflict and Development: An Interdisciplinary Journal, Vol.7 http://www.peacestudiesjournal.org [Accessed: 11/07/2018].

Yokwe, E. M. (1997) *Conflict Resolution in the Sudan: A Case Study of Intolerance in Contemporary African Societies'*, Africa Media Review, Vol. 11, No.3, pp. 80-103.

Young, C. (1976) *The Politics of Cultural Pluralism'*, Madison: University of Wisconsin Press.

Young, C. (1986) *Nationalism, Ethnicity, and Class in Africa'*, A retrospective, Cahiers d'Études Africaines, pp. 421–495.

Young, C. and Turner, T. (1985) *The Rise and Decline of the Zairian State'*, Madison: The University of Wisconsin Press.

Young, J. (2003) *Sudan Liberation Movements, Regional Armies, Ethnic Militias and Peace'*, Review of African Political Economy, No. 97, 423–434.

Young, J. (2005) John Garang's Legacy to the Peace Process, the SPLM/A & the South', *Review of African Political Economy*, No.106: pp. 535-548.

Young, J. (2006) The SSDF in the Wake of the Juba Declaration', HSBA Working Paper, No. 1, Small Arms Survey, Geneva.

Young, J. (2007) *Sudan IGAD Peace Process: an Evaluation'*, [online]. Sudan Tribune, http://www.sudantribune.com/IMG/pdf/Igad_in_Sudan_Peace_Pr ocess.pdf[Accessed: 9/02/2018].

Young, J. (2007) *Sudan People's Liberation Army: Disarmament in Jonglei and its Implications'*, Institute for Security Studies, Occasional Paper 137

Young, J. (2012) *The Fate of Sudan: The Origins and Consequences of a Flawed Peace Process*', Zed Books, London.

Yuar, A. (2014) *The polarised political dimensions in South Sudan's Conflict*', Sudan Tribune, online: www.sudantribune.com/spip.php?rubrique12 [Accessed 08/07/2016].

Yuval, D. (2003) *Belonging: from the Indigene to the Diasporic,*' In: U. Ozkirinli (ed.), Nationalism and Its Futures. Basingstoke: Palgrave Macmillan.

Zachariah, A.B and Mampilly, C. (2005) Winning the War, but Losing the Peace? The Dilemma of SPLM/A Civil Administration and the Tasks Ahead', *The Journal of Modern African Studies*, Vol. 43, No. 1, pp. 1-20.

Zambakari, C. (2013) South Sudan and the Nation-building Project: Lessons and Challenges', *International Journal of African Renaissance Studies*' Vol. 8, No. 1, pp.5-29.

Zambakari, C. (2015) *Sudan and South Sudan: Identity, Citizenship, and Democracy in Plural Societies, Citizenship Studies*', Vol. 19, No. 1, pp. 69-82.

Zambakari, C. (2016) The misguided and mismanaged intervention in Libya: Consequences for peace', *African Security Review*, Vol. 25, No. 1, pp.44-62.

Žarkov, D. (2008) *Gender, Violent Conflict and Development*', New Delhi: Zubaan (Imprint of Kali for Women).

Zartman, I.W. (1993) *The Unfinished Agenda: Negotiating Internal Conflicts*', in Stopping the Killing: How Civil Wars End, pp. 20–35.

Zartman, I.W. (1995) *Collapsed States: The Disintegration and Restoration of Legitimate Authority*', Boulder, CO: Lynne Rienner Publishers.

Zartman, I.W. (2003) *The Timing of Peace Initiatives: Hurting Stalemates and Ripe Moments. In Contemporary Peacemaking*', Springer pp. 19–29.

Zartman, J. (2008) *Negotiation, exclusion and durable peace: dialogue and peacebuilding in Tajikistan*', International Negotiation, Vol. 13, No. 1, pp. 55-72.

Zartman, W. and Touval, S. (1996) *International Mediation in the Post-Cold War Era*', In: Chester Crocker, Fen Hampson and Pamela Aall, (Ed.), Managing Global Chaos, (pp. 445-461). Washington, DC: United States Institute of Peace Press.

Zaum, D. (2012) *Review essay: Beyond the 'liberal peace' Global Governance*', Vol. 18, No. 1, pp. 121–32.

Zena, P. N. (2013) *The Lessons and Limits of DDR in Africa*', Africa Security Brief: A Publication of the Africa Centre for Strategic Studies', No. 24: pp.1-8.

Zürcher, C. (2007) *The Post-Soviet Wars: Rebellion, Ethnic Conflict, and Nationhood in the Caucasus*', New York: New York University Press.

ABOUT THE AUTHOR

Doctor Marial Mach Aduot is an extraordinary young talented political scientist, security policy strategies and international laws expert based in Melbourne Australia. He is currently an academic researcher at Deakin University in Melbourne, Victoria.

The End.

www.ingramcontent.com/pod-product-compliance
Lightning Source LLC
Chambersburg PA
CBHW070626260626
47161CB00007B/2598